St.Louis Community College

Library

5801 Wilson Avenue
St. Louis, Missouri 63110

HUMAN SEX DIFFERENCES

A Primatologist's Perspective

HUMAN SEX DIFFERENCES

A Primatologist's Perspective

G. Mitchell, Ph.D.

Department of Psychology
University of California, Davis
Davis, California

VNR VAN NOSTRAND REINHOLD COMPANY

NEW YORK   CINCINNATI   ATLANTA   DALLAS   SAN FRANCISCO
LONDON   TORONTO   MELBOURNE

Van Nostrand Reinhold Company Regional Offices:
New York   Cincinnati   Atlanta   Dallas   San Francisco

Van Nostrand Reinhold Company International Offices:
London   Toronto   Melbourne

Library of Congress Catalog Card Number: 80-28225
ISBN: 0-442-23865-7

Manufactured in the United States of America

Published by Van Nostrand Reinhold Company
135 West 50th Street, New York, N.Y. 10020

Published simultaneously in Canada by Van Nostrand Reinhold Ltd.

15 14 13 12 11 10 9 8 7 6 5 4 3 2 1

Library of Congress Cataloging in Publication Data

Mitchell, G.
   Human Sex Differences

   Includes Indexes.
   1. Sex differences (Psychology) 2. Personality and
culture. 3. Psychology, Comparative. 4. Primates–
Behaviour. I. Title, [DNLM: 1. Sex factors. 2. Sex
characteristics. 3. Identification BF 692.2.M681h]
BF692.2M57   305.3   80-28225
ISBN 0-442-23865-7

To My Brothers

Bruce Gordon Mitchell (Buzz)
John Philip Mitchell (Jack)
Roland Earl Mitchell (Rollie)
Mark Scott Mitchell (Mark)

Preface

I wrote this book in the Fall Quarter of 1979 while teaching a course entitled "The Psychology of Sex Differences." My intention was to develop a book which presented a broad and unbiased view of primate behavioral research as it applied to the subject of sex differences. This book has a companion volume by the same publishers entitled "Behavioral Sex Differences in Nonhuman Primates" which I also wrote. Both books are inventories or registers more than they are *integrative* reviews.

I wish to thank the many people who were of help throughout my academic development and the development of this book. George M. Haslerud and Harry F. Harlow, my academic advisors, have always been encouraging. William A. Mason, Donald G. Lindburg, and Robert Sommer have enlightened me concerning methodology in laboratory research, primate field studies, and human social behavior respectively. Joe Erwin, Nancy Caine, John Copp, Jody Gomber, Terry Maple, Bill Redican, and Barbara Sommer, all former graduate students under my supervision, have influenced my thinking on the current topic significantly. Terry Maple, in particular, has been focal in initiating the present project and in encouraging me to complete it.

Finally, I would like to thank my children and Patricia A. Jones who are always patient and helpful when I'm in the midst of a relatively long-term project. I would also like to thank Jacci Leger for an excellent and prompt typing service.

G. MITCHELL

Contents

HUMAN SEX DIFFERENCES

A Primatologist's Perspective

1
Biological Perspectives

A biological perspective on sex or gender differences means different things to different people. To some it implies resorting to the use of instinct as an explanatory principle. To others it may mean an emphasis upon hormones and/or upon suggestions regarding neurological differences. To still others it may imply an inordinate reliance upon evolutionary mechanisms as explanations for differences between males and females. Many feminists respond with horror at the mention of the word sociobiology (Wilson, 1975). The tack of the current deliberation does not depend on any single one of these, and, in fact, decries the inclination to espouse biology alone (of whatever ilk).

We, as a species, are characterized, even by some sociobiologists, as being organisms which have escaped from the control of the selfish gene. An understanding of biological principles, even of sociobiological principles, is necessary for a well-rounded explanation of what we know (or think we know) about human gender differences. We should know something about sociobiology if only to defend ourselves against its *possible* use in explaining away cultural determinants. There is more to our need than this, however.

SOCIOBIOLOGY AND GENDER

One of the best texts concerning sociobiology and gender is one by Daly and Wilson (1978). These authors explain sociobiological principles without making unwarranted claims concerning its use for

Homo sapiens. They point out, quite simply, that sexual reproduction is extremely important in evolution and that evolution has produced many different kinds of sexual behavior. Because sexual behavior is necessary for our own evolution to have occurred, it would seem that any understanding of the two sexes *must* include an understanding of natural selection. But a knowledge of natural selection alone is not enough. Knowledge of the ultimate adaptive significance of behavior and of evolutionary history must be supplemented by knowledge of physiology, developmental processes, self-awareness, culture, and other more proximate information.

Natural selection is a phenomenon involving gradual changes leading to more successful ("fit") genes. By success we mean reproductive success. Individuals differ in reproductive success and different *behaviors* differ in reproductive success. According to sociobiological theory, evolution, through natural selection, is a continuing process of producing organisms with "strategies" which serve to ensure or increase reproductive success.

Sexual reproduction itself is a result of evolution. Compared with asexual reproduction, it has advantages and disadvantages. Its main advantage over asexual reproduction is in the fact that it produces offspring (individuals) with greater interindividual genetic variability. Ultimately it produced *Homo sapiens,* a species which shows marked interindividual genetic variability *and* a degree of self-awareness or consciousness that changes the differences between individuals in ways which sociobiology has yet to explain. Each and every one of us is unique genetically, but then so are monkeys. Each and every one of us, however, has a unique self of which we are aware. Monkeys do not (although apes have the rudiments of self) (see Gallup, 1977). On the other hand, we are all easily classified, sometimes unjustly, into either the male or the female category. How are such categories defined?

Hampson and Hampson (1961) have listed seven different ways to define sex or gender. They are as follows:

1. sex of assignment
2. chromosomal sex
3. gonadal sex
4. hormonal sex
5. sex of internal accessory organs

6. sex of external genitalia

7. psychological sex (gender role)

Psychological sex may differ from assigned sex in individuals who are designated and reared as one sex but are psychologically inclined to be of the other sex (as in transexualism). It is obvious that the gender dichotomy is not a simple one. It is perhaps better defined as a continuum.

In sexual reproduction, more is involved than sexual behavior itself. In order to reproduce a new generation successfully, that new generation has to mature and reproduce itself. Sociobiologists deal with the whole process of replication through the use of several concepts. One of these is the concept of *parental investment.*

Among many mammals females generally invest far more time and energy in the rearing of each individual offspring than do males. Males, on the other hand, fight and die in order to inseminate females who are hardworking. Males, in most cases, are not as selective as are females in regards to a choice of a mate. There are, as always, exceptions to this general principle, both at the species level and at the individual level. Our purpose here is to simply define the sociobiological concept of *investment.*

In some cases males invest nearly as much or even more than do females. They are as selective as are their mates and/or they invest as much time and energy into each offspring. Often, in these cases, monogamous mating systems have evolved. Mating systems (e.g., monogamy, polygyny, polyandry) are the products of differing ecological variables, preadaptation, taxonomic constraints, and mating strategies.

Parental strategies differ just as do mating strategies. Each parent behaves to maximize reproductive success. To do this, he or she must raise offspring that also reproduce themselves. In some species, males do not participate in infant care, in others they do. In a few, the male is the primary caretaker because it is the best strategy for him in terms of improving his chance of getting his genes into the next generations. The mother, the father, and the offspring each have a strategy and frequently these strategies are not in agreement.

Sociobiological research on reproduction, including sexual behavior and infant care or parenting, has seldom included investigations of physiological or proximate developmental processes. Male and female physiologies differ in ways which often mesh with what one might expect on the basis of sociobiological theory, however. Physiology differs most when mating strategies and mating systems differ most. Anatomy has a similar correlation with mating strategy. Sexual dimorphism in size is often minimal in monogamous species.

Sociobiology deals with the ultimate (as opposed to proximate) causation of behavior. That is, sociobiology is more interested in the adaptive significance of behavior through evolution. We know, however, that more proximate developmental processes also influence behavior. The body, brain, and behavior of mammals develop in a masculine form, for example, if androgens are present in the individual's bloodstream early in life. If androgens are not present, female development results. Hence, physiological and early proximate developmental processes have organizing effects on body, brain, and behavior. In addition, children develop sexual identities and acquire sex roles through cultural processes often slighted in sociobiological treatises.

Even though sociobiology does *overemphasize* genetic determinants, many human behaviors and attitudes seem to be consistent with sociobiological predictions that we behave to maximize our genetic fitness. The concept of *inclusive fitness* has been particularly intriguing in analyses of human behavior. Inclusive fitness is . . . "the sum of an individual's fitness as a result of personal reproductive success and that of relatives weighted according to their coefficients of relatedness to the focal individual" (Daly and Wilson, 1978). From the point of view of the genes themselves, it is as important to help one's sibling as it is to help one's child. Inclusive fitness is a concept that improves upon personal reproductive success in explaining behavior genetically. What is being selected for is the gene's effect on its own numerical increase. Clearly then, assistance to kin can be adaptive. The more genes the focal individual and the relative have in common, the greater the selective advantage.

Marriage patterns, love and jealousy, birth spacing, birth control, infanticide, incest avoidance, and sexual behavior itself are often at least superficially consistent with sociobiology's investment and inclusive fitness predictions. Adult human males try to control women in order to prevent cuckoldry. Women select mates who command resources. The point made by sociobiology is that people have evolved in much the same ways as have other animals, at least up until we became more self-aware, linguistic, and culture-dependent.

Evolutionary biology should therefore have something to offer the sciences of human behavior. As Daly and Wilson (1978) suggest:

> ... emphases upon the reproductive consequences of behavior should be essential to an understanding of the specializations and adaptations of any species, including our own (p. 330).

Many sociobiologists go beyond this to affirm that morality and justice (and other distinctly human traits) evolved from our animal past and are rooted in our genes. They insist that without a consideration of evolutionary biology, concepts of morality and justice cannot be understood. It is at this juncture that some sociobiologists have implied that political science, law, economics, psychology, psychiatry, and anthropology will all become mere branches of sociobiology (Wilson, 1975).

The sociobiologists believe that it is not the *individual's* fitness that matters, it's the fitness of the genes themselves. The DNA sequences exist to protect themselves. This theory helps explain human altruism. According to the sociobiological approach, altruism is genetic selfishness, totaling up the genetic costs or benefits of helping out relatives who have many of the same genes. Organisms appear to behave as though they understood the underlying genetics. In evolutionary terms, sex is the focal point in life. The aim of all individuals is to get as many genes as possible into the next generations at the lowest cost.

Antisociobiological comment has come from Marxists, feminists, psychologists, and primatologists, among others. It is true that the discipline is long in theory and short on real proof. (Also, political misuse of genetic theories is dangerous.) The best arguments against sociobiology, however, concentrate on its failure to recognize the importance of the emergence of the human brain, consciousness, and culture.

BIOLOGICAL SEX DIFFERENCES

Few people doubt that there are at least *some* biological sex differences. However, the search for them has often been rooted in myth and prejudice. The search for evidence for a biological role in sex differences in general intellectual ability is an example of this. There is no good evidence for differences of this type. On the other hand there *is* reasonable evidence that sex differences in aggression are in part biologically influenced, as are differences in visual-spatial ability. However, experience can and *does* modify the genetic components of these traits and *drastically* alters their form (Deaux, 1976).

OUR PRIMATE HERITAGE

People are primates. Primates have, surprisingly, retained many of the generalized or primitive characteristics of the first mammals, particularly in regards to aspects of the skeletal structure and limbs. Primates, for example, have a mobile set of five grasping digits on the hands and feet, the digits having sensitive tactile pads and flattened nails rather than claws. Most primate forms have a reduced muzzle length, binocular vision, and a decreased sense of smell relative to other mammals. In correlation with the reduced muzzle they have fewer teeth.

Most important, however, primates have undergone a remarkable elaboration of the brain, particularly of the cerebral cortex. Associated with this change is a trend toward longer gestation, fewer infants per birth, greater nutrition for the fetus prenatally, and a prolonged dependency of the infant following birth. Bipedalism developed in the hominid line and, in conjunction with changes in the brain, language, consciousness, and culture evolved (Napier, 1967).

The living primates include 200 or so different species categorized into genera, families, and suborders, etc. Their diversity in terms of structure, size, behavior, ecology, and mating systems is truly incredible. We will refer to eight major types of living primates in our coverage of gender and behavior:

1. Prosimians (literally, premonkeys)
   A primitive suborder of primates showing extreme variability from species to species.
2. New World marmosets and tamarins
   Relatively primitive monkeys which live in monogamous family groups in which the father is the primary caretaker of infants. These species often show few if any sex differences in behavior.
3. New World cebids
   Monkeys which show great variability in social structure, in physical dimorphism and in sex differences.

4. Old World arboreals

   These are monkeys which are primarily leaf-eaters who live in the trees (e.g., langur). Sex differences vary.

5. Old World terrestrials

   These include the well-known macaques and baboons among others. Sex differences are pronounced.

6. Lesser apes

   These are not monkeys but retain monkeylike characteristics. They are monogamous and locomote by swinging through the trees via brachiation. They show few sex differences.

7. Great apes

   There are four species of great apes: the common chimpanzee, the pygmy chimpanzee, the gorilla, and the orangutan. There are sex differences here.

8. *Homo sapiens*

As we progress through the material on gender and behavior we will refer to members of each of these major primate groups. There is species variability within each group and each species, but some generalizations can be made at each level concerning sex differences (cf. Mitchell, 1979). We will start with sex differences in size and bodily structure and proceed toward differences in ability, achievement, and even consciousness. This comparative primate perspective may help us to see what kind of biological perspective might be most useful in our understanding of ourselves.

REFERENCES

Daly, Martin and Wilson, Margo. *Sex, Evolution and Behavior.* North Scituate, Mass: Duxbury Press, 1978.

Deaux, K. *The Behavior of Men and Women.* Monterey, CA: Brooks/Cole, 1976.

Gallup, G.G. Self-recognition in primates: A comparative approach to the bidirectional properties of consciousness. *American Psychologist,* 1977, 32, 329-338.

Hampson, J.L. and Hampson, J.G. Ontogenesis of sexual behavior in man. In Young, W.C. (Ed.) *Sex and Internal Secretions,* 3rd ed. Vol. II Baltimore MD: Williams and Wilkins, 1961.

Mitchell, G. *Behavioral Sex Differences in Nonhuman Primates.* New York: Van Nostrand Reinhold, 1979.

Napier, J.R. and Napier, P.H. *A Handbook of Living Primates.* New York: Academic Press, 1967.

Wilson, E.O. *Sociobiology: The New Synthesis.* Cambridge, MA: Harvard University Press, 1975.

2
Sexual Dimorphism: Phylogenesis and Ontogenesis

PHYLOGENESIS

Sexual reproduction, as opposed to asexual reproduction, produces diversity. Because of this diversity, sexually reproducing organisms have an advantage over those which do not sexually reproduce. If two sexes convey an advantage over one, why not three or more? Some fungi, in fact, have hundreds of sexes, but the two-sex system is the most prevalent because it is the most efficient (cf. Wilson, 1978).

In the two-sex system, the female manufactures the egg, the male makes the sperm. When the egg and sperm unite, a newly assembled mixture of genes results.

Anatomical differences between the male and female sex cells can be extreme. For example, the human egg is 85,000 times larger than the human sperm. A woman can produce only 400 eggs in her lifetime, with only about 20 of these resulting in infants. A man produces 100 million sperm with each ejaculation. It is little wonder that the woman has been assumed to have a greater investment in each of her sex cells. According to sociobiologists, conflict of interest between the sexes results directly from this primary sexual dimorphism (Wilson, 1978).

It pays males to be assertive, hasty, fickle and undiscriminating. In theory it is more profitable for females to be coy, to hold back until they can identify males with the best genes. In species that rear young, it is also important for the females to select males who are more likely to stay with them after insemination (Wilson, 1978, p. 125).

Before we can discuss behavioral differences we must examine anatomy. Anatomy has developed in accord with sociobiological principles in the primates, including humans. Sexual dimorphism in size has developed in most nonhuman primates. Reasons given by primatologists for this development have included: (1) A need for an optimal distribution of biomass (physical size); (2) Adaptation to the hazards of terrestrial life; (3) Tendencies toward larger species size and fewer offspring per litter; (4) Selection for fighting ability and strength in males to make them better adapted in competition with other males of their own species; (5) Selection for increased fighting ability and strength in males for group protection regardless of environment (terrestrial or arboreal); and, (6) Selection for increased attractiveness to females in males. Probably no one single factor can account for the size differences seen in all species.

Among the nonhuman primates, the most primitive show some sexual dimorphism in the expected direction. In the tree shrews, lemurs, bushbabies, and other prosimians, males are usually only slightly larger than the females.

Among primitive monkeys, like marmosets and tamarins, there is little or no sexual dimorphism. Females and males are, on the average, the same size. This is also true of some cebids (titi monkeys and night monkeys). However, in these two groups (marmosets and tamarins; titi monkeys and night monkeys) there is monogamy and the male invests as much in parental behavior as does the female.

The other groups of nonhuman primates to show minimal sexual dimorphism in size are the lesser apes—the gibbons and the siamangs. While the males of these two lesser apes do not display the quantity of parental investment displayed by the primitive marmoset and tamarin males, they *do* live in monogamous families in which they protect one female and her young (also his young).

All of the rest of the diverse species of nonhuman primates show physical sexual dimorphism in size to some degree. Among the rest of the South American monkeys, spider monkey and squirrel monkey males are only slightly larger than their female counterparts, but howler monkey males are substantially larger and heavier. All of the South American monkeys are arboreal. Living in the trees does not appear to ensure a low degree of dimorphism.

Among arboreal Old World monkeys, males are larger than females in proboscis monkeys, langurs, and vervets. Among terrestrial Old World monkeys, dimorphism is extreme in patas monkeys, macaques, mangabeys, and especially baboons.

All of the Great apes display sexual dimorphism favoring males. From least to most sexual dimorphism we have: pygmy chimpanzee, common chimpanzee, orangutan, and gorilla. The adult male gorilla is about twice the size of the adult female. The adult female common chimpanzee is about 88 percent the size of the male, a percentage similar to the human case.

In addition to sexual dimorphism in size, at least some primates show physical sexual dimorphism in shape, color, dentition, baldness, sexual swelling, shape of face, skeleton, and size of extremities (cf. Mitchell, 1979).

Among people, men are 20 to 30 percent heavier than women. Men are stronger and quicker; but, in regard to strength and speed, size is not the determinant, e.g., small male runners still have better average times than do women. In size, strength, and speed there is substantial overlap between the sexes. Women seem to be better than men in long-distance swimming, precision archery, and rifle shooting.

Although human males and females differ in size proportionally about the same as do male and female common chimpanzees, this sex difference changes with age. Nine to twelve-year-old girls grow faster than do boys and at these ages, they are often larger. But boys grow at least two years after girls stop their pubertal growth spurt (the same principles seem to apply for chimps and gorillas). There are large sex differences in human physique on such dimensions as hand width, chest circumference, head circumference, thoracic height, sitting height, foot length, and upper limb length, with males larger than females in all of these.

Humans, like some other primates, also show sexual dimorphism in shape. Females have larger breasts, more fat, and a different larynx. Males have facial hair and broader shoulders.

In summary, with respect to sexual dimorphism, people are intermediate between such species as baboons and gorillas, where males may weigh twice as much as females, and marmosets, titi monkeys, and gibbons, where males and females are nearly equal in size and appearance (Mitchell, 1979).

ONTOGENESIS

Structural sexual differentiation in mammals begins very early in development. Most cells of the human body have 23 pairs of chromosomes, 22 of which carry genes determining various features of the individual and one pair of which carries genes determining genetic sex. The sex chromosomes are designated XX in the female and XY in the male. Germ cells (ova and sperm), however, do not have 46 chromosomes, they have only 23; including only one X in the ovum and either one X or one Y in the sperm.

The X chromosome is one of the largest of all chromosomes, the Y is one of the smallest. Yet the Y chromosome, as we shall see, is more responsible for sexual differentiation than is the X. Testosterone, a male sex hormone which is most important in differential sexual development, is produced primarily by the male testes which are in turn differentiated from embryonic gonadal tissue via the action of the Y chromosome.

Genetic determination of sex by way of the Y chromosome merely initiates sexual differentiation. The continuation is completely under hormonal control, primarily under the control of testosterone.

Testosterone is an androgen. Androgens are predominantly but not exclusively male hormones produced by the testes and adrenal glands in males and, to a lesser extent, by the ovaries and adrenal glands in females. Males produce more androgens than do females. Dihydrotestosterone is another androgen so produced.

Estrogens are primarily female sex hormones produced by the ovaries and adrenal glands in females and, to a lesser extent, by the testes and adrenal glands in males. Females produce more estrogens than do males. Estradiol-17B and estrone are two different kinds of estrogen.

Progesterone is also primarily a female sex hormone produced by the ovaries and adrenal glands in females and, to a lesser extent, by the testes and adrenals of males. Females produce more progesterone than do males.

Gonadotrophins (FSH and LH) are *both* male and female hormones produced by the pituitary gland via releasing factors coming from the basal hypothalamus of the brain (the ventral portion of the diencephalon which is the second of the five primary divisions of the brain). There are two major gonadotrophins—FSH and LH. FSH stands for follicle stimulating hormone. It stimulates the growth of follicles which contain the ovum which in turn produces estrogen in females. It also stimulates the production of sperm in males. LH is luteinizing hormone (in the male it is called interstitial cell stimulating hormone or ICSH). LH (or ICSH) initiates ovulation and the formation of the corpus luteum in females. It leads to the production of testosterone and other androgens in males (see Table 2-1).

Of all these hormones, androgens are by far the most important as far as the development of structural sex differences are concerned. The male hormone testosterone determines the direction in which sexual differentiation will proceed.

Table 2-1. Sex Hormones, Primary Sources and Major Actions. (Jones, Shainberg, and Byer, 1977)		
Primary Source	Hormone	Major Action
Male testes	Testosterone	Male secondary sex characteristics
	Androgens in general	Male and female sex drive
Female ovaries	Estrogen	Female secondary sex characteristics; menstrual cycle
	Progesterone	Breast development at puberty; maintenance of uterine lining during pregnancy
Anterior pituitary gland	FSH (follicle stimulating hormone; a gonadotrophin)	Stimulates growth of follicles containing ovum and produces estrogen in females; stimulates production of sperm in males
(Hypothalamic FSH and LH releasing factors control the release of the gonadotrophins; estrogen, progesterone, and testosterone levels, in turn, control the releasing factors in a feedback system.)	LH (luteinizing hormone) often termed ICSH (interstitial cell stimulating hormone; a gonadotrophin)	Ovulation, formation of corpus luteum in females (as LH); production of testosterone and other androgens in males (as ICSH)

A critical period for the action of testosterone on the sexual differentiation of rhesus monkeys was discovered by Goy and Phoenix (cf. Phoenix, 1974). They injected pregnant female rhesus monkeys intramuscularly with testosterone proprionate during various stages of pregnancy. If the androgen was administered at between 46 and 90 days a *genetically* produced female fetus was born as a pseudo-hermaphrodite (having a mixture of male and female reproductive structures).

Pseudohermaphrodites have external genitalia that look like males', with a scrotum and small penis, but internal organs, including cycling ovaries, that are female. Menarche (first menstruation) arrives seven months late in the pseudohermaphrodites and the menstrual blood flows through the penile urethra. What is significant is that, if the fetus is a genetically produced *male*, it is not affected by the testosterone injections.

In addition to structural changes, there are also behavioral ones. Pseudohermaphroditic female rhesus monkeys threaten, play, and *initiate* more play than do nontreated females. Unlike normal females, they also develop a mature foot-clasp sexual mounting posture typical of normal adult males. Postnatal androgen administration does not produce such results. The differentiation, structurally and behaviorally, is clearly prenatal.

The commonsense notion that the sex of the individual is determined at conception is therefore only a half-truth at best. Sexual differentiation, whether structural or behavioral, takes time. It is a *process.* We begin life primarily as females. Something (Y chromosome, testosterone) must be added for the differentiation of a male. In the absence of a Y chromosome the embryo will develop into a female. The crucial *genetic* determinant is the Y chromosome, the crucial *hormonal* determinant is androgen.

The embryonic gonadal tissue is unisexual and undifferentiated. With a Y chromosome, the medulla (inside) of this tissue develops into testes. Without a Y chromosome the cortex (outside) develops into ovaries and the medulla becomes vestigial. Accessory sexual structures are affected similarly, as are the genitalia. Male development is a derivation from the female.

In humans, there are clinical examples of masculinization and feminization resulting from aberrant prenatal hormonal conditions. In what is called the androgen insensitivity syndrome, a genetic male (with a Y chromosome) is born with female genitalia and female secondary sex characteristics, yet with functioning testes which produce testosterone. A recessive genetic defect, however, makes the individual insensitive to androgens and, without androgens, the body follows the female line of development.

Another human clinical example demonstrating the principles

outlined above is the AGS syndrome. This syndrome (adrenogenital syndrome) is a rare condition in which there is a malfunction of the adrenal glands resulting in an *overproduction* of androgens. Not recognized until after birth, prenatal differentiation proceeds to masculinize the female fetus. Genetic females (having no Y chromosome) are born with male genitalia and display long-term "tomboyish" activity. A situation somewhat like AGS is said to occur among female fetuses whose mothers were given progestin in order to prevent miscarriage (progestin was discovered, too late, to have androgenizing effects).

Despite such clinical evidence, many people have been reluctant to accept the above comparative evidence for a biological contribution to sexual differentiation. And, in retrospect, it is probably wise to remain somewhat skeptical. The number of species of primates that have been studied with regard to prenatal androgenization is small. Almost *all* of the research has been done on the rhesus macaque, a species which shows extreme structural and behavioral dimorphism relative to people. The levels of hormones and the developmental patterns of hormonal production differ tremendously from species to species within the primate order. In regard to the hormones of pregnancy:

> ... the macaque, at least as evidenced by the patterns of pregnancy hormones, does not appear to be the best animal. By these limited criteria, either the chimpanzee or marmoset is closer to the human (Lanman, 1977, p. 36).

Prenatal androgenization studies have *not* been done on chimpanzees or other great apes. Facile generalization from macaque prenatal studies is *still* premature (cf. Mitchell, 1979). Recent studies on early androgenization in the marmosets (in species that do not show strong sexual dimorphism) suggest that postnatal, not prenatal, androgenization predisposes an individual toward masculine behavior (Abbott and Hearn, 1979). Moreover, postnatal processes involving the development of gender identity through reinforcement, modeling, and other more cognitive influences are also of major importance in primate, especially in human, sexual differentiation. We will discuss these influences in our next chapter.

REFERENCES

Abbott, D.H. and Hearn, J.P. The effects of neonatal exposure to testosterone on the development of behaviour in female marmoset monkeys. *Sex, Hormones and Behavior* (Ciba Foundation Symposium 62) Amsterdam: Elsevier-North-Holland (Excerpta Medica), 1979, pp. 299-327.

Jones, K.L., Shainberg, L.W., and Byer, C.O. *Sex and People.* New York: Harper & Row, 1977.

Lanman, J.T. Parturition in nonhuman primates. *Biology of Reproduction,* 1977, 16, 28-38.

Mitchell, G. *Behavioral Sex Differences in Nonhuman Primates.* New York: Van Nostrand Reinhold, 1979.

Phoenix, C.H. Prenatal testosterone in the nonhuman primate and its consequences for behavior. In Friedman, R.C., Richart, R.M., and van de Wiele, R.L. (Eds.) *Sex Differences in Behavior.* New York: Wiley, 1974, pp. 19-32.

Wilson, E.O. *On Human Nature.* Cambridge, Mass: Harvard University Press, 1978.

3
Postnatal Development

Apart from hormonal effects there are other factors affecting gender differentiation. Social or experiential variables strongly influence the behaviors which are expressed by either sex. In infant rhesus monkeys, for example, gender role is the result of behavioral predispositions induced by prenatal androgens *combined* with early social learning in interaction with the mother and among peers (Mitchell, 1968; Goldfoot, 1976). Social factors such as dominance rank among peers, for example, can modify prenatally determined tendencies.

Moreover, the interaction between hormones and experience continues after the animals have learned various roles. Androgens, for example, undoubtedly affect neural circuits that are involved in experience as well as those more directly involved in sex differences.

In addition, a minimal amount of social experience appears to be necessary for normal social gender differentiation. One needs to permit long continuous exposure to agemates in rhesus monkeys to guard against the development of high levels of social aggression between animals which can adversely affect the development of gender differences. For example, with high levels of aggression the use of the foot clasp in sexual mounting does not develop (Goy, et al., 1974). Obviously, behavioral sex differences do not depend on early hormones alone.

Postnatal hormone-experience interactive effects are seen in a study reported by Joslyn (1973). He injected androgen into infant female rhesus when they were 6½ to 14½ months old. The androgen increased the little females' aggressiveness so that they replaced the top males (also infants) in dominance. The females' dominance lasted for *one full year* after the last injection. Dominance was so well learned that it became independent of hormonal support.

Harlow and coworkers showed that normal infant male rhesus engaged in more rough-and-tumble play than did infant female rhesus (Harlow and Lauersdorf, 1974). Goy's (1966) prenatally androgenized pseudohermaphroditic females displayed play at a level that was *intermediate* between male and female levels. Clearly, prenatal androgens could not completely account for all structural and behavioral sex differences.

If we examine sex differences in play behavior at several taxonomic levels in the primate order, however, we can see evidence that the development of the greater intensity of male play is a general process among many higher primates. Among prosimians, adult play is common and early sex differences are not well established. Primitive New World monkeys, marmosets and tamarins, show few sex differences but, even here, play may occur more frequently in males than in females. In the more advanced New World monkeys as well (e.g., howlers, squirrel monkeys) males seem to play more than do females. However, the real sex differences in play are not seen clearly until we reach the more advanced forms of primates, the Old World monkeys and apes (Mitchell, 1979).

Juvenile males of the genera *Cerocopithecus, Erythrocebus, Presbytis,* and *Miopithecus* play more often, more intensely and longer than do their juvenile female counterparts. (There are some interesting ontogenetic reversals in at least one of these. *Miopithecus* males become *less* assertive than females after they reach puberty).

Among macaques other than rhesus, and among baboons, sex differences in play are much the same as Harlow had found for rhesus. Males play more frequently, initiate more play, play rougher, and play longer than do females. The ages at which the sex differences become apparent of course differ from species to species depending upon developmental rates (Mitchell, 1979).

An evolutionary explanation for these differences in play has been published by Owens (1975) who studied the ontogeny of play and aggression in *Papio anubis* (olive baboon). In the olive baboon, play is different from aggression in that the mean duration of body contact in play is greater than it is in aggression. Also, chases are longer in aggression, particularly in adult male aggression. In both male-male play and male-male aggression, roles are frequently reversed; whereas in female-female play and aggression, role reversals are uncommon.

Owens (1975) feels that play in males functions as practice for aggression. The prolonged contact of play facilitates the learning process. Selection pressures on females are different, however. Since females do not come into estrus at the same time, and are, from a sociobiological point of view, more selective because of greater parental investment (see Chapter 1), they do not compete for males. There is therefore a more stable dominance hierarchy in females and a selection *against* severe fighting which could injure the young (the female's investment). In pregnancy, as well, fighting could (and occasionally does) cause stillbirth. Clearly, according to these assumptions, if the males do not have early play *experience,* they will not develop into males which can compete for females. Once again it is obvious here that genes and hormones do not tell the whole story. Certain experiences, although close to inevitable, seem necessary.

No sex differences have been reported for play behavior in the lesser apes but several studies have reported sex differences in the great apes. Sex differences in infancy appear to be the same in the chimpanzees as they are in rhesus. Orangutans and gorillas show a similar pattern. The great apes differ somewhat from the terrestrial Old World monkeys in that adult females often play vigorously with infants. However, in infancy, and in the juvenile period, males play more than do females in all of the great apes (Mitchell, 1979).

In an article by Baldwin and Baldwin (1977), several fairly well substantiated sex differences in primate play were listed. They are as follows:

1. Prenatal androgens influence the development of sex differences.
2. Males are often physically larger and stronger than females.
3. Female play develops into "play mothering" directed toward smaller infants as the females approach puberty.
4. Younger ages of maturity in females than in males leads to an earlier diminution in active play in the former; and
5. There is a higher level of object manipulation play in females because objects are less arousing than social activities and because females *may possibly* have a lower tolerance for arousal.

PEOPLE

There are sex or gender differences in human play very much like those seen in other primates. These differences appear as early as social play begins, are particularly noticeable in play of the rough-and-tumble variety, and are reflected in toy preferences, in physical contact, and in *where* the two sexes play (cf. Mitchell, 1979). However, the human's special ability of being able to conceptualize the *idea* of gender puts matters of play into a different perspective than one sees in other primates.[1] Boys and girls as individuals, although perhaps primed in certain ways, often have a real choice about how they play, where they play, and how often. In addition, reinforcement, modeling, and other cognitive processes profoundly affect gender development in people.

Growing Up Human

Children develop a gender identity during their second year of life. By age three they know how to classify themselves and others by gender. This recognition of one's own gender becomes internalized in what is known as sex-role identification. Identification includes internalization of the sex role typical of the society in which one lives. It occurs somewhat like identification with a parent. In parental identification, however, the personality characteristics of the parent are internalized so that the individual responds in ways similar to that parent. In sex-role identification the personality characteristics of society's definition of each gender are inculcated and internalized so that the individual responds as society says a male or female should respond. Sex-role identification is assimilated through reinforcement and modeling as the child's cognitive development proceeds (Williams, 1977).

Sex-typed behavior can be acquired through *reinforcement* under a system of reward and punishment. However, reinforcement alone cannot account for all of the child's sex-role learning. The sex roles are learned so rapidly that surely something more than reward and punishment must be involved.

Several theorists have emphasized the role of imitation *(modeling)* which can occur as a result of observation without any direct reinforcement. However, the type of model the child will imitate varies with situational determinants. For example, children will imitate a more dominant model in one situation, yet a more nurturant model in another. If the father is dominant then one would expect *both*

---

[1]Although in the great apes there is also evidence of an animal's being able to conceptualize gender and, perhaps, even its own gender, the extent of this ability falls far short of the full development of gender identity seen in children and adult humans.

sexes to imitate *him* when the right circumstances prevailed. These situational differences do not account for the gender differences actually seen. The extant data do not corroborate the idea of parent-child similarity along a dimension of femininity to masculinity. The sex-typed choices of first-grade girls, for example, are often unrelated to the degree of femininity in their mothers. There is no evidence that feminine mothers have feminine daughters. Children do not consistently imitate the same-sex parent. The child's modeling is indiscriminate with regard to sex, although modeling *does* occur and so does sex-typing (Williams, 1977).

An important point to make here, also, is that what children *do* may be different from what they *believe* is appropriate. A girl may climb a tree yet believe that she is behaving in an unladylike fashion in doing so (Maccoby and Jacklin, 1974).

A third explanation of how children internalize sex roles is the cognitive developmental explanation. This theory argues that sex-typed behavior is acquired because the child develops rules or generalizations from observation and then applies these rules in very broad ways. Initially the rules are too simple and overgeneralization leads to mistakes. Eventually, however, the child changes and revises his/her ideas of what constitutes masculine or feminine behavior until they become "mature" rules. The rules do not develop in any particular sequence but their rigidity is very much affected by the society in which the child lives.

While this cognitive-developmental orientation seems to be most popular at the present time, it is likely that all three processes—reinforcement, modeling, and cognition—operate in the development of sex-role identification *and* that prenatal biological priming plays a part as well. In addition, a fourth model is gaining in popularity, the constraints-on-learning model. This model says that if one is male it may be easier to learn male things than female things, and vice versa. It may be easier to learn to be true to your own biological sex (cf. Nash, 1978).

Gender Preference, Adoption, and Identification

A child may prefer one sex and yet adopt the behavior of the other. A child may also adopt the behaviors of one sex yet identify his or herself as the other sex. Preference, behavior, and identity are separate processes.

By age three most children show a clear preference for the toys and activities of their own sex. However, in middle childhood, girls begin to show a preference for the masculine role while boys do not show a cross-sex preference. Girls *may* be perceiving the male role as having more status and/or girls may simply have more freedom in our society to make cross-sex choices.

In terms of identification, as opposed to preferences and behavior, *both* sexes identify more clearly with the mother than with the father, throughout childhood. The boy's identification with mother is revealed in personality variables which are not sex-typed, however. Boys must change their model, girls need not change. There is continuity in female development in addition to fewer restrictions regarding cross-sex behavior (Williams, 1977).

It is assumed by society that the best chance for healthy adjustment in girls is by identifying strongly with a feminine mother, and the best chance for healthy adjustment in boys is by eventually identifying with a masculine father. The evidence suggests that the first assumption is not true, but the second may be. Girls who identify with a masculine father might have a better level of personal adjustment than do girls who identify with a feminine mother. (This is the *opposite* of what is predicted by Freudian theory.)

The above paradox is particularly true if the masculine father (who is primarily instrumental as opposed to expressive) also behaves in an expressive, nurturant way toward his daughter. Daughters who develop both instrumental (active, doing-oriented life styles) and expressive life styles have more effective, healthy personalities than do those who develop expressive styles only. The *sex* of the parent is not important. What is important is that the parent be healthy—both effective (instrumental) and expressive (warm, nurturant).

Sex-typing is not sex-stereotyping. Stereotyping results from promoting societal beliefs about gender differences "to the point of caricature" (Williams, 1977, p. 172). Sex-typing can be healthy, sex stereotyping cannot. Fathers, and males in general, tend to be more extreme in their sex-typing than do mothers or females in general. This difference is seen in parental influences as early as the first few days of life (Williams, 1977).

But even with a nonsexist, warm, expressive father and/or mother, sex-stereotyping can adversely affect a developing child, limiting the potential growth of the personality and of ability. Television, books, school, and church all conspire to produce caricatures of the two sexes in the child's mind. It takes strong support indeed from an expressive-instrumental parent to counteract a sexist society. Regardless of the sex of the parent or the sex of the child, however, a nonsexist parent can promote the personal growth of a beautiful, productive person. Sometimes, however, what we *are* biologically is far more unique and filled with potential than whatever it is that results from societal or parental pressures. In any case, this overview of human postnatal development should remind us of how complex human gender differences are relative to those of nonhuman primates.

REFERENCES

Baldwin, J.D. and Baldwin, J.I. The role of learning phenomena in the ontogeny of exploration and play. In Chevalier-Skolnikoff, S. and Poirier, F.E. (Eds.) *Primate Bio-social Development*. New York: Garland, 1977, pp. 343-403.

Goldfoot, D.A. Social and hormonal regulation of gender role development in rhesus monkey. Paper presented at the *International Primatological Society* meeting, Cambridge, England, August 1976.

Goy, R.W. Role of androgens in the establishment and regulation of behavioral sex differences in mammals. *Journal of Animal Science*, 1966, 25, 21-35.

Goy, R.W., Wallen, K., and Goldfoot, D.A. Social factors affecting the development of mounting behavior in male rhesus monkeys. In Montagna, W. and Sadler, W.A. (Eds.) *Reproductive Behavior*. New York: Plenum, 1974, pp. 223-247.

Harlow, H.F. and Lauersdorf, H.E. Sex differences in passion and play. *Perspectives in Biology and Medicine*, 1974, 17, 348-360.

Joslyn, W.D. Androgen-induced social dominance in infant female rhesus monkeys. *Journal of Child Psychology and Psychiatry*, 1973, 14, 137-145.

Maccoby, E. and Jacklin, C. *The Psychology of Sex Differences*. Stanford, CA: Stanford University Press, 1974.

Mitchell, G. Attachment differences in male and female infant monkeys. *Child Development*, 1968, 39, 611-620.

Mitchell, G. *Behavioral Sex Differences in Nonhuman Primates*. New York: Van Nostrand Reinhold, 1979.

Nash, J. *Developmental Psychology: A Psychobiological Approach* (2nd Edition). Englewood Cliffs, NJ: Prentice-Hall, 1978.

Owens, N.W. A comparison of aggressive play and aggression in free-living baboons, *Papio anubis*. *Animal Behaviour*, 1975, 23, 757-765.

Williams, J.H. *Psychology of Women: Behavior in a Biosocial Context*. New York: W.W. Norton, 1977.

4
Puberty

We have followed an ontogenetic sequence in describing the relationship between gender and behavior (from prenatal androgen, to postnatal reinforcement, to modeling, to constraints-on-learning, and to cognitive developmental factors). We all know, however, that there are some discontinuities in human hormonal development that occur following childhood. At puberty, hormones once again become important determinants of behavior.

In physical and sexual maturation, the ontogeny of the pubertal processes vary temporally from species to species. The pubertal process in some species extends from birth to initial ovulation. Gender differences seen during development are not static patterns but are ever-changing processes (cf. Mason, 1976). Sex differences change with age as well as with the situation. Sometimes they even reverse (Wolfheim, 1977).

Prenatal hormones determine the path of development for the hypothalamus and pituitary gland at puberty. The mechanism that controls the onset of puberty is probably present during fetal development and is androgen dependent. Still, different behavioral sex differences develop at different times. Each species, each individual may have its own temporally consistent pattern (cf. Mitchell, 1979). Ontogenetic changes in the physiological processes that produce sex differences have not been studied very extensively.

Primitive primates mature more rapidly than do advanced primates. Tree shrews reach puberty in three (females) to four months (males). Certain behaviors are not seen prior to puberty but are seen following puberty. Some behaviors associated with tree shrew scent marking appear at puberty in males and castration reduces their frequency of occurrence. In the bushbaby (a prosimian), females (200 days) also reach puberty sooner than do males (one year). A bushbaby aggressive pattern including a special call and urine-marking is seen in adult males. Preadolescent males do not display the pattern.

Prosimian primates are different from monkeys and apes in that females past puberty do not menstruate. Among the primitive New World monkeys this is also true but among the more advanced New World monkeys, the females begin to show what looks like primitive menstruation at puberty (Mitchell, 1979).

In the primitive New World marmosets and tamarins, puberty develops between 300 and 500 days of age. Sexual play increases between pubescent males and females whereas in adulthood there is little play between the members of a monogamous pair. In pubescent play, males initiate and approach whereas females withdraw but encourage. Odoriforous glands in the skin of the circumgenital and sternal areas in both sexes develop at puberty (Mitchell, 1979).

As noted above, more advanced New World monkeys show primitive menstruation at puberty. In the female squirrel monkey the size of the pelvis increases at puberty; and, in both males and females a preference for same-sex clustering develops. Regardless of hormonal status, adult squirrel monkeys show a like-sex preference (see Mitchell, 1979 for primary references).

In capuchins of the New World, young pubescent males (but not females) may leave the natal group and join new groups. Solitary males are also seen. Females reach sexual maturity by the end of the third year, at which time they develop a very large clitoris. Spider monkey females also develop a large clitoris.

In New World howler monkeys, females do not reach maturity until four or five and males not until six or eight years. The more advanced the primate, the more prolonged the period of immaturity. Overall life spans also increase in the more advanced forms (Mitchell, 1979).

All Old World monkey females menstruate at puberty. Among the Old World arboreal Colobinae, the transition from adolescence to adulthood is accompanied by a substantial amount of aggression for males. Young subordinate males frequently start territorial clashes in some species and wounding is common in pubescent males. In many species, vocalizations change at puberty so that calls are emitted by adult but not by preadult males. Subadult males do not emit certain loud calls until they leave the natal troop at maturation.

In the talapoin *(Miopithecus talapoin)*, already mentioned, sex differences seen prior to puberty reverse following puberty. Preadolescent males are more aggressive, assertive, and active than are females, but adult males are, if anything, less aggressive, assertive, and active than their female counterparts.

Most Old World monkey males leave their natal groups after puberty and live either a solitary existence or join all-male groups. This seems to be a normal developmental phase for males but not for females. There are also coloration changes seen at this time. For example, in the patas monkey *(Erythrocebus patas)*, the scrotum becomes blue and the perianal skin scarlet (resulting in the so-called red, white, and blue display).[1] At the onset of puberty young patas so adorned are often attacked by adult males. Typically one does not see Old World adult females attacking pubescent females (Mitchell, 1979).

Hormonal correlates of behavior at puberty have been evaluated most completely in the terrestrial rhesus monkey *(Macaca mulatta)*. As we have already seen, many sex differences, including some appearing at puberty, are preset by prenatal androgens. Postnatally castrated rhesus males still show mounting and the normal pubertal decrease in play. However, postnatal castrates do not display penile erection, aggression and yawning as frequently as do noncastrates. The increases in these behaviors seen in intact male rhesus *do* depend upon increasing androgens at puberty. Adding androgens to rhesus castrates before puberty produces physically precocious two-year-old males (see Mitchell, 1979).

Pubescent male rhesus are more aggressive toward infants than are pubescent females. Aggression (of all kinds) shows a sharp increase at puberty in both sexes, but it increases more in males than in females.

Female rhesus in the wild reach puberty at around one year earlier than do males. Up to puberty and following puberty females emit more clear calls for social contact than do males. However, when females have already reached puberty and the males have not, the sex difference disappears, primarily because such vocalizations decrease at puberty in both sexes but in females first (see Mitchell, 1979). Male puberty in captivity may be seen somewhat earlier, however, because males in the wild may be prevented from expressing it by the older males.

As in many Old World arboreal species, wounding in rhesus peaks

---

[1]Vervet males also have a red, white and blue display.

during the transition months between puberty and adulthood, particularly in the mating season. Wounds are more serious in males but young females are also sometimes hurt. Intertroop interaction *increases* at puberty in males, but *decreases* at puberty in females.

Male rhesus monkeys develop huge canines at maturity, females do not. Males also become much larger. Sexual maturity in some rhesus males in captivity occurs by three years of age.[2] At approximately three, the concentration of testosterone in the male reaches the adult blood level, but shows no seasonal fluctuation for the first 1½ years. The sexual performance of the young male remains well below that of the adult. Especially in males there is a prolonged transition period to adulthood. At four or five years of age they join all-male peripheral groups, become solitary, or join new groups.

Females remain with the natal group. In some females, puberty can occur as early as age two years. Sexual swelling is prominent at puberty. With increased estrogen levels at puberty in the females, responses to stress begin to change. Estrogens can exert sensitizing or stimulating effects in the pituitary-adrenal system while testosterone inhibits this system. Sex differences in ACTH-response (adrenocorticotrophic hormone) become more pronounced as subadult females approach sexual maturity (Sassenrath, 1970, p. 296).

As females become adult, they hold a dominance rank just below that of their own mothers. Males initially rank near the mother but then either gain in rank, drop in rank, or leave the group.

Other species of macaques show changes similar to those outlined for the rhesus, although there are some slight species differences in ages of maturity. In addition, in the bonnet macaque *(M. radiata)*, males do not leave the natal group and become solitary. In the toque macaque *(M. sinica)*, males change troops, but do not become solitary. Some male macaques change troops five to six times in a lifetime. Surprisingly, there are occasional "tradition drifts" in regards to sex differences in peripheralization. For example, in the present-day Barbary macaques *(M. sylvana)* on Gibraltar, it is the adolescent females that are largely peripheralized or isolated from other troop members. This is in contrast to all other studies of macaques (see Mitchell, 1979 for primary references).

In baboons *(Papio spp.)*, sexual maturity is reached at about four

---

[2]The age of menarche in female macaques born in captivity and perhaps the age of puberty in males has steadily declined through a period of years in captivity. This may be a change due to diet or an adaptation to "domestication" (Boice, 1973).

years of age for both sexes, but males are not physically or socially mature until almost eight. Social structure varies considerably from species to species. Some baboons live in harems, others in multimale troops.

The monogamous lesser apes *(Hylobates spp., Symphalangus spp.)* have developmental rates like those seen in Old World monkeys but they show little physical sexual dimorphism in size. However, some species are sexually dimorphic in coloration. *Hylobates lar pileatus* (a subspecies of gibbon) have dark colored adult males and pale colored adult females. Both sexes are pale at birth and darken with age, but only the females revert to pale coloration at puberty. Both siamangs and gibbons show peripheralization of both sexes at puberty.[3]

The great apes (common chimpanzee, pygmy chimpanzee, gorilla, and orangutan) also show behavioral and structural changes at puberty. FSH levels for female infant chimpanzees are cyclical; for males they are not. In the juvenile period this sex difference disappears, but reappears at puberty. Common chimpanzee menarche begins at six to eight years at which time sexual swelling occurs. Female chimpanzees remain with their mothers throughout adolescence, give birth to their first infants at approximately 13 years of age, and return to stay with their mothers between estrus periods for life.

The male common chimpanzee reaches puberty at seven to eight at which time the male begins to travel away from the mother but not for more than a few days until he is ten. Social maturity in the male is reached at 15 years of age.

Lowland and mountain gorillas reach puberty at 5½ to 8 in females and five to nine years for males. An accompanying pubertal growth period lasts much longer in males than in females. Females show only slight swelling. During the gorilla's puberty, heterosexual sexual play occurs frequently, with the female initiating most of it. First babies are delivered at over 11 years in most gorillas, but one female in captivity gave birth as early as eight. Puberty in captivity may occur earlier than it does in the wild. There is true menstruation in all lesser and great apes.

---

[3] Monogamy often exists because: (1) A female cannot rear her young without the aid of conspecifics, and/or (2) the carrying capacity of the habitat allows for only 1 adult female in the same home range. In such cases, the young often exhibit delayed sexual maturation in the presence of the parents so that only the adult pair breeds and the older juvenile aids in rearing younger siblings (babysitting) (see Kleiman, 1977).

HUMAN PUBERTY

There has been a debate in the literature concerning whether or not the term *menstrual* cycle should be used to describe the cycles of monkeys, apes, and humans, or be reserved for humans. Some prefer to use the term *estrous* cycle for nonhuman primates. We see no need to use different terms.

With regard to onset of puberty, there is increased delay as we ascend from prosimians, to monkeys, to apes, to humans. In some nonhuman primates in captivity, animals are reaching puberty at earlier and earlier ages. This finding is similar to what has been termed the "secular trend" in humans. Throughout the world today, people are becoming sexually mature at younger ages, possibly as a function of better diets, but also probably because of an adaptation to "domestication" (Boice, 1973).

There are also some similarities between nonhuman primates and people with regard to sex differences in growth rates. Females mature earlier and males have a more prolonged pubertal growth spurt than do females in many species of primates including people.

Another similarity between people and other primates concerns increased aggression in adolescents, particularly in males. This has been attributed at least in part to dramatic increases in androgens. Androgens sharply increase in both boys and girls at eight to ten years of age, but in boys they reach *twice* the level of girls. Estrogens increase dramatically in girls at age eleven but do not become cyclical until 18 months prior to menarche. A growth spurt accompanies this change in estrogen.

Peripheralization of males at puberty is common in primates and this is to some extent also true of people. There is a greater relative frequency of exclusively subadult human male groups compared to subadult human female groups.

Human mating systems are somewhere between the polygyny of macaques and the monogamy of gibbons, although we are probably more monogamous than polygynous. The tendency toward delayed sexual maturation and baby-sitting seen in monogamous nonhuman primates is also seen in humans. Of course, political and economic factors become important in human marriages.

Puberty is a process during which hormonal events regulated by the hypothalamus result in a rapid acceleration of growth, the appearance of new secondary sex characteristics, and the maturation of the reproductive systems. Menarche occurs late in this process, usually after the peak of the growth spurt. The timing of puberty is controlled by the hypothalamus. In females, hypothalamic action is cyclic, in males it is not. The *innate potential* for cyclicity in the mammalian brain is preserved in the female and destroyed by prenatal androgen in the male. The onset of the process of puberty cannot be dated precisely, the changes occur gradually over several years beginning prenatally. In the United States, the average age of *menarche* is thirteen.

Menarche and menstruation are related to fear and mistrust of women in the male human being. Historically speaking, women have been hidden at such times, e.g., menarcheal girls must not touch the earth or see the sun. (see Williams, 1977).

We will not go into the physiological details of control of the human menstrual cycle here. Suffice it to say that the cycle is controlled by a feedback system involving the hypothalamus, the pituitary gland, the ovaries, and their hormones. Important points to be made are: (1) That the menarcheal event has great significance for human females, and (2) that this event is somehow related to distrust of women by males. An analogous critical event in males does not exist, unless "wet dreams" or first ejaculations could be considered such. As far as we know, however, the latter have not been given a negative symbolic significance. At this level of comparison, the pubertal process of females *is* marked by a unique event, while that of the male's *is not.*

REFERENCES

Boice, R. Domestication. *Psychological Bulletin,* 1973, 80 (3), 215-230.

Kleiman, D.G. Monogamy in mammals. *The Quarterly Review of Biology,* 1977, 52, 39-69.

Mason, W.A. Primate social behavior: Pattern and process. In Masterson, R.B., et al. (eds.) *Evolution of Brain and Behavior in Vertebrates.* Hillsdale NJ: Lawrence Erlbaum Associates, 1976, pp. 425-455.

Mitchell, G. *Behavioral Sex Differences in Nonhuman Primates.* New York: Van Nostrand Reinhold, 1979.

Sassenrath, E.M. Increased adrenal responsiveness related to social stress in rhesus monkeys. *Hormones and Behavior,* 1970, 1, 283-298.

Williams, J.H. *Psychology of Women: Behavior in a Biosocial Context.* New York: W.W. Norton, 1977.

Wolfheim, J.H. Sex differences in behavior in a group of captive juvenile talapoin monkeys *(Miopithecus talapoin). Behavior,* 1977, 63, 110-128.

5
Private vs. Public Attention

We noted in the last chapter that at puberty, male primates of many species tend to become peripheralized from the core of the group, become solitary, or join new groups more than do females. These differences between males and females, as we shall see, develop out of the following tendencies (from Mitchell, 1979): (1) The tendency for males to seek more active and rougher playmates (away from mothers with infants); (2) the tendency for mothers to permit their male infants greater independence; (3) the tendency for mothers to punish, reject, or withdraw from male infants more than they do from female infants; (4) the tendency toward competition-aggression in males which is not as strongly developed in females; and (5) the evolutionary "need" for outbreeding to encourage genetic variability.

As we will also see, the overall sex difference in peripheralization seen in nonhuman primates is also evident in such important evolutionary developments as those involving gender differences in infant care, in social spacing, in vigilance, in group protection, in territoriality, in interactions with strangers, in travel, in predation (hunting), in grooming, in vocalization, in visual communication, in responses to stress, and in vulnerability and mortality (Mitchell, 1979). The pattern of gender differences seen in the primate order appears to be consistent. Gender differences in peripheralization and related behaviors are produced by biological-experiential factors interacting to evolve and develop females who direct their attention centripetally (into the social group) and toward *private* interpersonal events and males who direct their attention centrifugally (out of the natal group) and toward strangers or toward *public* intergroup events.[1]

---

[1]A book dealing with primate social structure and attention has been published by Chance and Larsen (1976). The reader may wish to consult this or Mitchell (1979) for evidence concerning the primate gender differences alluded to above.

In humans, too, there is said to be a peripheral subadult male stage of development analogous to that seen in many other primates. Lockard and Adams (1977) analyzed the various age/sex groupings in *public* places in over 10,000 different groups of people. They reported a greater relative frequency of exclusively subadult male groups when compared to subadult female groups.

The ontogenetic beginnings of these peripheralization tendencies are seen in early sex differences in human play. There is more rough-and-tumble play in young boys than in young girls, as early as three years of age. Moreover, boys perform more play *outdoors* than do girls (Sanders and Harper, 1976). One does not *have* to invoke socio-biological or even biological explanations for such differences, but the fact is, they do exist.

Perhaps the reader has already anticipated where the above information *could* lead us. If males are inherently or experientially more public than females, this may account in part for their greater success in the working and political world and for the inequality seen in regards to employment, salaries, etc. But patterns of gender differences, especially those seen in nonhuman primates, cannot justify sexism and misogyny. It is one thing to show that differences exist, it is another to assume that such patterns *have* to exist. It is still something else to place more value on one pattern than on the other. Before discussing whether the patterns *have* to exist or considering the question of values, we should look at human cross-cultural data on the private vs. public dichotomy. Are there societies, unlike our own, where women are publicly recognized as equal to or more powerful than men?

Most (perhaps all) contemporary societies are characterized by some degree of male dominance. While women have received considerable recognition in some societies, they have not had publically recognized power surpassing that of men. Sexual asymmetry, in this regard at least, appears to be a universal fact of human life (Rosaldo and Lamphere, 1974).

Such cross-cultural evidence does *not* mean that anatomy is destiny, or that gender tells us all about our social world. For aware humans, biology is *interpreted* by norms and by cultural or societal expectations. People, unlike nonhuman primates, can (and do) alter their biological constitutions through symbolic forms like language. "Human biology *requires* human culture" (Rosaldo and Lamphere, 1974, p. 5). Even the behavior of the two sexes within a single sexually dimorphic nonhuman primate species varies depending on the environment in which the species is observed (Mitchell, 1979). Non-human primates display impressive potentials to adopt new forms of social relationships. What does this augur for *Homo sapiens?* Biological evidence taken from primate studies cannot shed light on contemporary human forms of social life unless we recognize the true potential for variability in the primates. Just as human biology requires culture, so does nonhuman primate biology require variability, potential for alternate social roles, and in some species, self-awareness and culture.[2]

Given these tenets, we should not be quick to let our sciences—be they primatology, sociology, or whatever—be swayed by societal stereotypes. Rather, our sciences (and our societies) should celebrate the potential of each individual, regardless of gender. After all, it is the potential of the individual which has made it possible for both nonhuman and human primate forms to evolve.

It is our view (via Rosaldo, 1974) that it is not necessary (or natural) to accept that in every human culture women must or should be subordinate to men. The "domestic" (centripetal, non-peripheralized) orientation of women and the "public" ties of men have and still do reinforce domination by men. Women are tied to domestic activities because they are mothers. However, birth control, the women's movement, and other contemporary factors (which are new examples of primate variability, potential and culture) have probably set human society moving in a direction heretofore not taken in the history of humanity. We do *not* feel that sociobiology will phagocytize the cultural sciences. The hallmark of the primates, especially the human primates, is that they control biology, not the other way around. Once beyond domestic limits, women gain in sense of value. Once within the home, men recognize the value of the private sphere.

---

[2]The evidence for this assertion will be seen in subsequent chapters.

REFERENCES

Chance, M.R.A. and Larsen, R.R. (Eds.). *The Social Structure of Attention.* London: Wiley, 1976.

Lockard, J.S. and Adams, R.M. Peripheral males: A primate model for a human subgroup. Paper presented at the *Animal Behavior Society* meeting, University Park, Pennsylvania, June, 1977.

Mitchell, G. *Behavioral Sex Differences in Nonhuman Primates.* New York: Van Nostrand Reinhold, 1979.

Rosaldo, M.Z. and Lamphere, L. (Eds.). *Woman, Culture, and Society.* Stanford CA: Stanford University Press, 1974.

Rosaldo, M.Z. Woman, Culture, and Society: A theoretical overview. In Rosaldo, M.Z. and Lamphere, L. (Eds.). *Woman, Culture and Society.* Stanford, CA: Stanford University Press, 1974, pp. 17-42.

Sanders, K.M. and Harper, L.V. Free-play fantasy behavior in preschool children: Relations among gender, age, season, and location. *Child Development,* 1976, 47, 1182-1185.

6
Sex Hormones in Adulthood

As we have seen, prenatal male sex hormones (androgens) are important in sexual differentiation. Sex hormones also play a role in behavioral development at puberty, including increased peripheralization of males. In adulthood, too, sex hormones affect the behaviors of male and female nonhuman and human primates. The effects are often cyclical, but we will reserve the discussion of cyclicity for a later chapter.

All primates, including people, have essentially the same basic sex hormones. These were listed and defined in a previous chapter (see Table 2-1). How are these hormones related to adult behavior?

PROSIMIAN BEHAVIOR

As in birds and small mammals, sex hormones are concentrated and retained in certain neurons of the prosimian brain, especially in the basal hypothalamic and amygdaloid areas. Increased output of male sex hormones at puberty in male prosimians increases scent-marking behavior associated with territoriality. Also, in prosimians, as in other small mammals, there is a definite relationship between hormones and reproductive behavior. Mating is often restricted to brief periods coinciding with vaginal estrus. Relative to more advanced primates, prosimians show minimal emancipation of sexual behavior from adult hormonal influences (see Mitchell, 1979).

NEW WORLD MONKEYS (SEE MITCHELL, 1979)

At puberty, sex hormones increase dramatically in the marmoset and tamarin; however, with adult animals present there is a suppression of testosterone in juvenile males and a suppression of progesterone in juvenile females.

Male marmosets carry and care for infants regularly. Castration has no effect on this behavior. In the hormones of pregnancy, marmosets have a hormonal pattern closer to the human's than do macaques.

In squirrel monkeys, estrogen increases affiliative behavior, social contact, and grasping of males in females. Estrogenized females elicit more male following and approaching than do nonestrogenized females. Progesterone has the reverse effect.

There are neurological sex differences related to sex hormones in the squirrel monkey (e.g., differences in the size of neurons in the amygdala). Estrogen increases the responsiveness to vaginal stimulation of some cells in the central nervous system. Biogenic amines (e.g., dopamine, epinephrine, etc.), serving as neurotransmitters, are differentially affected by different sex hormones. The distribution of sex hormone-concentrating cells in the squirrel monkey brain is like that reported for prosimians and other small mammals.

Squirrel monkey males (and some other New World monkey males) have higher absolute levels of testosterone than do rhesus monkey males. There is a correlation between dominance and testosterone in squirrel monkeys but the evidence for it is not as good as the evidence for the correlation in macaques.

RHESUS MONKEYS (SEE MITCHELL, 1979 FOR PRIMARY REFERENCES)

Male rhesus who are defeated in fights show testosterone levels which are lower than they were prior to the fight. Victorious males show up to a threefold increase in plasma testosterone. There is some evidence that changes in physical secondary sex characteristics affect dominance but structural changes are not necessary once the dominance rank has shifted. The androgen DHTP (dihydrotestosterone propionate) seems to be particularly implicated in dominance change.

Sexual behavior is also affected by testosterone. There is often an *overall* positive correlation between rhesus dominance, rank, and ejaculatory mounts. However, there is no consistent relationship between an *individual's* testosterone levels and his level of sexual activity.

The potential for rhesus bisexual behavior persists even in those males with the highest testosterone levels. However, the castration of a subadult male rhesus decreases ejaculatory performance more than does the castration of a full adult male. In full adults, ejaculation continues for two years following castration. Testosterone administration cannot completely compensate for castration because the testes also produce androgens other than testosterone (e.g., dihydrotestosterone for one).

Play behavior is apparently diminished by the large increase in testosterone at puberty. If castrated prior to puberty, male rhesus continue to show high levels of play into their sixth and seventh years.

Testosterone levels in rhesus are directly related to levels of aggression in adulthood. That is not to say that testosterone causes aggression; however, it does facilitate it. In rhesus, testosterone and DHTP are implicated in behavior aimed at achieving and/or maintaining dominance but not in dominance status itself.

Although not completely dependent upon sex hormones, male rhesus behavior is sensitive to them. However, the male rhesus also shows independence from hormones to some degree. For optimum playful, sexual, dominant, aggressive performance, hormones alone are not enough.

In the rhesus female, copulation is seen during pregnancy. Even though there are high levels of gonadotropic hormones during pregnancy, factors other than hormonal ones are often at work. On the other hand, outside of pregnancy, estrogen-sensitive vaginal secretions in the female rhesus are said to be smelled by males and to increase sexual activity, a pheromonal effect (see Michael, 1969).

But some females are sexually attractive to males regardless of pheromonal effects, even though they may be rendered even *more* attractive by estrogen. Female receptivity and initiative are affected somewhat differentially by sex hormones. In *proceptivity,* the female actively seeks the male; in *receptivity,* she accepts the approaches of the male but does not initiate; in *attractivity,* she is attractive but not receptive or proceptive. Proceptivity is increased by both androgen and estrogen; receptivity is increased by estrogen, is unaffected by progesterone and testosterone but is decreased by DHTP. Attractivity is increased by estrogen and decreased by progesterone. Presumably, many of these effects are somewhat affected by pheromonal processes. However:

> the particular odor of a partner is not the determining characteristic which initiates sexual activity. Rather, either by innate mechanisms, or, much more likely, by associative learning, particular odors may be one additional cue, not always reliable, which tells the male something about his chances of success with a potential sexual partner (Goldfoot et al., 1976, p. 27).

Still, hormones do affect adult female rhesus behavior. Sexual solicitations peak at midcycle and the female sexual skin reddens at this time. Aggression between the sexes becomes redirected if estrogen levels are high, but does not become redirected if progesterone is high. Estrogen administration increases a female's lever pressing for males, progesterone decreases it.

Female hormones also affect the rhesus female's libido. A clutching reaction seen in adult female rhesus sexual behavior has been shown to be homologous to the human female orgasm. Estrogen increases this response, progesterone decreases it. Testosterone also increases female libido while DHTP decreases it.[1] DHTP increases female aggressiveness, female dominance, and female weight.

The testosterone in the intact female rhesus comes primarily from her adrenal cortex. It is known that adrenalectomy decreases female sexual responsiveness in the rhesus. Testosterone from the female adrenal increases libido by affecting the female's central nervous system via the biogenic amine neurotransmitter serotonin. After adrenalectomy, when female libido goes down, serotonin can reverse the effects of the operation on sexual responsiveness (see Mitchell, 1979, for many primary references).

There is an interesting difference between the effects of the male and female sex hormones on the rhesus female. Estrogen increases receptivity, proceptivity, and attractivity. Testosterone increases only her receptivity and proceptivity. An androgenized rhesus female is not attractive to the male. Estrogen affects attractiveness through

---

[1]It is interesting that in studies of the prenatal effects of androgens, DHTP produces less genital virilization but just as much behavioral masculinization as does testosterone. Also, in dominance studies DHTP increases dominance but not sexual behavior.

external changes in the female's genitalia, coloration, and appearance.

There are sex differences in rhesus monkeys in regards to the way the brain responds to hormones. Depending upon early prenatal androgen, the hypothalamus is organized with built in cyclicity or with no cyclicity. The metabolism of female hormones by the hypothalamus and pituitary gland changes at puberty in the female rhesus; it does not change with maturity in males. There is also evidence that there are sex differences in the amygdala. Lesions there decrease aggression in males yet increase aggression in females. Rhesus have sex-hormone-concentrating neurons in the same preoptic hypothalamic and limbic neural structures as do prosimians and squirrel monkeys (see Mitchell, 1979).

RESEARCH ON OTHER OLD WORLD MONKEYS

One hormone studied in *Macaca nemestrina* females (pigtail monkeys) has not been discussed as yet. Following the birth of her infant, the pigtail female shows increased levels of plasma *prolactin* (a hormone important in nursing). Behavioral preference for her infant apparently coincides with the increased titers of prolactin, particularly at around ten days following delivery.

Testosterone has been linked to baldness in adult males of the stumptail species (*M. arctoides*). In this species, testosterone is retained less by hair follicles above the forehead than by terminal follicles. Stumptail behavior seems to be less dependent on hormones than is that of rhesus.

In many other Old World monkeys there are also structural and coloration changes which are correlated with differing hormonal levels. In mangabeys *(Cercocebus albigena)* there is sexual swelling. There is a change in the nose patch from black to white in female patas monkeys *(Erythrocebus patas)* (see Mitchell, 1979).

GREAT APES

During pregnancy the female chimpanzee (*Pan troglodytes*) is said to be more gentle than when she is not pregnant. Estrogen treatment increases her aggressiveness, her dominance, and causes a reddening and swelling of her sex skin. There is also some evidence that testosterone in males is positively correlated with dominance changes.

Very little research has been done on the great apes with respect to hormones and behavior.

HOMO SAPIENS

At puberty, girls begin to produce male sex hormones as well as female sex hormones, though not as much as do boys. Androgens from the human female's adrenal glands are responsible for the growth of pubic and underarm hair in girls. Androgenic hormones are at their highest just after sunrise for both men and women. At this time many men and women have increased sexual feelings. Estrogen, however, is also highest in the morning in both sexes. Androgens may be more important for sexual desire. In humans, removal of the ovaries does not affect desire, removal of the adrenals does.

In humans, there is some evidence that androgens also play a role in the status processes of both males and females. Testosterone has been related to human aggression, particularly in adolescent males. Interestingly enough, despite the strong evidence of a link between androgens and aggression in male animals, it has rarely occurred to researchers that *male* mood swings could be hormonally caused, although, as we will see, it has often occurred to them that *women's* moods are so caused. Some men *do* have testosterone cycles, ranging in length from eight to 30 days.

Many physical and psychological changes have been related to the human female's menstrual cycle and to the relative amounts of estrogen and progesterone in a woman's bloodstream. How correct these observations are is the subject of much current debate. A sharp drop in the levels of both estrogen and progesterone occurs at menstruation, at childbirth, and at menopause. Premenstrual depression, postpartum depression, and menopausal depression have been said to stem directly from hormonal changes. However, *all three* of these events are also associated with strong social-emotional pressure. Menstrual myths and taboos, the myth that all mothers should immediately love their babies, and the myth that a non-reproductive woman is somehow not a whole person give reason enough to be depressed, irritable, or weepy without having to look to raging hormones for the answers.

Even if hormones are implicated each woman differs from every other woman in the way she responds to each hormone. *Average* responses mean very little when we are talking about complicated, intelligent, conceptually self-aware individuals. As we noted in our last chapter when discussing sex differences in public vs. private orientation, for aware humans, biology is interpreted by norms and by societal expectations.

The most likely outcome of most of these biology vs. culture debates will probably be that *both* evolutionary-hormonal and societal expectations and pressures are involved, but that the importance of each will depend upon the individual *person* and the *situation* (see Deaux, 1976).

Overall, the evidence for an influence of the human adult sex hormones on sex-typed behavior is good enough to deserve some attention. The evidence for animals is better, however. High testosterone does not make all men violent or sex-crazed maniacs. Nor does low estrogen and progesterone make all menstruating, postnatal, or menopausal women depressed, irritable, or weepy (see Tavris and Offir, 1977).

The evidence for a differential influence of the sex hormones on the central nervous system of humans is also substantial enough to warrant serious consideration. The same areas of the brain implicated in nonhuman primate research are involved in humans. Complete neural sexual dimorphism certainly does not occur, even though human brains do appear to be affected by prenatal testosterone. Most female neural mechanisms appear to be protected from the early androgenic effect in males.

There are target sites in the human hypothalamus for progesterone, estrogen, and testosterone and it is highly likely that human biogenic amine neurotransmitters are affected differentially by sex hormones. Drugs other than sex hormones which affect neurotransmitters also influence sexual and aggressive behaviors. Mood is also affected by the same drugs. Sex hormones are therefore probably of *some* importance to human mental health and emotion. Evidence for a role for sex hormones in thinking, intelligence, etc., is not as good and is controversial, to say the least. Two things are clear with regard to sex hormones and the brain:

1. There are biologically based sex differences in the brain, but
2. Sex or gender differences in behavior cannot be explained solely in these terms.

Simple explanations cannot account for differences seen in all individuals, in all situations, at all times. Even rats, guinea pigs, and beagles show individuality in behavior that is situationally dependent.

REFERENCES

Deaux, K. *The Behavior of Women and Men.* Monterey, CA: Brooks/Cole, 1976.

Goldfoot, D.A., Kravetz, M.A., Goy, R.W., and Freeman, S.K. Lack of effect of vaginal lavages and aliphatic acids in ejaculatory responses in rhesus monkeys: Behavioral and chemical analyses. *Hormones and Behavior,* 1976, 7, 1-27.

Michael, R.P. The role of pheromones in the communication of primate behavior. *Recent Advances in Primatology,* 1969, 1, 101-107.

Mitchell, G. *Behavioral Sex Differences in Nonhuman Primates.* New York: Van Nostrand Reinhold, 1979.

Tavris, C. and Offir, C. *The Longest War: Sex Differences in Perspective.* New York: Harcourt Brace Jovanovich, 1977.

7
Sexuality in Nonhuman Primates

A useful concept for sexual behavior analysis advanced by Beach (1976) is the *principle* of S-R *complementarity* which states that, independent of the genetic sex of an animal, a masculine stimulus will elicit a feminine response and a feminine stimulus will elicit a masculine response. If a male primate sees another male primate presenting, he is likely to mount (the complementary behavior). In both sexes there are neural representations for both male and female sexual behavior patterns (Beach's hypothesis of neural bisexuality). Prenatal androgen does not completely do away with a male's potential for female sexual behavior.

The sexual present in nonhuman primates, however, has come to have nonreproductive as well as reproductive meaning. The sexual present is used as a sign of submission, appeasement, or of friendship. The hypothesis of neural bisexuality also encourages us to think in terms of varying degrees of masculinity and femininity in sexual behavior within the same individual. Male presenting is viewed as normal, as is female mounting.

Among most nonhuman primates, the adult female is said to be in *estrus* when she is physiologically and behaviorally ready for mating, usually during that part of her monthly cycle when she is fertile. Each species of primate has its own set of reproductive postures and communicative acts, however.

PROSIMIANS (SEE MITCHELL, 1979, FOR PRIMARY REFERENCES)

Many prosimian females show a postpartum estrus. In the days directly before a female gives birth, the male shows increasing sexual interest. The female becomes receptive to this attention, however, only after she has delivered her infant. Precopulatory displays of prosimians include short, darting runs by females, male "courtship dances," circling, stamping, and vocalizations. Play-grappling between the sexes also often precedes copulation. Licking of the female's vulva by the male may occur before coitus, during which the male usually mounts and grips the fur on the female's neck with his mouth. The female arches her back (lordosis) to permit intromission. Female prosimians are usually attractive to males long before and long after they are receptive. Some aggression typically occurs between the two sexes toward the end of estrus. Estrous females, on the other hand, show proceptivity to the extent that they will sometimes mount both males and females.[1]

In some prosimians there is a foot clasp during the sexual mount. In the foot clasp, the male's feet grasp the female's ankles in order to get up high enough for intromission. In some species there are many mounts to ejaculation (MME—multiple mount ejaculators). in others there may be only one mount (SME—single mount ejaculators).

Prosimian males and females frequently scent-mark with sexually different scents. Estrus includes female sexual swelling, flushing or coloration changes, vaginal opening and vaginal discharge. While mounting, males often emit loud and/or excitable vocalizations, particularly at the time of ejaculation. Genital self-grooming follows copulation for both sexes.

The above are typical prosimian patterns. There are exceptions to these. For example, the estrus female slow loris *(Nycticebus coucang)* hangs upside-down under a branch as she presents. Copulation also takes place upside-down.

---

[1]The appearance of female mounting in tree shrews has also been related to high stress levels under crowded conditions.

NEW WORLD MONKEYS (SEE MITCHELL, 1979, FOR PRIMARY REFERENCES)

The monogamous marmoset female shows no obvious signs of swelling. She has a postpartum estrus like the prosimians. Courtship displays include mutual following, arched backs, extended limbs, and piloerection. There is scent marking, after which the male approaches, the female crouches, and the two lipsmack at each other, making contact tongue-to-tongue and licking each other's faces and genitals (this is not true of tamarins). Tongue movements occur throughout copulation which occurs in an SME mount.

Dominant heterosexual pairs of marmosets will interfere with the sexual activity of subordinate pairs. Brothers or sons of a female are reproductively inhibited by the female. Thus, there is an incest avoidance which is primarily a matter of female choice.

In monogamous and monomorphic species like marmosets, males and females perform many of the same displays. There are fewer sex differences in sex itself when compared to dimorphic species. In addition, sexual behavior in monogamous species occurs *less* frequently while grooming and sleeping together occur *more* frequently than in nonmonogamous species.

In more advanced monogamous New World species like the titi monkeys *(Callicebus spp.)*, or night monkeys *(Aotus spp.)*, there is also no external sexual swelling. The courtship display is absent but the marmosetlike SME pattern still prevails. In these monogamous Cebids there is a strong emotional bond between the male and female. Titi monkeys show clear evidence of "jealousy", particularly the males. Sexual behavior in an established pair is much less frequent than it is in a pair just forming a bond (see Cubicciotti and Mason, 1977).

The nonmonogamous New World monkeys show irregular menstruation. There are vaginal changes in the female but little external swelling. The squirrel monkey female sometimes shows swelling of the external genitalia, however. Courtship displays in males of this species include repeated jumping, opening of the mouth, contraction of abdominal muscles, chasing, tail biting, and genital inspection. Females abduct the thigh, displaying an erect clitoris and emitting some urine.[2] The female initiates by presenting the anogenital region toward the male and looking back over her shoulder toward him.

---

[2]The clitoris of some of the nonmonogamous New World monkey species (e.g., spider monkeys) is huge and pendulous, often making it difficult to tell the sex of the animals.

Squirrel monkeys form *consorts* (temporary mating pairs) which remain together for varying lengths of time. The male displays a foot clasp when mounting and he mounts ten to 25 times before ejaculating (an MME species). Squirrel monkeys have a three-month-long mating season.

Brain-stimulated females often display the same sexual behaviors normally seen in males. This is good support for Beach's "hypothesis of neural bisexuality."

In other nonmonogamous New World monkeys, sexual behavior is very much like that described for squirrel monkeys. In some of these species (e.g., howler monkeys) the mounted female looks back at the mounting male and may reach back to touch him with her hand. Menstruation occurs every 24 to 28 days.

RHESUS MACAQUES (SEE MITCHELL, 1979, FOR PRIMARY REFERENCES)

Rhesus monkeys, like some New World monkeys, form consort pairs. Some bonds are short in duration and weak, others are strong. Female rhesus initiate 70 percent of all close physical contact. The mount includes a foot clasp. Grooming by both the female and the male is seen between mounts. The rhesus is an MME species. Grooming displays affection, strengthens the consort bond, and sexually arouses the partner. Reaching and looking back by the female is common during an ejaculatory mount. When the male ejaculates, he bares his teeth and squeals. The female sometimes squeals and clutches at him.[3]

The male yawns frequently between mounts and eats any ejaculate remaining on his genitals after the ejaculatory mount. Rhesus copulation is primarily seasonal but can occur throughout the year (even during pregnancy).

Bisexuality in rhesus is extensive, especially in males. Ambisexual (bisexual) behavior is also seen in females. At times during homosexual interactions there is a clear preference shown for one individual of the same sex over another individual of the same or other sex. Female homosexuality occurs less often than male homosexuality (cf. Carpenter, 1942).

---

[3]Michael and Zumpe (1971) and others believe that this display is homologous to the human female's orgasm. Symons (1979) disagrees. Goldfoot, et al. (1980) show conclusively that it is an orgasm.

Rhesus monkeys masturbate in the wild as well as in captivity. Males sometimes masturbate even when females are in estrus. Males masturbate more often than do females.

Among rhesus there is an inhibition of mating between mothers and sons, that is, mother-son mating is rare. The incidence of brother-sister mating is also low. As relatedness decreases, sex increases; however, even uncles and nieces show less sex with each other than do unrelated individuals. The avoidance of mating with kin is also maintained by male peripheralization, and by the migration of males away from their natal troops.

OTHER MACAQUES (SEE MITCHELL, 1979, FOR PRIMARY REFERENCES)

Like rhesus monkeys, most other female macaques have 28-day (or longer) menstrual cycles. Consort pairs are formed, but not *all* macaques show the MME pattern (the Japanese and pigtail macaques do, the bonnet and stumptail macaques do not). In the SME species, the male is more likely to initiate contact. In the MME species, the female initiates.

Japanese and pigtail macaque males are peripheralized, may become solitary, and usually change troops. Bonnet males do not.

Females occasionally mount males, but not often. Pigtail macaques display a unique facial expression called the "len" (or "flehmen") in which the male retracts his ears and protrudes his muzzle and lips prior to displaying sexual behavior. Pigtail monkeys have a diurnal sex hormone pattern like that of people. In the pigtail there is conspicuous female swelling.

The stumptail macaque *(M. arctoides)* shows the most variability in sexual behavior in this genus. The stumptail is an SME species but there is much foreplay with mouth and hand prior to a mount. Subadult and juvenile stumptails also harass an older copulating couple.[4]

Stumptails are also unique in that they appear to display a "tieing" at ejaculation, but not to the degree that domestic dogs do. The female stumptail displays orgasm and is often quite active in sexual interactions, especially with younger inexperienced males. An adult female may actively aid such a male by inserting his penis into her vagina.

---

[4]Of course, harassment of copulation by younger animals is not unique to stumptails. It is seen in gorillas and some other primates as well.

Homosexuality is frequently seen in stumptail macaques, including anal intromission and oral-genital sex. These behaviors can be seen in either heterosexual or homosexual behavior. Orgasms in females are especially obvious in homosexual interactions. Homosexuality and heterosexuality occur between animals of all ages. In closed captive colonies the avoidance of incest does not occur.

When the female takes a more active role, she is more likely to have an orgasm. Females (and males) sometimes engage in mutual vaginal or penile masturbation to orgasm. There is also mutual fellatio.

BABOONS AND OTHER OLD WORLD MONKEYS (SEE MITCHELL, 1979, FOR PRIMARY REFERENCES).

Baboons *(Papio spp.)* have a 31- to 32-day menstrual cycle. Their mounts are dorsoventral with foot clasp much like the macaques, and they occur in consort pairs. The chacma baboon *(P. ursinus)* is an MME species but the olive baboon is an SME species.

The hamadryas baboon *(P. hamadryas)* is interesting because mating takes place within stable one-male groups called harems. Mounting is of the MME variety.

Mangabeys *(Cercocebus spp.)* are MME species and breed much as do rhesus. Vervets *(Cercopithecus aethiops)* are SME. Talapoins *(Miopithecus talapoins)* are unique in that the adult female is more aggressive than is the adult male.

One-male groups are frequently seen among many varieties of Old World monkeys (e.g., gelada baboons, patas, langurs, etc.). The patas monkey *(Erythrocebus patas)* is an MME species. Langurs live in the trees but still display the same basic Old World mounting pattern as do rhesus, including the MME sequence.

APES (SEE MITCHELL, 1979, FOR PRIMARY REFERENCES).

Gibbons *(Hylobates spp.)* and siamangs *(Symphalangus spp.)* are monogamous arboreal Asian lesser apes. Their sexual behavior is rich and varied but infrequent compared to rhesus. Mating postures, however, are either dorsoventral or ventroventral (face to face). In the siamang, at least, the male appears to be a multiple mount ejaculator (MME).

Common chimpanzees *(Pan troglodytes)* show pronounced mid-cycle swelling in the females. They are an SME species in which the female crouches and the male thrusts dorsoventrally.

Adult-infant and infant-adult sex is seen, particularly between infants and adult females who are *not* their mothers. Masturbation is frequently seen in both sexes. Tools are used in autoeroticism. Mother-son copulation is infrequent. In sex play, young animals kiss each other, manipulate each other's genitals with hands or mouth, and thrust at one another. Sometimes a male mounts another male's head and thrusts into his face.

Pygmy chimpanzees *(P. paniscus)* are much more variable in their sexual behaviors than are common chimpanzees. Their sex is more likely to occur away from the time of ovulation; in fact, the female's genitals remain swollen even following menses. Mounts are either dorsoventral or ventroventral. Female homosexual ventroventral thrusting bouts are common in which clitoral erection, gestures, and vocalizations are obvious. Copulation is often associated with food sharing. Mutual face-peering or eye-to-eye contact is common in ventroventral copulation. Both the male and the female show thrusting.

Both male and female gorillas *(Gorilla spp.)* masturbate. Sexual behavior is rarely seen between adults and immatures. Female swelling is slight and the cycle is 28 days. Females will copulate when pregnant; and, females, in general, initiate most of the sexual contact. Female orgasm has been said to occur. Both sexes thrust. Females initiate sex by playing with slow, gentle, caressing, wrestling, kissing, and sometimes by sticking their tongue into the male's mouth. They also "back ride" the males. Often they lie on their backs while thrusting, looking at the male, and reaching toward him with one hand held palm up.

Ventroventral (as well as dorsoventral) copulation has been observed in orangutans *(Pongo spp.)*. There is no obvious sexual swelling in the female. Mother-infant sexual behavior, however, is very common in this species. Mothers establish genital contact, mount, and thrust at their infants (male or female) as early as the second week of life. They also provide oral-genital contact for the infant. The female orangutan shows proceptive behavior but is also at times taken by force by the adult male. Orangutans have an extremely diverse and creative sexual repertoire. The duration of each copulation is longer than for other primates and a variety of positions and postural adjustments occur during each copulatory event. Orangutans are unpredictable, tending toward extremes, first lethargic and then almost constantly copulating. Their lethargy, however, may be at least partly an artifact of unstimulating captive environments (Maple, personal communication). Usually, in the wild, males will copulate with a female on sight. Orangutans also masturbate occasionally and use inanimate objects in sex, especially the females.

The sexuality of nonhuman primates is indeed varied, like that of their human cousins which we will discuss next.

REFERENCES

Beach, F.A. Cross-species comparisons and the human heritage. *Archives of Sexual Behavior,* 1976, 5, 469-485.

Carpenter, C.R. Sexual behavior of free-ranging rhesus monkeys *(Macaca mulatta).* II. Periodicity of estrus, homosexual, autoerotic and nonconformist behavior. *Journal of Comparative Psychology,* 1942, 33, 143-162.

Cubicciotti, D.D., III and Mason, W.A. A comparison of heterosexual jealousy responses in *Callicebus* and *Saimiri.* Paper presented at the *American Society of Primatologists* meeting, Seattle, Washington, April 1977.

Goldfoot, D.A., Westerborg-van Loon, H., Groeneveld, W., and Koos Slob, A. Behavioral and physiological evidence of sexual climax in the female stump-tailed macaque *(Macaca arctoides) Science,* 1980, 208, 1477-1479.

Michael, R.P. and Zumpe, D. Patterns of reproductive behavior. In Hafez, E.S.E. (Ed.) *Comparative Reproduction of Nonhuman Primates.* Springfield, Ill: Charles C. Thomas, 1971, pp. 205-242.

Mitchell, G. *Behavioral Sex Differences in Nonhuman Primates.* New York: Van Nostrand Reinhold, 1979.

Symons, D. *The Evolution of Human Sexuality.* New York: Oxford, 1979.

8
Human Sexuality

PRIMATE SIMILARITY

Monkeys differ considerably from humans in their sexual behaviors. The sexual behaviors of the great apes and of humans, however, are remarkably similar. In the courtship patterns of both apes and humans there is eye contact, and nongenital and genital foreplay. The copulation thrusting patterns of both male and female apes are similar to those of humans, although all patterns vary according to the species of ape. There is privacy-seeking in consort relationships and repeated selection of preferred partners in both apes and people. Copulating pairs are harassed by juveniles and there is inhibition of sexual behavior in a male when a more dominant male is present (Gordon Jensen, personal communication). People, however, do not have an estrus so that their sexual activity is less periodic than is that of the great apes. In addition, humans make use of language and fantasy.

With regard to cyclicity, however, apes are *not* totally bound to a sexual cycle. They do copulate during pregnancy and outside of estrus. Even in the rhesus monkey, there is often sexual arousal at menstruation. Moreover, there is some evidence for sexual cyclicity in people, although rising levels of circulating sex hormones are probably not as involved in the human's desire for initiating sexual activity as in the ape's.

In human infancy, sexuality is much like that of infant ape sexuality. At less than one year of age female humans masturbate by using friction of the thighs, objects, or by using direct manipulation. These episodes, with clitoral erections, include grunting, flushing, orgasm, relaxation, pallor, and sweating followed by deep sleep. Male infants also masturbate to orgasm (with no ejaculation). One eleven-month-old boy had 10 orgasms in one hour (see Bakwin, 1973).

As we have seen many primates show incest avoidance (see Demarest, 1977). There is active avoidance of mother-son incest in chimpanzees, primarily by the mother. Overall, in most primates, the chances of mating taking place among kin are much lower than the chances of it occurring outside a geneology.

Among people it is, for the most part, considered boring or dull to marry a brother or sister. Even unrelated children growing up together in the Israeli kibbutzim almost never marry their artificial "sibs." Sometimes, apes captured at infancy and raised together also fail to breed in captivity (Maple, 1980). Thus, there is some evidence for a stimulus saturation or habituation theory of incest avoidance. However, there is also a possibility that incest avoidance in humans may be more a matter of role conflict than of stimulus saturation. If the individual is already a sibling, a parent, or one's child, how can s/he also be a lover? Or, perhaps an element of fear and aggression is important in sex and these are socialized out in normal contacts with kin.

In addition, in people, incest avoidance becomes an incest *taboo.* There is a proscription against inbreeding. People have rules, nonhuman primates do not. Of course, it could still be true that the behaviors are the same but people label them and other primates do not.

Postpartum estrus is also common in nonhuman primates, particularly in the more primitive species. Even in rhesus monkeys and in orangutans, however, the male frequently becomes sexually interested in the female at the time of delivery. In people there is also some recent evidence for sexual arousal at the time of birth. In the so-called natural methods of childbirth (Lamaze, Read, etc.), women often report peak experiences and orgasms while delivering their babies in the presence of their husbands (Tanzer, 1973; Newton, 1973).

As we have seen in previous chapters, the primate order is remarkable for its diversity. Facile generalization from one species of nonhuman primate to another is risky to say nothing of generalization from nonhumans to humans. The best way to learn about a particular species of primate is to study *that* species. People are at least as different from other primates as the other primates are from each other.

HUMAN SEXUALITY IN RECENT HISTORY

Men and women are more alike sexually than was once thought. Both men and women have strong sex drives. The differences between the two appear in the meanings attached to the sexual act (Tavris and Offir, 1977).

Even in Victorian times, with all their rules and taboos, people actually behaved sexually much as they do today, although fewer people participated. They were prudent more in word than in deed. As a consequence, they felt guilty about sex. Freud brought sex out in the open—but *only for men, not for women.*

Kinsey et al. (1948, 1953) and Masters and Johnson (1966) pioneered the scientific study of human sexuality. Kinsey's data were weak in that he slighted poorly educated, rural, and black people. However, Kinsey[1] made it known that so-called perversions were actually quite common and that some of these practices were almost universal.

Kinsey also found that men were more sexually active than were women—they had more partners, more orgasms, more homosexuality, more sexual fantasies, and masturbated more. This was not because men had a stronger sex drive as much as it was a reflection of the greater freedom for males.

Over half the women who had sex before marriage in Kinsey's sample had only one partner (the fiancé). Premarital sex occurred for these women in the context of a serious relationship. Between the 1950s and 1970, however, there was a two-to threefold increase in premarital sex among women, and this increase has continued into the seventies. Despite these increases, men are still more likely to have premarital sex than are women (Tavris and Offir, 1977); and a fourth of the women who have premarital intercourse say that they yielded because of force or a sense of obligation rather than because of desire. They used sex to *prove* their love. "Women . . . use sex to get love; men use love to get sex" (Tavris and Offir, 1977, p. 68). Even today, both sexes still feel that sex without affection is all right for males but not for females. The double standard survives.

Men are also currently more likely to have sex outside of marriage (when married) than are women. However, extramarital sex has increased in both sexes over the last three decades. As in premarital

---

[1]Kinsey was an entomologist. Interestingly enough, so is Sociobiology's E.O. Wilson. An evolutionary-biological background cannot help but predispose one to an interest in sex differences and in sexual behavior itself.

encounters, it may be that many women have extramarital affairs for love rather than for sex. Even mate-swapping is usually at the instigation of the husbands (Tavris and Offir, 1977).

In Kinsey's studies men reported having more sexual fantasies than did women. Women *are* aroused by fantasy. However, they seem to be more susceptible to ordinary movies, romance, and emotion than men, whereas men are more susceptible to pornography. The majority of *both* men and women show physiological signs of sexual arousal to erotica. Men and women are becoming more alike in their responses as women feel more free to respond. It is more permissible for women to enjoy such things today than it was in Kinsey's time (Tavris and Offir, 1977).

Males masturbate more than do females. Female masturbation has, historically, been punished by approved medical practices as severe as clitoridectomy and cauterization. Not so for male masturbation. In recent years, women have begun to masturbate at younger ages and with greater frequency. The practice appears to play a great role in the *normal* sexual development of both males and females. Female orgasms during coitus are dependent to some extent on previous female practice in orgasm in masturbation. Masturbatory orgasms are the easiest kind for women to have. Nine women in ten in Kinsey's sample eventually responded with orgasm to some kind of sexual stimulation (Kinsey, 1953). Despite these data accumulated almost 30 years ago, some gynecology texts still claim that most women are "frigid" (see Tavris and Offir, 1977).

Masters and Johnson (1966) demonstrated that male and female orgasms are physiologically quite similar. In both sexes, arousal leads to genital vasocongestion, muscular tension, and irregular muscle twitches which become rhythmic. Skin flushing, heart pounding, and heavy breathing occur in both males and females. Variability in orgasmic response, however, is greater in women than in men (see Katchadourian, 1974).

The four phases of the orgasmic response are as follows: excitement, plateau, orgasm, and resolution. After ejaculation, males have a refractory period during which they cannot have another erection; women do not have a refractory period. Some women can have as many as 50 orgasms in a row (Masters and Johnson, 1966).

Female orgasms are clitoral. That is, the main site of arousal is the clitoris (which contains as many nerve endings as does the penis). The clitoris is the only organ of any animal that has as its *only* purpose sexual arousal. Despite there being no *physiological* need for a partner, most women still prefer a partner to masturbation. There is more to sex than mechanics and physiology (see Tavris and Offir, 1977).

Girls have historically been less likely to learn about orgasm than have males. Instead, they have learned about romance, beauty, and "catching a husband". Because of social differences, females have come to enjoy sex at later ages than have males. As the double standard gives way, women too become able to enjoy sex at young ages. Women of Mangaia, a South Pacific Polynesian island, have intercourse at 12 or 13 years of age, with several partners. Here the two sexes are much more alike in their orgasmic development than they are in America (see Tavris and Offir, 1977). Orgasms are of some importance to the well-being of women in general. *Willing* involvement in sex is more characteristic of orgasmic females than of non-orgasmic. They do not give in to male pressure, rather, they have a mutual interest in sex with the male. They therefore have a freedom of action and autonomous consent not seen in nonorgasmic females (Williams, 1977). Of course, being orgasmic is also situational.

GETTING THE PARTNERS TOGETHER

Despite the similarities between the two sexes in regard to physiology and orgasmic experience, men and women *do* react differently in heterosexual situations. Even before they become close enough to make love, men and women are attracted to each other for different reasons. Men *say* it is important that their date be *attractive.* For women, the *stated* ideals of intelligence, status, race, religion, character and values, seem to be more important. Assertiveness and dominance are important *stated* characteristics of the ideal date of many women. Many men *say* they have as an ideal a woman who is high on dependency. But when a particular man and a particular woman get together in a particular situation, what they *say* may be very different from what they *do* (Deaux, 1976).

When a date must be arranged, both men and women are inclined to consider their own attractiveness relative to their dates. People prefer to date those of similar physical attractiveness, similar attitudes, and similar values. For men, similar sexual values seem to be especially important; for women similar religious values are important. There is some evidence that the woman plays the greater role in making decisions about similarity of values (Deaux, 1976).

In the beginning of a relationship, women make more eye contact than do men. When a woman does not make eye contact, her male partner views her as less attractive (Deaux, 1976).

Because of social reasons given earlier, one would expect that women would be more romantic than men. Not so. Men are more likely to believe that they would marry their lover regardless of her social position. Women, on the other hand, carefully consider economic security. Women are pragmatic *before* their decision (perhaps marriage, for example) and romantic *after* their decision. Men may operate in exactly the opposite way. In terms of "liking," rather than "loving," women *like* their male lovers more than men like their female lovers (Deaux, 1976).

The chances of a heterosexual relationship developing are improved if there is: (1) Geographical proximity; (2) similarity in attitudes and values; and, perhaps, (3) complementarity of *needs.* We say *perhaps* complementarity of needs because so often this comes to mean that the man is *instrumental* and the woman is *expressive* (see Chapter 1). In an androgynous marriage, however, both partners fulfill both roles. In addition, the factors that keep couples together early in a relationship are often not the same factors which keep them together later in a relationship. People become more alike the longer they are together. Recall that even monogamous marmosets behave differently when the "honeymoon" is over (Deaux, 1976; Mitchell, 1979).

HOMOSEXUALITY

As we have seen, nonhuman primates frequently engage in homosexual behavior. Less frequent among nonhuman primates, however, is a quantitative preference in adults for same-sex vs. different-sex copulation and/or other sexual activity (although Erwin and Maple [1976] have reported on what appears to be a same-sex preference in two rhesus monkey males). What is even less likely among nonhuman primates is an *exclusive* preference for the same sex where all (or nearly all) of the social sex is directed toward a *same*-sex rather than opposite-sex partner.

As in nonhuman primates, homosexual encounters occur very early in the lives of people. Sex play and genital exploration are very common after two or three years of age. At age five, according to recollections of the adults involved, girls are more likely to engage in sociosexual play than are boys. However, by age 12, boys engage in sociosexual play four times as much as girls (Williams, 1977).

Childhood sociosexual activity involves (most commonly) exhibiting and handling the genitals. Most of this is homosexual (60 to 70 percent of it). Homosexual play decreases sharply after puberty, but many adult homosexuals discover their sexual preference in the childhood years (Williams, 1977).

Males are more apt to try a homosexual experience and to be exclusively homosexual than are females. Approximately 4 percent of American adult males and only 1 percent of American adult females are *exclusively* homosexual. Fifty-two percent of the males and 34 percent of the females have had at least one homosexual experience. Males tend to have more short-term homosexual relationships than do females (Tavris and Offir, 1977).

No one knows why some people are homosexual and others are not. Some would say that there is really no such dichotomy. But for *some* people there clearly is. For most people, however, sexual behavior falls on a continuum, with exclusive heterosexuality at one end and exclusive homosexuality at the other (Tavris and Offir, 1977).

Homosexual behavior is no longer viewed as being symptomatic of an illness. Homosexuals engage in all of the same sexual behaviors as do heterosexuals, except with someone of the same sex. They do not fit any stereotypes of personality or appearance—this is particularly true of young, modern homosexuals (Williams, 1977).

Despite increasing acceptance of homosexuality, its incidence has not increased. Homosexuals also exhibit the same range and kinds of psychological disorders as heterosexuals do. Sexual response cycles or orgasms are no different from those seen in heterosexuals. Societal prejudice, persecution, and discrimination *do* cause problems for them, however. Concealment, secrecy, and alienation can hardly be healthy for anyone regardless of sexual preference. Interestingly enough, archaic laws against behavior associated with homosexuals are not enforced even-handedly. However, in this case it is not women who are most often discriminated against, it is men. Kinsey found that, in over a decade in New York City, thousands of males were arrested *and convicted* for homosexual acts while only three females were arrested and *none* convicted (Tavris and Offir, 1977). There are not thousands of male homosexuals for every one female homosexual. The cry of the male in this injustice is particularly in need of being heard by society. This is but one example of many which demonstrate that male liberation from stereotype is as important as is female liberation. Gradually, sometimes very gradually, men and women are realizing this.

REFERENCES

Bakwin, H. Erotic feelings in infants and young children. *American Journal of Diseases of Childhood,* 1973, 126, 52-54.

Deaux, K. *The Behavior of Women and Men.* Monterey, CA. Brooks/Cole, 1976.

Demarest, W.J. Incest avoidance among human and nonhuman primates. In Chevalier-Skolnikoff, S. and Poirier, F.S. (Eds.) *Primate Biosocial Development.* New York: Garland, 1977, pp. 323-342.

Erwin, J. and Maple, T. Ambisexual behavior with male-male anal penetration in male rhesus monkeys. *Archives of Sexual Behavior,* 1976, 5 (1), 9-14.

Katchadourian, H. *Human Sexuality: Sense and Nonsense.* San Francisco: W.H. Freeman, 1974.

Kinsey, A.C., Pomeroy, W.B., and Martin, C.E. *Sexual Behavior in the Human Male.* Philadelphia: Saunders, 1943.

Kinsey, A.C., Pomeroy, W.B. , Martin, C.E., and Gebhard, P.H. *Sexual Behavior in the Human Female.* Philadelphia: Saunders, 1953.

Maple, T. *Orang-utan Behavior.* New York: Van Nostrand Reinhold, 1980.

Masters, W.H. and Johnson, V.E. *Human Sexual Response.* Boston: Little, Brown, 1966.

Mitchell, G. *Behavioral Sex Differences in Nonhuman Primates.* New York: Van Nostrand Reinhold, 1979.

Newton, N. Trebly sensuous woman. In Tavris, C. (Ed.) *The Female Experience.* New York: Ziff-Davis, 1973.

Tanzer, D. Natural childbirth: Pain or peak experience. In Tavris, C. (Ed.) *The Female Experience,* New York: Ziff-Davis, 1973.

Tavris, C. and Offir, C. *The Longest War: Sex Differences in Perspective.* New York: Harcourt Brace Jovanovich, 1977.

Williams, J.H. *Psychology of Women: Behavior in a Biosocial Context.* New York: W.W. Norton, 1977.

9
Birth Control

In most parts of the world human population is still growing at intolerable rates. While from a sociobiological point of view this growth can be viewed as proof of reproductive success, our growing energy and nutritional needs are beginning to tell us that fertility control of some kind is a must. Sex can no longer be justified or explained in terms of reproduction even though it has developed through millennia for that purpose. Sex and/or gender differences of today are indeed ultimately related to human courtship and mating. Sex and/or gender differences of tomorrow may also be ultimately guided by the sexual act itself. But the sexual act will not be as closely linked to reproduction in the future.

A recent popular survey of the sexual attitudes and behaviors of American women and men (Hunt, 1974) noted freer attitudes and an increase in knowledge concerning sexual pleasure or satisfaction in American adults. Correlated with those changes were increases in better birth control methods and the growing women's liberation movement. Women especially were becoming more active and more interested in sex for its own sake rather than for reproduction alone. In fact, along with the woman's increasing interest in sexual pleasure there has been her equally increasing interest in birth control. Fertility potential, in the women's movement, has become contingent upon individual *choice*. Biology as destiny no longer applies. Social pressure as destiny is decreasing. *Individual* decision as a determinant of sexual and reproductive events is ascending, although not in all quarters.

A human female can produce 20 children in her lifetime. In the United States the average woman produced 7.0 in 1800, but only

2.3 in 1971. Increasing participation by women in nondomestic service has helped produce this change. Birth control methods do not account for all of it. Most women of today are choosing to spend only *part* of their adult lives caring for young children. Not only do small children take time away from the nondomestic growth of women as individuals, but successive pregnancies in a very short time are also telling from the perspective of good health. Family size is, of course, also related to standard of living.

Birth control has permitted potential carriers of genetically transmitted disorders to marry and/or have sexual relations without fear. Huntington's chorea, cystic fibrosis, and some anemias are now more likely to be under some degree of *individual* control. Most societies still leave birth control up to the individual. Birth control among the unmarried, particularly among the very young unmarried, is still not extensive. Teenage pregnancies and births are not decreasing as are adult pregnancies and births. In fact, some have likened teenage pregnancies to a modern epidemic (Konner, 1977).

Methods of birth control currently practiced range from complete abstinence from heterosexual genital intercourse to infanticide, the latter of course being illegal and morally repugnant. Abstinence for fertility control need not mean abstinence from sex. Petting, masturbation, and oral-genital sex are still available to one who abstains. A type of partial abstinence called the *rhythm* method, involves abstaining from coitus at around the time of ovulation. Unfortunately, this time varies considerably and rhythm is therefore inaccurate. Even with temperature measurements (A woman's temperature drops then rises a degree at ovulation), the rhythm method is unreliable.

Coitus interruptus, the withdrawal of the penis before ejaculation, is also ineffective. Men frequently do not withdraw in time, pre-ejaculatory secretions of the Cowper's glands can contain viable sperm, and even sperm on the outside of the vulva can find their way into the vagina (Williams, 1977).

Sterilization renders males or females unable to reproduce. Women are surgically sterilized by removal of the uterus (hysterectomy) or ovaries (oophorectomy), or by interruption of the Fallopian tubes (tubal sterilization, tubal ligation). Reversible sterilization can be accomplished by putting small clips on the Fallopian tube which can be removed by surgery. Sterilization in the male is accomplished by making two small incisions in the scrotum to cut, section, or tie the vas deferens (the two sperm-carrying ducts). This is safer and simpler than the female tubal methods and is called vasectomy. A possible problem with surgical sterilization for both sexes is its potential for psychological side effects, none of which are uniform for all people. However, there are not *widespread* emotional aftereffects.

Contraceptives include condoms, diaphragms, intrauterine devices, douches, foams, jellies, and oral contraceptives. Oral contraceptives come in many forms but they all inhibit ovulation by changing normal hormonal blood levels in the woman. Most pills contain a combination of synthetic estrogen and progesterone and act by mimicking pregnancy. Women take the pill for 20 days, then stop. They menstruate about three days later, then resume pill usage on the fifth day of menstruation. This makes a 28-day cycle. There are of course other kinds of pills including *minipills* (only a little progesterone and no estrogen), *morning-after pills* (large amounts of estrogen following possible exposure to pregnancy), *progestagen injections* and *skin implants* for longer term release of hormones, a *monthly pill,* and postcoital pills. Male hormonal pills are in the experimental stages.

Pills produce symptoms associated with elevated hormonal levels. These symptoms include increased breast size, water retention, weight gain, headaches, nausea, and vaginal discharge. Pills produce more regular cycles, however, and they reduce acne. High estrogen pills tend to create feelings of well-being, whereas high progesterone pills sometimes induce feelings of depression. Estrogen has been implicated in thromboembolic disorders (blood clotting). One in 10,000 women on the pill are admitted to hospitals for blood clotting. With regard to both physical and psychological effects, the pre-existing personality pattern of the woman determines consequences of pill use (see Williams, 1977).

Intrauterine contraceptive devices (IUD's), which are small devices of plastic or metal inserted into the uterus to prevent implantation of the zygote or fertilized ovum, also produce side effects. The uterus may reject the IUD and expel it, and there may be cramps or bleeding. About 2 percent of the women on IUDs become pregnant. Perforation of the uterus is possible, though not common.

Diaphragms are thin rubber shallow cups that cover the cervical opening. They have a failure rate of from 5 to 20 percent, and the woman must interrupt love-making to insert it. Otherwise, however, there are no side effects.

Condoms are penile sheaths made of thin rubber or sheep intestine. They sometimes break or slip off and therefore should be supplemented with the use of contraceptive spermicidal creams, jellies or douches. Condoms are the most widely used contraceptive in the United States. They are also the best way, other than abstaining, to prevent the spread of venereal disease.

Spermicidal creams, jellies, and foams when used alone are relatively ineffective birth control methods. They have a failure rate of 25 percent. Douches have a failure rate of 35 percent (Williams, 1977).

Lactation or breastfeeding has often been put forward as a method of birth control in humans. There is indeed a positive correlation between the intensity and duration of lactation and the length of postpartum sterility in human and in other primates. However, *very* little is known about the quantitative degree of this relationship and little is known about the quantitative relationship between nursing and delay to the start of ovulation. Social factors may also be involved. One should be cautious in assuming that breastfeeding causes postpartum anovulation. The major research on this has *not* yet been done (see Masnick, 1979).

Abortion, the termination of unwanted pregnancy, is found among illiterate people everywhere. In the United States it has become an emotional, moral, and legal issue. Before the Supreme Court decision of 1973 over one million illegal abortions per year were performed in the United States (one in five pregnancies were so terminated). Legal methods of abortion today include the *vacuum suction* method, in which the cervix is dilated and a sterile tube aspirator is inserted into the uterus to withdraw the fetus. In this method, hospitalization is not required, although local or general anesthesia is. The entire procedure takes only a few minutes to complete. *Menstrual extraction* uses the suction method if a woman has missed a period and thinks she's pregnant. D & C (dilation and curettage) involves dilation of the cervix and the cleaning of the walls of the uterus with a small spoon on a long handle (a curette). Dilation and curettage requires hospitalization for a day or two because of a greater chance of physical trauma to the uterus.

Saline injection via hypodermic needle through the abdomen, uterine wall, and amniotic sac kills the fetus and induces labor in a few hours. Hysterectomy is also sometimes performed if a tubal sterilization is planned. This is major surgery and requires hospitalization. There are also other abortive techniques which are less often used than those discussed above.

At one time it was believed that abortion *had* to produce serious psychological problems for the woman. This is no longer held to be true. Women's freedom to define their own life roles has changed the attitudes of many people. The legalization of abortion has taken away much of the mystery and with it the myths. Guilt undoubtedly produced emotional disorder in prelegal abortions. According to some, adverse psychological reaction to abortion is simply psychoanalytic and societal myth (see Williams, 1977). In one study, 94 percent of the women who had an abortion felt relieved and satisfied. Those who had regrets said: (1) They were influenced by others, and (2) the regrets were mild and they did not require professional help. Women with severe emotional problems *before* abortion are those who have them later. "Healthy women are in no way harmed by being able to choose whether or not they wish to have a child." (Williams, 1977, p. 257)

Love and/or need for the release of sexual tension is the basis for most sexual intercourse. This is true for monkeys and apes as well as for people. The desire for pregnancy and children is certainly not the most common goal (see Jones, et al., 1977). If, however, a man and woman *do* want children, they want the assurances of family stability, personal contentment, physical health, financial security, and good living conditions. Their ideal is parenthood by *choice.* In this realm the human primate is a unique one.

In today's world, for most men and women, fertility control is a question of which method to choose, not whether or not to choose one. Few women want 10 to 20 children. Birth control methods are selected on the basis of safety, effectiveness, ease of use, medical history, religious and cultural attitudes, reversibility, expense, effect on libido, and compatibility of each couple with regard to all of the above factors. It is not surprising, given all these factors to consider, that the choice is not always an easy one to make. Unfortunately, some people avoid careful consideration, or fail to choose a method of fertility control altogether (Jones et al., 1977).

One group of people who are often quite likely to fail to use birth control are adolescents. Konner (1977) has spoken eloquently in their behalf. In recent history, there has been a decrease in the age of puberty in the United States and elsewhere. There has also been an increase in teen-age pregnancy. Among the !Kung San, primitive African hunter-gatherers, age of first menstruation is 16½. Among girls in the United States menarche occurs at age 12 (Konner, 1977).

American births in the 15-19 maternal age group doubled from 1940 to 1960. In 14-17 year range, births rose from 1960 to 1973. Teenage pregnancy today continues to rise at one million a year, and the fastest rate is in the youngest group, 11-13 years (Konner, 1977). In such young mothers, mortality risk is high for both mother and child and there is a high probability of birth defects. Even if mother and child are unaffected physically by the pregnancy and birth, poverty, divorce, child neglect, and child abuse are more frequent in teenage parents than in older parents. It could be argued that denying a junior high school girl an abortion is itself a kind of child abuse. In court we say she is not responsible, in the maternity clinic she is.

These are *new* and younger teenage pregnancies. Old moral and sometimes ignorant sanctions are of little help. We may be moving slowly toward a system of children born to children and the inadequacies of pregnancy and parenthood accruing to that situation. Foster care does not balance the increased dangers of prenatal abnormality associated with immature reproductive systems. Konner (1977) has reminded us that as adults we should provide some protection for our children, and especially for our pregnant children who may deliver those even more in need of special care.

REFERENCES

Hunt, M. *Sexual Behavior in the Seventies.* Chicago: Playboy Press, 1974.

Jones, K.L., Shainberg, L.W., and Byer, C.O. *Sex and People.* New York: Harper & Row, 1977.

Konner, M.J. Adolescent pregnancy. *New York Times,* Saturday, September 24, 1977, p. 21.

Masnick, G.S. The demographic impact of breastfeeding: A critical review. *Human Biology,* 1979, 51 (2), 109-125.

Mitchell, G. *Behavioral Sex Differences in Nonhuman Primates.* New York: Van Nostrand Reinhold, 1979.

Williams, J.H. *Psychology of Women: Behavior in a Biosocial Context.* New York, W.W. Norton and Co., 1977.

10
Pregnancy and Birth

After ovulation, the egg goes from the follicle in the ovary to the fimbria (extensions of the fallopian tubes) and starts down the fallopian tube. Its journey is largely passive. The fallopian tube sucks the egg in, and through a peristalticlike action, pushes the egg toward the uterus. Cilia in the tube also aid in the movement. The egg takes three to four days to reach the uterus, during which time it may be fertilized. If fertilized, it begins to develop before reaching the uterus; if not fertilized it is dead by the time it reaches the uterus (Jones et al., 1977).

Sperm reach the fallopian tubes within 15 minutes following ejaculation. Theirs is an active movement, although the muscular movements of the female tract do help them. Only a few hundred out of 500 million sperm in one ejaculation reach the site of fertilization. Only one sperm penetrates the egg while others in the vicinity produce the enzyme hyaluronidase to aid in penetration. A fertilized egg is called a *zygote* and is one-celled. Once it starts dividing it is called an embryo (Jones et al., 1977).

As it develops, the embryo moves toward the uterus (which is about the size and shape of a pear). The embryo is a small, hollow, fluid-filled ball as it attaches itself to the lining of the uterus. Implantation is usually in the upper part of the pear-shaped uterus. From the outside of the embryo (called a blastocyst at this stage) villi begin to grow into the uterine lining and maternal blood surrounds the villi forming transfer tissue which becomes the placenta. The embryo becomes attached to the placenta by the umbilical cord and the new organism develops within a double-layered membrane in amniotic fluid (Jones et al., 1977).

After eight weeks of pregnancy, the embryo is known as a fetus. Pregnancy lasts for 266 days from conception to birth. By 28 days the heart is beating and eyes, nose, ears, and brain begin to appear. The embryo is only ¼-inch long at this stage. The woman has, by now, missed her first period, begun to urinate more frequently, and may feel a tenderness of the breasts. By eight weeks (56 days), the nervous system has begun to coordinate bodily function and the embryo is 1 inch long (½-inch of which is head). It is now a fetus. Many women report morning sickness at this time (Jones et al, 1977).

At three months (90 days), fingers and toes are evident as the fetus develops in cephalo-caudal (head to feet) and proximo-distal (trunk to periphery) directions. External genitalia are formed and the sex of the fetus is evident. At 120 days the fetus is 6 inches long and covered with downy hair (lanugo). The mother is aware of its movements and the mother's breasts may begin to secrete colostrum (a yellowish fluid). (Jones et al., 1977).

Fetal heartbeats can be heard through the mother's abdomen at 140 days. The breasts begin to enlarge at this time. At 170 days eyebrows and eyelashes appear on the fetus. The fetus sucks its thumb and may get the hiccups. Fetal movements are frequently felt by the mother. If the fetus is delivered at this time it almost never survives. At 190 days the fetus averages 14 inches in length and is capable of hearing and tasting *in utero.* Many seven-month-old fetuses survive if delivered at this time (Jones et al., 1977).

By eight lunar months (240 days) the fetus weighs about 3½ pounds and is about 15 inches long. The lanugo has disappeared from its face. At nine lunar months it is 18 inches long or more and weighs 5 to 6 pounds. It begins to look plumper and less wrinkled. The mother urinates much more often because of fetal pressure on the bladder. By 10 lunar months, most of the lanugo has disappeared, nails are well-developed on the digits, and the fetus is 20 inches long and weighs about 7 pounds. Males weigh slightly more than females. This is true of almost all of the nonhuman primates (Jones et al., 1977).

PHYSIOLOGY OF BIRTH

Oxytocin, a hormone produced in the supraoptic and paraventricular nuclei of the hypothalamus of the brain, passes within axons to the posterior pituitary gland where it is released into the circulatory system of the mother. Oxytocin stimulates uterine contractions during the last four weeks of pregnancy. Before this, the uterus is influenced by progesterone from the placenta which effects a direct local block of uterine smooth muscle activity. Throughout gestation, estrogen distends and continuously stimulates the uterus but the uterine contractions do not trigger labor until the progesterone block is removed and oxytocin is released. The initiation of birth is also affected by the volume of amniotic fluid, the increasing size of the fetus, and pressure by the fetus against the cervix. These mechanical factors are implicated via a nervous reflex in the release of oxytocin from the neurohypophysis (pituitary). Recent data also suggest that tissue hormones from the placenta called prostaglandins and the fetal pituitary as well as fetal estrogens may also be involved in the instigation of labor (Mitchell and Brandt, 1975, Resko, 1974; also Bo, 1971).

Labor proceeds in four stages: (1) Effacement or flattening of the cervical muscle; (2) opening of the cervix to permit passage of the baby; (3) expulsion of the baby, and (4) delivery of the placenta. The same four stages apply to all nonhuman and human primates.

BIRTH IN NONHUMAN PRIMATES

Primate-like insectivores (tree shrews) deliver a litter of two or three young, usually in the early morning and in the summer. Gestation is 40 to 50 days at most and may be significantly less than this because of delayed implantation. Tree-shrews show a clear postpartum estrus. They also display nest-building. The mother eats the placenta and occasionally, especially in captivity, there may be cannibalism of the young. Delivery takes only a few minutes.

Prosimian primates vary considerably in gestation length (lorises 160-170 days; bushbabies 120-145 days; dwarf lemurs 60-70 days; other lemurs 120-135 days). Among prosimian primates there is often, but not always, more than one baby delivered at a time. A nest may be built by either a female or a male. Labor is short, postpartum heat occurs, cannibalism in captivity is common, and placenta-eating by the mother is the rule (Brandt and Mitchell, 1971).

In the tree-shrew, occasionally another female will protect the mother while the latter is in labor. Following delivery the tree-shrew mother leaves her infants and returns to the nest every 48 hours to nurse them. Lorises also deliver in the presence of others, although some mothers actively avoid males. Sometimes another female watches and carries the babies away from danger, grooms the mother, and may even help her eat the afterbirth. All members of most lemur groups take a great interest in the birth process. Among prosimians, birth is not a private matter (Mitchell, 1979).

New World monkey births take place after a gestation period of from 160-180 days (in the squirrel monkey). Labor lasts 1 to 2 hours and birth is usually at night. The mother licks the neonate immediately and eats the placenta. Twins and triplets are common among the monogamous species, and, in these, the father usually takes possession of the infant quite soon after birth. In fact, the father frequently assists at birth by receiving and washing the babies. (Occasionally, however, cannibalism also occurs in marmosets.) All group members of monogamous New World monkeys take an interest in the birth. There is also a sexual interest in the delivering mother by the father (postpartum estrus). The male does not help eat the placenta but he does groom the female. Many marmoset males carry the infant at birth, tamarins wait three weeks before taking over infant-carrying chores. Lion tamarin males present food to their offspring during these three weeks (Mitchell, 1979).

In the nonmonogamous New World monkeys, adult females and juveniles of both sexes surround the mother at delivery. Males show much less interest, except for the woolly monkey (where the adult male takes a great interest and protects the delivering mother) and the saki where males may steal infants. (It is said by Kleiman [1977] that the saki may be monogamous, however.) Squirrel monkey males *retreat* from a female in labor (Mitchell, 1979).

Old World monkey deliveries have been very well studied. The mother is usually quite active for a time as birth becomes imminent. At delivery, she squats and pushes. The discharge of mucus from her vagina is removed manually by the mother and her fingers are licked. As the baby emerges, usually after from 20 minutes to two or three hours, the mother supports it and pulls on it. The baby clutches at her as soon as its arms are free and may aid in its own delivery. Most Old World monkey mothers eat the placenta, although some do not. The infants are born at night after a 5-6 month gestation. Twinning is rare (Mitchell, 1979).

Female Old World monkeys do not isolate themselves from the group as was formally believed. Among gelada baboons, others withdraw from her somewhat but watch intently. Adult females and juveniles approach following parturition. Adult males show a passing interest and may approach and touch the infant. The same is true for vervets. Among langurs, *(Presbytis entellus)*, at times another female is permitted to hold the infant, sometimes as long as an hour or two. Some langur males appear to be indifferent, others show some interest. Immature males and females, especially females, also occasionally touch and even handle the newborn.

Sexual arousal is seen in some Old World monkey males and females when a female delivers an infant. Stumptail and rhesus macaque males may attempt to copulate *during delivery.* * The mother withdraws and screams. Male yearling rhesus (siblings to the neonate) have been known to aid their mothers and lick the afterbirth; but young females are generally more interested in birth than are young males (Mitchell, 1979). Primiparous females are much more clumsy and anxious at birth than are multiparous females (Mitchell, 1979).

Great ape gestation lasts 7 to 8½ months. Impending delivery is often difficult to detect but discharge of fluid is a telling sign in chimpanzees and orangutans. Chimpanzee females crouch, gorilla females support themselves on knees and elbows, and orangutan females often recline during delivery. Only about 50 percent of the chimpanzee mothers eat the placenta. Extremely complex maternal behaviors following delivery have been seen in great ape mothers and males. Chimpanzee and orangutan mothers sometimes place their mouths over the nose and mouth of their offspring and blow conspicuously *as if* administering artificial respiration. However, the mother's motives are not clear here. While lesser ape males pay little attention to their neonates, an orangutan male in captivity was reported to aid in delivery. Again, the animal's motives were not clear. One orangutan male in captivity ate but regurgitated the placenta. Sexual interest in the birthing female by males has been reported for the great apes (see Mitchell, 1979).

An overview of the primate parturitive patterns reveals that:

1. The more advanced the primate the longer the gestation period.
2. The more advanced the primate the fewer the offspring delivered per birth.
3. The more advanced the primate the more complex are the nurturant and protective behaviors.

---

*Females who watch sometimes arch their backs and finger their vaginas.

4. The more advanced the primate the less the chance of nest-building at birth.
5. The more advanced the primate the less the chance of placenta eating, although it still occurs in the great apes 50 percent of the time.
6. The more advanced the primate the more likely there is to have been a change from a specific, rigid postpartum estrus to a generalized sexual arousal on the part of those watching the birth (both males *and* females).
7. Monogamous primates in which males show a lot of infant care display more male "midwife" help at birth.
8. Close kin and siblings aid at birth quite frequently.
9. Females, except in the monogamous species alluded to above, are more interested in birth and in the neonate than are males.
10. Births take longer, are more difficult, and the mothers are more clumsy and nervous during first deliveries than during second or subsequent deliveries.

BIRTH IN HUMANS

The pregnant woman experiences back pains and irregular uterine contractions toward the end of pregnancy. "False labors" are common because labor does not happen all at once. The woman, in a sense, has a chance to get used to the hormonal and physical changes in her body which are later responsible for triggering labor.

Labor itself first involves regular uterine contractions every 15 to 20 minutes. At first these last only a few seconds and are mild. As labor proceeds they become stronger and last longer. After the cervical plug is expelled ("showing"), the rupture of the amniotic sac (bag of waters) is usually not far behind. Before birth may proceed, the cervix must dilate enough for the baby's head to pass. This effacement and dilation may take 12 to 16 hours in a first birth (Williams, 1977).

During expulsion of the baby, there are powerful uterine contractions (via cervix-oxytocin reflex) which push the baby through the cervix and vagina and into the world. What the baby and the mother experience during this whole process depends upon the birthing method agreed to beforehand.

Given what we know about nonhuman primate birth, isolation of the mother from close kin does not seem like the right or "natural" way to do things. But in the United States at least, people grow up having little or no exposure to child birth. Birth control and the trend toward smaller families are making experience with parturition even less likely. Women, and potential fathers, often enter their first parental experience with little understanding of the birth process. At the end of pregnancy, when the woman begins labor, she is whisked away from kin and friends, receives general anesthesia, and is either terrified or has no memory at all of her birth experience until she sees her baby hours later. The sterile, impersonal separation, the treatment of birth as though it were an illness, and the removal of choice and control from the mother and her loved ones can all be frightening and demoralizing.

In the last decade or two there have been trends toward:

1. Instructional preparation for birth of the mother and father.
2. Presence of the father at delivery.
3. Minimal or no anesthesia to permit full active participation by the mother.
4. Immediate contact between mother and neonate following delivery.
5. Prolonged "rooming-in" of the neonate with the mother during the days following birth.
6. Home deliveries or deliveries under home-like conditions.

All of these changes seem to be advantageous for the infant, the mother, the father, and for the emotional bonds between the three. Preparation before birth increases knowledge about the birth process and the birthing situation and reduces anxiety in the mother. Presence of the father reassures the mother when she is frightened, sometimes leading her to report peak experiences and even orgasms during delivery. Fathers who are present tend to feel closer to both mother and infant after the birth. Lowered use of general anesthesia is correlated with the delivery of more alert infants who breathe sooner and suffer fewer neurological and behavioral deficits. Immediate contact between mother and infant (and father and infant) takes advantage of strong bonding potentials that have been ignored in the past, decreases uncertainty concerning ownership of the infant, and helps establish early individualistic nursing patterns. Home deliveries or deliveries in homelike situations increase the participation of other family members, siblings, grandmothers, sisters, etc., and surround the whole event with love and celebration. These trends may not be making births more "natural" but they are making them more like those seen in our primate cousins, the monkeys and the apes.

REFERENCES

Bo, W.J. Parturition. In Hafez, E.S.E. (Ed.) *Comparative Reproduction in Laboratory Primates.* Springfield, Ill.: Thomas, 1971.

Brandt, E.M. and Mitchell, G. Parturition in primates. Behavior related to birth. In Rosenblum, L.S. (Ed.) *Primate Behavior* Vol. II New York: Academic Press, 1971, pp. 177-223.

Jones, K.L., Shainberg, L.W., and Byer, C.O. *Sex and People.* New York: Harper & Row, 1977.

Kleiman, D.G. Monogamy in mammals. *The Quarterly Review of Biology,* 1977, 52, 39-69.

Mitchell, G. *Behavioral Sex Differences in Nonhuman Primates.* New York: Van Nostrand, 1979.

Mitchell, G. and Brandt, E.M. Behavior of the female rhesus monkey during birth. In Bourne, G.H. (Ed.) *The Rhesus Monkey* Vol. II. New York: Academic Press, 1975, pp. 231-244.

Resko, J.A. Sex steroids in the circulation of the fetal and neonatal rhesus monkey: A comparison between male and female fetuses. *International Symposium on Sexual Endocrinology of the Perinatal Period,* 1974, 3, 195-204.

Williams, J.H. *Psychology of Women: Behavior in a Biosocial Context.* New York: W.W. Norton, 1977.

11
Infant Care in Primates

Not only are nonhuman and human primate sex differences influenced by early prenatal hormones and by later hormones of adulthood, but they are also a function of early and later experience. In the current chapter we will be concerned with the role of mothers, adult males and other significant individuals in the development of behavioral sex differences. Infants, both nonhuman and human, receive care from adoptive parents, from close kin, and even from immature individuals. In general, in most primates, there are sex differences in infant care, with females providing more of it than males. There are also differences in the way caretakers respond to male as opposed to female infants.

Among most primates, males usually defend females and young but are less inclined than are females to offer direct care. Redican (1976) and others, however, have emphasized the great variability in male care within nonhuman primate societies. Apparently male primates respond to sex differences in the infants more than do females. Male care is also a function of maternal restrictiveness of the infant. If a female permits other females to contact her infant, a male is likely to contact it also, although usually at lower frequencies and for shorter periods of time. The probability of nonhuman primate male care of an infant increases when:

1. The male is related to the infant.
2. The male is familiar with the mother.
3. Conditions of captivity (crowding, stress, etc.) permit it.
4. The mother is in estrus.
5. The group is a stable one.

6. The infant is a male.
7. The mother is a dominant female.
8. The infant is old enough to initiate contact with others.
9. There is a "cultural tradition" of male care in the male's group.
10. The birth season arrives and the mothers have new infants to care for.
11. An infant is orphaned.
12. There are many males and infants in a group.
13. The male and the infant are properly socialized, e.g., not raised under deprived conditions.
14. The male is interested in the center of a troop "in order to" increase status.
15. The male is a monogamous New World primate (marmoset, tamarin, titi monkey, or night monkey).

The variability in male care from species to species and within a species is greater than is the variability in female care. Female interest in infants is usually strong and persistent (Mitchell, 1979). This is not to say that there is not a great range in maternal care in the primate order. There is. Among prosimians alone, female care of infants ranges from visiting a litter of two or three infants for an hour or so every two days (tree shrews) to almost constant mother-infant contact where the infant develops very slowly and is carried clinging tightly to the mother's waist (monkey lemur) (Mitchell, 1979).

Male care in the primitive prosimians ranges from infanticide with cannibalism of infants, through indifference, to nest building, to playing with infants, holding them, and cuddling them. Overall, however, female prosimians provide much more care for infants than do male prosimians. There are probably no species of these primitive primates which show more male care than female care (Mitchell, 1979).

In contrast to the prosimian pattern, infant care in the monogamous New World monkeys (marmosets, tamarins, titi, night monkey) is primarily but not exclusively a male prerogative. All members of a monogamous group will carry infants—the male, the female, and juveniles. The male, however, usually does more carrying than do the others. It is interesting that most of the male care is calm carrying and grooming rather than play. We will see a different pattern in other primate groups (Mitchell, 1979). In those monogamous species which have large infants, the male starts carrying the infant sooner.

In the nonmonogamous New World primates, females definitely care for infants more than do males, although adult males will occasionally carry infants dorsally and ventrally and will sometimes play vigorously with them. In some species (howler), males make a bridge with their bodies between trees so that infants can cross from one tree to another. "Aunting" behavior is seen in females who are friends or relatives of the mother. Juvenile females show a greater interest in infants than do juvenile males. Baby-sitting is seen in adult males, adult females, and juveniles of both sexes. Even here, however, females surpass males. Infants of the nonmonogamous New World monkeys usually sleep with females. Males sleep alone.

Rhesus monkeys, as we know, show sex differences in infancy with males displaying more threats, play, and sexual mounting. These differences are, recall, related to prenatal androgen. Since the two sexes of infant behave differently it is not surprising that adults treat them differently. Mother rhesus are more passive toward, and restrain and retrieve their female infants more than they do their male infants. Mothers withdraw from, play with and present more to male infants. Male infants bite and pester their mothers more than do females. They are therefore punished more than are female infants (Mitchell, 1979). These sex differences in care according to the sex of the infant probably produce differences in independence and activity at a distance from the mother. Male infants seem to achieve greater independence.

Immature rhesus, especially immature female rhesus, are very attracted to infants and display what has been called "play mothering" (see Lancaster, 1971). Female rhesus preadolescents in the laboratory show four times as much positive social behavior toward month-old infants as do males. Male *infants* elicit more play from juveniles and preadolescents than do female rhesus infants (Mitchell, 1979).

As we have already seen, adult female rhesus show more interest in newborns than do males. Adult females respond to infant vocalization more than do males. Some females even kidnap infants from their mothers.

Even though there are evidently strong biological predispositions toward sex differences in rhesus parenting or infant care, some parts of infant care behavior are undoubtedly learned. Female rhesus raised in isolation do not make good mothers and primiparous females are more awkward and anxious with their infants than are multiparous (experienced) mothers. There is less behavioral variability in maternal behavior and in the behavior of the offspring of multiparous mothers than in the behavior of the young of primiparous mothers (Mitchell, 1979).

Despite these sex differences in actual behavior, adult males have the potential for very strong and enduring emotional attachments to infants. When given tiny infants, apart from adult females, adult males can rear the infants and become very attached to them. They do not permit nearly the quantity of ventral contact; however, they play with "their infants" much more often and much more intensely than do mothers (Redican, 1976; Mitchell, 1979).

Other species of macaques like pigtail monkeys and crab-eating monkeys display sex differences in infant care somewhat like those described for the rhesus. Japanese macaques and Barbary macaques show a lot more male care than does the rhesus but, even here, females surpass males in infant care. In some Japanese macaque troops there appears to be a "tradition" of male care (see Mitchell, 1979).

Baboons differ tremendously from one species to another. Females perform most of the infant care but males are usually quite tolerant, protective, and playful toward infants. Some mangabey males also form fairly close ties to infants.

In general, however, in Old World monkeys it is a *matrifocal* core that provides most of the infant care. In some Old World monkeys, like the patas monkey, male care is minimal. In others, like the spectacled langur, it is quite extensive. Adult male spectacled langurs carry infants and kiss their backs as an adult female would. Occasionally these males even sleep with older infants and juveniles (Mitchell, 1979).

Lesser apes, siamangs and gibbons, are monogamous like South American marmosets, titi monkeys, etc. However, unlike the New World monogamous primates, these primates do not show more male care than female care. In the lesser apes, the father *does* show paternal behavior, but usually toward an offspring in its second year when the mother is busy with her younger infant. The infant sleeps with the mother, the juvenile with the male. Males probably play more with the juvenile than females do with the infant (Mitchell, 1979).

Among chimpanzees, daughters remain closer to their mothers throughout life than do sons. Family units are matrifocal; the father is usually not identifiable. Siblings often help with infant care; indeed, orphaned infants are sometimes even adopted by older siblings.

Adult and adolescent males tend to do more traveling than do females, hence females are responsible for most of the infant care. An interesting new development at the great ape level is that mothers and adult females play *more* with infants than do adult males. Even though females show the most infant care, adult and immature males do show a great deal of potential for it, and occasionally do play with and carry infants. The best guess, based upon meager data regarding infant sex differences, is that male infants tend to be more aggressive toward their mothers than do female infants, whereas female infants initiate more grooming bouts with their mothers. Mothers tend to play with other infants more than with their own. Kinship plays a factor in infant care for females, for juveniles, and even for males. Close kin are cared for more than are unrelated infants. Overall, males are rougher with infants than are females when they do interact with them. Some juvenile males occasionally harass infants by pinching or biting them. There is some evidence that these behaviors can be somewhat disadvantageous for the male since some researchers believe that chimpanzee females select males as mates according to the males' caretaking abilities (see Mitchell, 1979 for primary references).

As in the chimpanzee, adult females display most of the infant care in gorillas. They also answer infant calls more than do males. Adult male gorillas sometimes groom infants, however, and infants often play on and around a male. An adult male gorilla will occasionally carry an infant for short distances and has more potential for infant care than he typically displays. One adult male gorilla took a large infant, left the main group, and the two went on an excursion by themselves for almost a month (Mason, 1964). Maple and Hoff (1981) have described gorilla males in captivity who carry infants. Males accept "babysitting" duties, and tolerate up to four infants climbing all over them. Infants show interest in the adult male by the time they are seven months old.

Infant gorillas display a sex difference in play and in independence, with males playing more and achieving independence earlier than females. Occasionally a male gorilla will take an infant from a mother and carry it (often awkwardly). In one such male, infant males were more attractive than an available female infant. If the infant is young it whimpers and the mother follows and retrieves it (see Mitchell, 1975, for primary references).

Orangutans are unique. The female and her infant(s) live alone and the adult male travels by himself. In captivity, a female orangutan may occasionally give her infant to an adult male. The male tolerates infant contact and as the infant matures in such a situation there may be extensive play between the adult male and the infant. In the wild, juvenile females remain with their mothers much longer than do males. Solitary juvenile male orangutans are probably seen in the wild more than are solitary juvenile females. Play occurs more frequently in infant males than in infant females, but play *is* seen in females and even in adult females.

Most orangutan infant care comes directly from the mother. Infants learn many things from the mother such as nest building, tool-using, and sexual behavior. Mother orangutans share food with their infants and sometimes actively feed them. From a very early age the mother has ventro-ventral sexual behavior with her infant (mother thrusting on top while holding the infant down) whether the infant is male or female (see Mitchell, 1979 for primary references; also Maple, 1980).

Older siblings, particularly older female siblings sometimes hold an infant, but they rarely carry it or groom it. Contact between adult males and infants in the wild is rare. When copulating with a female a male usually ignores her juvenile although he will occasionally attack it (see Mitchell, 1979 for references).

The range of female, sibling and juvenile, and male care of infants in the primate order is great indeed. One cannot generalize from prosimian to monkey, from monkey to ape, from monkey to monkey or even from great ape to great ape with regard to the nature of infant care systems. Orangutan males in Borneo have little or no contact with infants, yet in captivity they may show extensive and gentle male care of infants. Rhesus monkey males display almost no male care in the wild, yet they are capable of raising normal infants by themselves in captivity. The potential which exists in practically all primates for increases in infant care in males or for the development of totally different infant care systems, makes one especially cautious about generalizing from non-human primates to people, from one kind of people to another, or from the most important perspective, from one person to another.

THOUGHTS ABOUT HUMANS

Only in recent years have there been major publications on the role of the human father (cf. Biller, 1971; Lynn, 1974; Lamb, 1976). Now there are research reports on the human adult male's response to birth (Tanzer, 1973), and on the father's response to neonates and to infants in the first year of life (Lamb, 1977; Freudenberg and Driscoll, 1976; Parke and O'Leary, 1975; Sternglanz, et al., 1977).

From classic biological perspectives, Man the Hunter has dominated evolutionary speculation. This orientation toward the male and away from the female has distracted us from the role of infant care in the evolution of humanity. Tanner and Zihlman (1976), however, have recently attempted to reorient us by emphasizing women's role in evolution. They surmised that mothers have had an *innovative* economic role in evolution through their *gathering* with tools and in *sharing* food with their offspring. These behaviors have made the female *socially central*. She has been the *primary socializer* and essential for kin selection, sexual selection and *cultural transmission*. More importantly, for the topic of the current chapter, her social centrality and long parental investment in her children has brought her to choose a mate she considers to be suitable for sexual interaction and for *infant care*. Most probably these have been *nonaggressive males*.

Through this line of thought Tanner and Zihlman (1976) lead us to the idea that human males have become closely integrated into kin groups and toward "fatherhood." Thus, men were selected for non-aggression and nurturance and became culturally institutionalized as parents. This is but one evolutionary speculation, but an interesting one from the point of view of our present topic. In the next chapter we will examine human infant care from a cross-cultural, developmental, and social psychological perspective to compare human sex differences in infant care to those seen in the versatile and plastic nonhuman primates.

REFERENCES

Biller, H. *Father, Child, and Sex Role*. Lexington, Mass: Heath, 1971.

Freudenberg, R. and Driscoll, J.W. Reactions of adult humans to cries of normal and abnormal infants. Paper presented at the *Animal Behavior Society* meeting, Boulder, Colorado, June, 1976.

Lamb, M.E. (Ed.) *The Role of the Father in Child Development*. New York: Wiley, 1976.

Lamb, M.E. Father-infant and mother-infant interaction in the first year of life. *Child Development*, 1977, 48, 167-181.

Lancaster, J.B. Play-mothering: The relations between juvenile females and young infants among free-ranging vervet monkeys *(Cercopithecus aethiops)*. *Folia primatologica*, 1971, 15, 161-182.

Lynn, D.B. *The Father: His Role in Child Development.* Monterey, CA: Brooks-Cole, 1974.

Maple, T. *Orang-utan Behavior.* New York: Van Nostrand Reinhold, 1980.

Maple, T. and Hoff, M. *Gorilla Behavior.* New York: Van Nostrand Reinhold, 1981.

Mason, W.A. Sociability and social organization in monkeys and apes. In Berkowitz, L. (Ed.) *Recent Advances in Experimental Social Psychology* (Vol. 1) New York: Academic Press, 1964, pp. 277-305.

Mitchell, G. *Behavioral Sex Differences in Nonhuman Primates.* New York: Van Nostrand Reinhold, 1979.

Parke, R.D. and O'Leary, S. Father-mother-infant interaction in the newborn period: Some findings, some observations, and some unresolved issues. In Riegel, K. and Meacham, J. (Eds.) *The Developing Individual in a Changing World* (Vol. 2): *Social and Environmental Issues.* The Hague: Mouton, 1975, pp. 653-663.

Redican, W.K. Adult male-infant interactions in nonhuman primates. In Lamb, M.E. (Eds.) *The Role of the Father in Child Development.* New York: Wiley, 1976, pp. 345-385.

Sternglanz, S.H., Gray, J.L., and Murakami, M. Adult preferences for infantile facial features: An ethological approach. *Animal Behaviour,* 1977, 25, 108-115.

Tanner, N. and Zihlman, A. Women in evolution Part I: Innovation and selection in human origins. *Signs: Journal of Women in Culture and Society,* 1976, 1 (3), 585-608.

Tanzer, D. Natural childbirth: Pain or peak experience. In Tavris, C. (Ed.) *The Female Experience.* New York: Ziff-Davis, 1973.

12
Infant Care in Humans

If we examine sex differences in infant care in *Homo sapiens* cross-culturally, we see that men are found less often with children than are women, even when males are free to be available to children. Groups of men with children tend to be smaller groups than do groups of women with children. Older children are more likely to be found in same-gender groups. Older boys are seen in men-only groups more than are younger boys (Mackey, 1977); men show a preference for the cute look of the infant face (small chin, large forehead, large eyes) (Sternglanz, et al., 1977); and, male teenagers in the United States baby-sit as much as do female teenagers.

Human infants show no preference for either parent until they are 13 months of age. They actually respond *more* positively to *play* with the father than to play with the mother. Women seem to have more of a caretaking function in *holding* infants whereas men more often play (Lamb, 1977). When rooming-in following birth in a hospital, the infant is actually held and rocked by the father more than by the mother. If the mother is not present the father is much more likely to interact with the infant than if she is present (Parke and O'Leary, 1975). Even in the Israeli kibbutzim, fathers' visits are long, especially with older boys (Gewirtz and Gewirtz, 1968). In addition to all of the above, there is a growing trend associated with the women's movement toward a greater part in child rearing for the modern father.

On the other hand, if pupil dilation is used as an index of preference, adult females respond more than do men to infant faces (Sternglanz, et al., 1977). Moreover, mothers of newborns smile at infants more than do fathers (Parke and O'Leary, 1975). Mothers, however, may smile at *any* person more than do fathers.

Let us now look more deeply at the more traditional sex roles with regard to infant care. After all, regardless of what nonhuman and human primate research tells us about the potential of the male, we all know that, *in fact,* infant care is primarily a woman's role.

Parents say they see different qualities in girls and boys from birth onward. Even when male and female babies are alike in weight, length and physiological conditions at birth, daughters are described as little, beautiful, and delicate, while boys are described as firm, alert, and strong. Fathers are more extreme in such sex-typing than are mothers (Williams, 1977).

By the time a child is six, the effects of this early bias in interaction with developing biological predispositions lead parents to describe their boys as rougher, noisier, more competitive, and more likely to do dangerous things. Girls are seen as being helpful, neat, clean, quiet, sensitive, and more easily upset. Parents value *both* groups of qualities for both sexes, but think it quite unlikely that they could achieve neatness in their boys or competitiveness in their girls. They firmly believe that they are starting from different points with different beings (Williams, 1977).

Throughout early development, parents provide different toys for boys than for girls. Toys are sex-typed, so are clothes. Girls receive dolls and aprons—tools for infant care and domestic duty.

Although parents value initiative and competitiveness, they do not value aggression *in either sex.* Prior to the preschool years, independence is encouraged in both sexes. But in kindergarten, parents begin to become more protective and restrictive with girls than with boys. Boys receive more punishment than do girls, primarily because they do more to encourage parental wrath (Williams, 1977).

With regard to differences between mothers and fathers on the factors discussed above, parents are most permissive with the child of the other sex. Mothers are more tolerant of sons, fathers are more tolerant of daughters, particularly with regard to angry behavior directed toward the parent by the child. Overall, however, boys receive more discipline than do girls (Williams, 1977).

With regard to discipline, Baumrind (1972) has studied four different patterns: authoritative, authoritarian, permissive, and harmonious (see Table 12-1). The permissive and authoritarian styles do not encourage independence, competence, or instrumental behavior in girls. Both of these parental patterns overprotect the girl, one (permissive) by demanding nothing, the other (authoritarian) by overstructuring so that she makes none of her own decisions. In harmonious and authoritative situations the child experiences nonconformity and autonomy, and the child's individual personhood is valued.

Table 12-1. Baumrind's (1972) Four Patterns of Parental Authority (Also see Williams, 1977).

Authoritative	Exercises firm control, sets limits, but values autonomy and individuality.
Authoritarian	Values obedience, restricts autonomy, uses punitive control. Parent is final authority.
Permissive	Accepting, affirmative. Parents are a resource for the child. Child should be free of all restraints unless it physically harms her/him.
Harmonious	Parent has control but does not exercise it. The child knows intuitively what the parent wants so that no strict command is necessary.

The same principles apply for boys but society has not conspired as much against the growth of competence in boys as it has against similar growth in girls. In recent years, however, more conscious attention has been given to teaching girls how to compete (e.g., in sports) and how to win and lose. Assertiveness training for adult women is also becoming a part of the women's movement. In the future perhaps girls will more often be socialized to assert their individuality; if so, it's unlikely that authoritarian or permissive *parenting* will help.

Despite new options for women, most women still live a large portion of their lives in the home and with children. Jobs outside the home are still largely secondary, i.e., the women with a strong interest in *both* home and career are still in the minority.

The average age for marriage for females in the United States is 20. The woman's life span is getting longer, but her child-bearing years (apart from potential) are becoming shorter because of increasing use of birth control. The American woman of today usually aims to have her first child at 21, her last at 26. This leaves twenty childbearing years which she may spend without becoming pregnant, a state of affairs quite different from that at the turn of the century. Women with small children drop out of the nondomestic labor force only to join it again at a later time in life (see Williams, 1977).

But housework and child care can be done by either females *or* males. We know from our review of primate parenting that even the *least* paternal of primate males has the potential to rear normal young (and sometimes has the opportunity to do it). One problem with infant care and with work in the home is that they are not looked upon as being as important as they actually are. What work could be more important for humanity than the normal, loving, rearing of the offspring of the next generation? It is strange that no particular qualifications are required, no instruction given, and no money paid that is commensurate with its importance. Marxists would suggest that women are domestic *slaves* (Williams, 1977).

To glorify the roles of mother and housewife does no good. Economic gain must be a part of the package, as must proper training. Women often become housewives and mothers the day after they are married, having no training (some would say warning) whatsoever. When they do well at it (despite no training) they are often not rewarded. In fact, they may be punished. They are, after all, *just housewives.* This is taken as meaning that they are not employed, not skilled, and *not* respected as competent adults (Williams, 1977).

The role of mother cannot be described in the same terms as can the role of housewife. Women usually *gain* in self-esteem as a result of the feeling of importance associated with being a mother. These feelings are not universal, but they *are* typical. Eighty-three percent of the women in the United States still experience the role of mother. Feminism will not change these percentages as much as will birth control methods and environmental concern over a growing population. The increased self-esteem associated with the maternal role is *probably* not the result of any "maternal instinct." Society still respects motherhood—not the housewife—but motherhood. And most people still believe that the mother is the best primary caretaker for a child. The corollary of this belief, of course, is the belief that if something goes wrong with a child, it's the mother's fault.

Becoming a mother means abandoning one's own self-interests and becoming "tied down" (at least to a degree). However, it also means growth away from childishness and toward responsibility. In a housewife role, children are both the biggest joy and the biggest pain. Perhaps that is what life is all about. The other parts of being a housewife, domestic duties, general family relations, husband and happy marriage, and the house itself pale before the extremes of parenthood. These other roles of a housewife are relatively mundane, not respected, and not as deeply rewarding (or disappointing) to most women (Lopata, 1971).

Children *are* extremely important in ratings of personal happiness. Surprisingly, however, 88 percent of childless wives, but only 65 percent of mothers of children under six, say they are generally happy with life (see Williams, 1977). Contentment drops as soon as a child is born and does not increase again until the child grows older and leaves home. Parents are the *least* happy when children are young. This is often because of stresses which are due to economics, in-laws, and/or attributable to immaturity on the part of the parents (Cameron, 1974).

Aside from domestic duties and parenthood, marriage and the monogamous family are also topics of current interest in the women's movement. Many feminists believe that marriage is oppressive for women. It is in fact true that traditional marriage is healthier for men than it is for women. In health matters, single women fare far better than do single men, married men, and even married women.

The women's movement favors educational, sexual, and economic freedom for women. Open marriage, multilateral marriage, group marriage, and/or communal living have often been put forward as alternatives to an oppressive monogamous union involving sexual possessiveness and exclusivity. Single life and dual-career marriage are less extreme alternatives. In 1976 the first drop in the number of marriages in the United States in 30 years occurred. The decline was only 3 percent; however, the proportion of women remaining single until after age 20 has increased by over 30 percent in the last 20 years, and the number of unmarried men and women living together has increased *800 percent* (Williams, 1977).

Women delay marriage when there are alternatives open to them. The higher the income of a woman, the lower her chances of becoming married. Unmarrieds living together are usually *both* working. It is possible in these situations to have children without being married (even by adoption). The roles of the man and the woman in infant care are probably going to be somewhat different in such situations than they are in the traditional monogamous nuclear family. After all, many couples who live together believe that: (1) The ultimate goal of marriage is not necessarily to have a child; (2) both partners will change and grow with time; (3) each will take full responsibility for herself (or himself); and (4) children are not necessary as proof of love.

In *open* marriage or *open* cohabitation (living together can also involve traditional roles and hence be closed) couples believe in equality (respect for the equal status of the other); role flexibility (sharing or exchange of household and economic work); open companionship (freedom to relate to males or females outside the home); identity (personal growth, autonomy); privacy (time and space to be alone); communication (honesty with the other about real feelings); living in the present (too many reflections on the past or fixations on the future can be destructive of the here and now); and trust (respect for the integrity of the other) (Williams, 1977). The commitment in such cases is more personal than legal. "The trend is for increasing freedom and flexibility of choice of life styles on an individual basis" (Williams, 1977, p. 309).

Technology, birth control, divorce and abortion laws, the changing sexual morality, and the women's movement are working to free women from the parental role. The parental role, however, is still of tremendous importance to our species. Feminists believe that: (1) Women will always have babies but men will probably become more involved in their care; (2) women will gain in "male strength", men in "female nurturance"; (3) infant care will become a true skill for which people are prepared; and (4) people will *want* their children and will love them, be they male or female parent, male or female child. In addition to the above, feminists believe that informal and formal child care by nonparents (friends, siblings, grandparents, institutions) is probably going to have to increase.

But how much role adaptation in infant care has actually occurred? In families where the woman works outside the home, (1) children are seen as the responsibility of the mother, (2) children themselves have more household chores, and (3) husbands help more with some household chores but *not* with child care (see Williams, 1977). Sociobiologists, being believers in gender differences in human parental investment, might say, "We told you so." The women's movement, however, is still new. So also are technological advances in the home (microwave ovens, home computers, etc.), birth control methods, abortion and divorce laws, and the changing sexual mores.

Patterns of infant care may still be altered significantly enough to show new sex differences. The present writer is not convinced that the genetic contribution to this sex difference in infant care is large enough to preclude significant increases in *paternal* investment in people.

The Social Science Research Council (SSRC) recently held a workshop on biological and social determinants of parenting in which I was privileged to participate. Parenting was examined from both a cross-species and cross-cultural perspective. Parenting was seen as involving protection, training, feeding, the encouragement of independence, and discipline. Parenting was also viewed as a means of achieving adult status by the parents. In agreement with trends seen in primate species, cross-cultural data suggested that in nonindustrial societies where infants sleep with their mothers for longer periods of time than they do in the United States, the children grow up to be less attention-seeking, easier to discipline, and are less indulged in terms of their expecting material goods (LeVine, 1979).

The cross-cultural data also suggested that age-segregated children (large birth-spacing) tended to be *less* sympathetic and considerate than did children born closer together. The children tended to socialize each other and come to expect less. Perhaps family planning is producing generations of people who are making a "me first" society (SSRC, 1979).

In *all* human societies, females do most of the infant care. Particularly in polygynous societies, however, males show very little parental investment. This agrees well with the primate data. In addition, the more hunting there is, the less the male care of children (SSRC, 1979). When human males do show nurturance toward children it tends to involve: (1) More play than in mothers, and (2) more sex stereotyping than in mothers (SSRC, 1979).

Human sex differences in sensory ability may be involved in sex differences in parenting. Adult females have better auditory acuity and there is evidence for more verbal behavior in mothers than in males. In addition, there is faster verbal development in female children and better communication in general in females. Females are said to have more empathy and this may account in part for their greater orientation toward child care (SSRC, 1979).

In a learning orientation, mothers seem to be more *contingently* responsive to the needs of the male infant than to the needs of the female infant. The key word here is contingently. This difference might lead to a more instrumental orientation in male children than in female children. Mothers also leave boys alone to experiment but tend to interfere prematurely with girls. There is therefore more active engagement with the environment by boys. The proximity vs. peripheralization dichotomy may start with these seeds. Boys have more freedom, less structure, and their games are less predictable. Public or private orientations may therefore begin very early (SSRC, 1979).

Most nonhuman primate mothers discipline their children. They tend to discipline males more than females but they also permit the males to wander further from them. (The orangutan mother probably disciplines the least of all nonhuman primates but *she* lives *alone* with the infant.) (Mitchell, 1979).

In the United States many facets of human parenting are being lost. For example, children see less and less of old age and death. Women and men are spending an increased amount of time with an empty nest. There is thus an absence of the reverse of parental responsibility; that is, there is an absence of filial responsibility for the parents in their old age. In a related trend, there are also more parents who survive their children, especially parents of sons. Very little is known about parenting patterns beyond age 40 or so (SSRC, 1979).

Other trends in the United States include lower marriage rates, more single parents, and more divorced parents. There is some evidence that daughters of divorced parents are more likely to become promiscuous (this is *not* true of daughters of widows or widowers) (SSRC, 1979).

World-wide, the family (where there is one) tends to remain in the area of the adult male or father. Around 90 percent of the societies of the world are patrilocal, only 10 percent are matrilocal. In the United States, however, strong emotional bonds tend to go along mother-daughter lines. These tendencies have not been studied enough (SSRC, 1979).

Infant care by siblings or other nonadult individuals is another type of care which has rarely been the subject of study in humans. Nonhuman primate sibling care is common. With more working mothers there may be increased responsibility for older siblings. Babysitting may be increasing. Sibling care may have the effect of *increasing* empathy on the caretaker. In those societies where sib care is frequent, there seem to be fewer individual differences in the children than in those cultures where sibling care is infrequent (SSRC, 1979).

Nonhuman primate parents sometimes punish their infants but they are rarely abusive unless the parents themselves have been reared in social isolation or other stresses of captivity have made them behaviorally abnormal. Child abuse in human parents is more common than it is in nonhuman parents, but the causes seem to be similar. Inadequate socialization is certainly of importance in the etiology of child abuse as we will see in our chapter on pathology.

The definition of abuse is often difficult. Intent and consequence are often unrelated. Sampling problems are also difficult to overcome in the study of such morally repugnant behavior. Only 3.8 percent of abusive parents will admit they are so. There are 2½ million abused children over the age of three in the United States. If we add neglect cases, the number increases to 12 million out of a total of only 50 million children. Almost one child in four is abused or neglected between birth and 17 years of age. In older children there is sometimes reciprocal or parent-directed violence, and there is a correlation between child abuse and neglect, and spousal abuse and neglect. It is of significance to know that *exposure* to violence in the home is even more important in producing violence than is being the victim. Mothers are implicated more than are fathers, although mothers are probably overblamed. About 50 percent of abused children become abusive parents (Gelles, 1979). Males are abused more than are females, so it is likely that the principle that violence begets violence is more applicable to male children and fathers than it is to female children and mothers. Violence in the home in the United States is a real problem and one that is difficult to do anything about without major changes in individual decisions about if, when, and how many children we are going to have. Technology, birth control, abortion and divorce laws, and the women's movement are all of direct relevance to child and spousal abuse. Each of them may help or actually make worse some of the underlying pressures which sometimes almost force people to abuse each other (Gelles, 1979). With regard to violence against children, in 1970, according to Gil (1970), a high proportion of households headed by women but with no biological father present were involved in child abuse. At that time more mothers than fathers killed their own children. In one twenty-five-year study of homicides involving preadolescent children (Myers, 1967), nearly half of the children were killed by their mothers, the other half by males, including their fathers. Gelles (1979) has reported essentially the same thing in a more recent summary of these unfortunate cases. In addition, Gelles (1973) reported that mothers were slightly more likely to use abusive violence on their own children than were fathers, probably because the women were more often with the children than were the men.

REFERENCES

Baumrind, D. From each according to her ability. *School Review,* 1972, 80, 161-197.
Cameron, M. Family relationships. In *No Longer Young.* Work group reports from the 26th annual conference on aging, Institute of Gerontology, University of Michigan and Wayne State University, 1974.
Gelles, R. Child abuse as psychopathology. *American Journal of Orthopsychiatry,* 1973, 43 (4), 611-620.
Gelles, R. Personal communication, 1979.
Gil, D.G. *Violence Against Children.* Cambridge, Mass.: Harvard, 1970.
Gewirtz, H.B. and Gewirtz, J.L. Visiting and caretaking patterns for Kibbutz infants: Age and sex trends. *American Journal of Orthopsychiatry,* 1968, 38, 427-433.
Lamb, M.E. Father-infant and mother-infant interaction in the first year of life. *Child Development,* 1977, 48, 167-181.
LeVine, R. Personal communication, 1979.
Lopata, H.Z. *Occupation: Housewife.* New York: Oxford University Press, 1971.
Mackey, W.C. The adult male-child bond: A cross-cultural analysis. Paper presented at the *Animal Behavior Society* meeting, University Park, Pennsylvania, June, 1977.
Mitchell, G. *Behavioral Sex Differences in Nonhuman Primates.* New York: Van Nostrand Reinhold, 1979.
Myers, S.A. The child slayer: A 25-year study of homicides involving preadolescent victims. *Archives of General Psychiatry,* 1967, 17, 211-213.
Parke, R.D. and O'Leary, S. Father-mother-infant interaction in the newborn period: Some findings, some observations and some unresolved issues. In Riegel, K. and Meacham, J. (Eds.) *The Developing Individual in a Changing World: Social and Environmental Issues* Vol. 2: The Hague: Mouton, 1975, pp 653-663.
Social Science Research Council, Committee on Parenting: Workshop #2. New York City, September, 1979.
Sternglanz, S.H., Gray, J.L., and Murakami, M. Adult preference for infantile facial features: An ethological approach. *Animal Behaviour,* 1977, 25, 108-115.
Williams, J.H. *Psychology of Women: Behavior in a Biosocial Context.* New York: W.W. Norton, 1977.

13
Social Spacing and Social Structure

NONHUMAN PRIMATES

In general, the larger the male of a primate species relative to the female, the more females there are to each male in a group (cf. Mitchell, 1979). There are exceptions to this rule, of course. For example, the orangutan male is very large relative to the female, yet there are *no* females that live with the orangutan male. Each orangutan male lives alone. In general, sexual dimorphism also correlates positively with group size and with terrestrial living (the orangutan, the howler monkey, and several other species are exceptions here). Another general rule is that where there is no monogamy, but there is strong sexual dimorphism, adult females are usually more closely *spaced* than are adult males. Males are forced away from their mothers to the periphery of the group where they may become solitary or join a different group (see Mitchell, 1979).

Prosimian primates can be polygamous, solitary, or even monogamous. Some live in "spatial harems" in which several females live in individual territories within the larger territory of a single male. In some species, sleeping groups may form at night which are larger and more closely spaced than are the groups seen during the day. Nocturnal, diurnal, and crepuscular species have quite varied social structures. In general, however, female prosimians are more closely spaced than are male prosimians (Mitchell, 1979).

New World monkeys show as much diversity in social structure as do the prosimians. They, too, can be polygamous, solitary, or monogamous. There is like-sex clumping in some of the New World monkeys (e.g., the squirrel monkey). As in prosimians, however, females tend to be more closely spaced than males. Males are more loosely attached to the troop than are females. Even at night males in a troop usually sleep alone and away from matrifocal groupings. Solitary males are seen, but solitary females are not seen (Mitchell, 1979).

The Old World macaques like the rhesus *(M. mulatta)* also have spacing arrangements in which females remain closer together than do males. Males sometimes remain solitary or form all-male groups. In laboratory research it has been found that partner preference in terms of proximity varies with the age of the animal. Up to seven months of age neither male nor female rhesus monkeys show any preferences for interacting with their own gender. After seven months, both sexes begin to show a preference for proximity with individuals of their own gender. Before puberty, however, there is a shift toward other sex preferences. After three-and-a-half years there is another shift back toward like-sex preferences. This last shift coincides with the age at which males become peripheralized, join all-male groups, begin to become solitary, or change troops. Bonds between females are stronger than are bonds between males (Mitchell, 1979).

In most macaques there is a tendency toward avoidance of contacts between adult females and young males. Sometimes, "satellite" males are seen. Such males are essentially solitary but may stay near a troop (between 20 and 200 meters) without joining it (Mitchell, 1979).

Among some macaque species (e.g., bonnets, toque macaques), exclusively male groups are rarely, if ever, seen and solitary males are practically never seen. However, even in these species, at night males are not as closely spaced as are females. Clasping-while-sleeping positions, seen very frequently in adult females and immatures, are rarely seen in adult males. Males sleep alone (Mitchell, 1979). Throughout life, female pigtail macaques *(M. nemestrina)* stay more closely spaced than do males (Bernstein, 1972).

Hamadryas baboons *(Papio hamadryas)* live in one-male, several-female harems which gather in herds. Hamadryas females are more intimate with each other than are the males. This intimacy can be seen in their closer inter-individual distance, their higher frequency of friendly interactions, more touching and less fighting.

Gelada baboons *(Theropithecus gelada)* also live in harems which come together to make herds. Female gelada like-sex dyads are more compatible than are male like-sex dyads. Mandrills *(Papio sphinx)* show a similar sex difference within a harem structure (Mitchell, 1979).

Other baboons *(Papio spp.)* live in multimale troops. But even here males are more loosely attached to the troops than are the females. Males sometimes leave the troop to hunt, females do not.[1] Only the males sleep alone (Mitchell, 1979).

There are many other species of Old World monkeys that could be discussed here. Each of them is somewhat unique but the same gender difference reported above appears to be the rule in all of them. In those species which live in multimale troops (e.g., manga-beys, vervets) females seem to space themselves closer together than do males. Even in the talapoin, where sex differences in aggression in adulthood are surprisingly in favor of females, adult males do not show the close spacing and proximity seen in females. Among other Old World species that live in one-male groups (e.g., patas, colobus) females are more closely spaced and more intimate with one another than are males. Langurs are found in both one-male and multimale groups, but in both types females show more proximity and contact with one another than do males (Mitchell, 1979).

Lesser apes, of course, live in monogamous family groups. Im-matures of both sexes, however, are peripheralized starting at around two-and-a-half years of age. The adult male is occasionally found alone, but when in a family group he does not sleep alone. The mother sleeps with the infant and the male with the juvenile. Sex differences in spacing are minimal in both gibbons and siamangs (Mitchell, 1979).

The great apes (chimpanzees, gorillas and orangutans) are quite different from one another in social organization. When it comes to sex differences in spacing, however, they have something in common. Among chimpanzees *(Pan troglodytes)*, males leave their mothers earlier, become more peripheralized, are solitary more, and sleep alone more than do females. Females are occasionally solitary, however. Gorilla males travel more than do gorilla females, and they are also more often solitary than are females. However, as in chim-panzees, females are sometimes solitary; and, most gorilla females

---

[1]Females sometimes hunt, but they do *not* leave the troop to do so.

change groups before or at maturity. Orangutan males cover greater distances and have larger inter-individual distances between them than do orangutan females. Adult female orangutans can get along with one another, adult males seem to be unable to get along with each other. As in chimpanzees and gorillas, both male and female orangutans are solitary at some time in their lives, but males are definitely alone more than are females (Mitchell, 1979).

HUMANS

Sommer (1969) has written extensively about human social spacing patterns. People from different cultures show different patterns of inter-individual distances. Among preschool children, as we have seen in previous chapters, boys play outdoors and at the periphery of social groups, more than do girls (Harper and Sanders, 1978). There is also a tendency toward larger same-sex groups in males and a tendency toward the peripheralization of human males in adolescence (Mitchell, 1979).

HUMAN INFANCY

In regard to sex differences in infant human *proxemics* (the study of social spacing and social distance), some research on infants' responsiveness to adult females (mother vs. female strangers) has been reported. Among 12-month, 18-month, and 24-month-old babies, girls show more social initiative than do boys, and this difference increases between one and two years of age. At 24 months of age, girls exceed boys on all social behaviors with female adults including approach and proximity, whether these behaviors are directed toward adult female strangers or toward their own mothers (Bretherton, 1979).

HUMAN CHILDHOOD

Three-year-olds keep less distance from their age peers than do five- and seven-year-olds. There is a very early tendency to keep less distance from girls than from boys (Lomranz, et al., 1975). The older the boy, the greater the distance from other boys. Even *four-year-old* and *five-year-old* boys differ in distancing, with four-year-olds staying closer together (Melson, 1977). However, in the school years, both sexes place themselves closer to same-sexed peers in the early grades and to opposite-sexed peers in the later grades (Meisels and Guardo, 1969).

The sex difference in social spacing seen in dyads of human *children* is greater among friends than among strangers. Girls who are friends stand closer together than do boys who are friends (Aiello and Cooper, 1972).

In humans, spacing patterns change somewhere between the sixth and eighth grades. Sixth graders maintain greater distances from opposite-sexed peers than they do from same-sexed peers. Eighth grade *females,* however, allow closer approach by males than by females (Whalen, et al., 1975). With regard to personal space, up to *puberty,* boys and girls apparently prefer similar distances between themselves and others. By the age of puberty, however, girls permit people to get closer to them than do boys (Price and Dobbs, 1974).

Male-male adolescent pairs are found to not only stand at greater distances from one another but also at greater angles than female-female pairs (that is, the female-female pairs stand more face-to-face) (Aiello and Aiello, 1974).

ADULT HUMANS

According to research reported in Deaux (1976), adult males (age forty-five) in the United States seem to have about the same numbers of close friends as do adult women (same ages), although the women tend to show a stronger tendency toward same-sexed friends than do males. In addition, the bonds between women seem to be stronger, more spontaneous, and more open in terms of confiding in each other. Women friends also spend more time together (Deaux, 1976). Data on human adults of different ages, however, may not agree with these data reported on those 45 years of age and older.

In same-sex groups, *middle-aged men* seem to get together for a reason; women simply get together. When together, men tend to make instrumental comments while women make expressive or socio-emotional comments. In mixed-sexed groups, however, women become more instrumental while men become more expressive. Men are friendlier in mixed-sexed groups than they are in same-sexed groups; women, however, are friendlier in same-sexed groups (Deaux, 1976).

Spacing itself tells us about sex differences in proximity and may give us clues about social bonding. However, two individuals or more may be close together and yet have little affection for one another or little commitment. Women, in general, seem to report more positive feelings about being close to others, even about physical contact, than do men. Men in the United States *prefer* greater distances between themselves and another person than do women. As reported in Deaux (1976), there are data showing that women stand closer to other women than men do to other men when viewing public exhibits. They also: (1) Sit closer in experimental laboratories; (2) walk up closer to a person of the same sex who has her/his eyes closed; (3) prefer a face-to-face approach more; and (4) disclose more about themselves in social interaction than do men (Deaux, 1976).

The sexual composition of *adult* groups affects the spacing preferences of the people in those groups. Women, when in mixed-sex groups, prefer that the group be large and that there be crowded rather than uncrowded conditions. Women prefer much smaller and uncrowded groups if the people in those groups are all women (Marshall and Heslin, 1975).

Just as in children, adult strangers respond differently than do friends. Among strangers, the sex difference may not be as great and, in some situations, may actually reverse. For example, in adult stranger dyads in London, England, females stand at significantly greater distances from one another than do males (Heshka and Nelson, 1972).

People also apparently use *visual* marking in much the same way as many primitive primates use scent marking to delay invasion of marked locales (for territoriality). Regardless of the "gender" of the marker (e.g., purse vs. pipe), the markers *are* effective in "delaying invasion." However, masculine items are more effective in reserving space than are feminine items (Shaffer and Sadowski, 1975).

In general, the data on intragroup spacing in humans are not very different from those on intragroup spacing in nonhuman primates. At least the sex differences appear to be quite similar. Females are usually more closely spaced than are males. While there are age differences, cultural differences, differences which depend upon sexual composition, and situational differences, in *most* cases human females seem to be more tolerant of personal physical proximity. As we will see, this tendency is part of an overall general sex difference in social communication.

REFERENCES

Aiello, J.R. and Aiello, T.D. The development of personal space: Proxemic behavior of children 6 through 16. *Human Ecology,* 1974, 2 (3), 177-189.

Aiello, J.R. and Cooper, R.E. Use of personal space as a function of social affect. Proceedings of the 80th *Annual Convention of the American Psychological Association,* 1972.

Bernstein, I.S. Daily activity cycles and weather influences in a pigtail monkey group. *Folia Primatologica,* 1972, 18, 390-415.

Bretherton, I. Beyond wariness: Infants' spontaneous approach to and proximal interaction with unfamiliar adults. Paper presented at the biennial convention of the Society for Research in Child Development, San Francisco, CA, March, 15-18, 1979.

Deaux, K. *The Behavior of Women and Men.* Monterey, CA: Brooks/Cole, 1976.

Harper, L.V. and Sanders, K.M. Sex differences in preschool children's social interactions and use of space: An evolutionary perspective. In McGill, T.E., Dewsbury, D.A., and Sachs, B.D. (Eds.) *Sex and Behavior.* New York: Plenum, 1978, pp. 61-82.

Heshka, S. and Nelson, Y. Interpersonal speaking distance as a function of age, sex, and relationship. *Sociometry,* 1972, 35 (4), 491-498.

Lomranz, J., Shapira, A. Choresh, N., and Gilat, Y. Children's personal space as a function of age and sex. *Developmental Psychology,* 1975, 11, 541-545.

Marshall, J.E. and Heslin, R. Boys and girls together: Sexual composition and the effect of density and group size on cohesiveness. *Journal of Personality and Social Psychology,* 1975, 31 (5), 952-961.

Meisels, M. and Guardo, C.J. Development of personal space schemata. *Child Development,* 1969, 40, 1167-1178.

Melson, G.F. Sex differences in proxemic behavior and personal space schemata in young children. *Sex Roles,* 1977, 3 (1), 81-89.

Mitchell, G. *Behavioral Sex Differences in Nonhuman Primates.* New York: Van Nostrand Reinhold, 1979.

Price, G.H. and Dobbs, J.M. Sex, setting, and personal space: Changes as children grow older. *Personality and Social Psychology Bulletin,* 1974, 1 (1), 362-363.

Shaffer, D.R. and Sadowski, C. This table is mine: Respect for marked barroom tables as a function of gender or spatial marker and desirability of locale. *Sociometry,* 1975, 38 (3), 408-419.

Sommer, R. *Personal Space.* Englewood Cliffs, NJ: Prentice-Hall, 1969.

Whalen, C.K., Flowers, J.V., Fuller, M.J., and Jernigan, T. Behavioral studies of personal space during early adolescence. *Man-Environment Systems,* 1975, 5 (5), 289-297.

14
Status, Alliances and Leadership in Nonhuman Primates

In nonhuman primates, status in a group is usually referred to as dominance or rank. The definition of the word dominance is fraught with difficulties if not with controversy. Dominance is an intervening variable, an abstract term which is operationalized by the different ways in which it is assessed or measured. Sometimes these different assessments do not agree with each other. When they do, the intervening variable itself becomes useful (Hinde, 1974).

Dominance is not the same thing as aggressiveness. A dominant animal need not be aggressive and an aggressive animal is not necessarily dominant. Dominance must also be differentiated from leadership. In addition, alliances between nondominant individuals can overcome single animal dominance. Friends, kin, or sexual partners of dominant individuals often obtain derived dominance from their higher status companions. On the other hand, dominance is something which can be characteristic of individuals even though an individual may not be dominant in all situations (Mitchell, 1979).

In behavioral primatology, dominance is assessed by priority of access to an incentive like space, food, water, a sitting place, a sexual partner, or grooming. Dominance is correlated with many kinds of behaviors and it may be a dimension which is more obvious in some primates (e.g., baboons) than in others (e.g., spider monkeys).

In species of primates where relatively unidimensional dominance orders exist, the status hierarchy may not be apparent as long as the number one or alpha animal is present. If that animal is removed, social instability, aggression, and increased "dominance displays" may result. Such alpha animals often perform a "control role" in maintaining group stability.

Dominance displays in primates include branch shaking, jumping and roaring, and chest beating. Aggression need not be shown.

Sexual interactions *are* affected by dominance relations but subordinate males occasionally impregnate females by sneaking in when the male animals of higher status are busy elsewhere. Within-sex interactions are affected differently by dominance than are between-sex interactions. Males and females may have separate dominance hierarchies, although this point of view may have been, to an extent, generated by a history of sexism in the biological sciences, reflecting, of course, the values of the society at the time (Shields, 1975). Biological science is certainly not alone in having shown sexism, nor is it by any means the most repugnant source of sexism in society.[1]

With regard to other sex differences in dominance, we already know that sex hormones, primarily testosterone, are important in dominance attainment, at least in some species. We also know, however, that testosterone alone does not cause dominance. In addition, social and situational factors have been implicated.

Not only sex hormones but also sexual behaviors are related to dominance. Many social signals used in sexual reproduction, including sexual mounting and sexual presentation themselves, are used as signals of dominance and/or subordination. A mount can be a sexual mount, a dominance mount, or both. An erect penis is a dominance display in the squirrel monkey (cf. Wickler, 1967). Sex itself is extremely important in primate status systems, including those of human primates. Social scientists cannot ignore this.

Aside from these more directly biological contributions to dominance relations, dominance can also be learned. Males, in particular, seem especially liable to learn dominance, particularly in sexually dimorphic species. There is some evidence for protocultural and/or genetic effects as well. Infants of dominant mothers often become dominant themselves (cf. Mitchell, 1979).

The dominant individual also does not, in fact, cannot, always take advantage of her/his own status. In troops of Japanese macaques, for example, dominant males are rarely the first to explore

---

[1] It would be interesting to debate this question. Religion, schools, government, and the family are certainly obvious sources.

new objects. They are, in fact, quite conservative in this regard. Subordinates and/or juveniles often test out new situations, after which dominant individuals displace them. Dominance is quite complex indeed.

In summary, dominance is an intervening variable which must be differentiated from aggression, leadership, alliance, and even sexual behavior. Dominance is situation-specific and is usually defined by priority of access to some desired incentive. Dominance relations help to maintain group stability. Displays of dominance include both sexual-like and nonsexual displays. Dominance can be learned; and, dominant animals can be very conservative in some regards. Let us now review sex differences in dominance relations in the primate order.

PROSIMIANS

Male dominance over females is apparently characteristic of bushbabies. Adult male bushbabies in their home territories dominate those not in their own areas. If a female bushbaby becomes dominant, however, she becomes quite aggressive relative to a dominant male bushbaby. Male dominance over females is more often than not the rule for prosimian primates, although females of some species of lemurs are dominant over males.

NEW WORLD MONKEYS

Among monogamous species of the New World, male dominance over females is not necessarily the rule. Among golden lion marmosets, there is equal dominance between male and female. In the pygmy marmoset, the female is dominant over the male. Titi monkey males are somewhat dominant over their female mates, however (Fragaszy, 1976; Mitchell, 1979).

Nonmonogamous squirrel monkeys show two separate dominance hierarchies, one for males and one for females. A male is usually the most dominant member of a group, regardless of how the group is formed. Erect penile displays are directed toward females more than toward other males. Sprawling and back-rolling are shown only by dominant males. Female squirrel monkeys living together without males display hierarchies similar to male hierarchies. Thus they have the potential to display male-like dominance in the absence of males, just like rhesus males have the potential to display femalelike infant care in the absence of females. This is additional evidence for Beach's hypothesis of neural bisexuality in primates alluded to earlier.

Other New World monkeys vary from species to species in regards to dominance systems. In cebus monkeys (organ-grinder monkeys), males are dominant over females. The sexually dimorphic howlers show the same pattern. But, in spider monkeys, which are mono-morphic, but not monogamous, mounting and presenting are not used in dominance-related situations and males are not particularly dominant over females. Thus, both the use of sexual posturing in dominance *and* male dominance over females may be a function of sexual dimorphism more than of monogamy. The reports of lower frequencies of sexual behavior in monogamous relative to non-monogamous species may actually be a reflection of this relative absence of the use of sexual posturing in dominance relations in the monogamous species when compared to nonmonogamous ones. These views may help to shed some light on the human situation which we will discuss later (cf. Mitchell, 1979).

OLD WORLD ARBOREAL SPECIES

Sacred langur females have less rigid dominance hierarchies than do males, yet it *is* clear that a female's dominance or status does in-crease when she gives birth. This may remind us of the increased feelings of self-esteem surrounding the achievement of motherhood in human females. Male sacred langur dominance hierarchies are rigid and males are dominant over females. Even subadult males are dominant over adult females. Despite this male dominance over females, in many langurs female-female encounters create more tension, more excitement, and more loud vocalizations than do male encounters. Perhaps this is so because of the central social importance of the females relative to the males. It is unlikely that this would be true of humans indicating that even langur females may be taken more seriously in their groups than human females are in theirs (cf. Mitchell, 1979).

In African arboreal monkeys, males are dominant over females, although in some cases they do not exert a very strong dominance over them.

OLD WORLD TERRESTRIAL MONKEYS

As we have already seen in Chapter 7, there is a role for the sex hormone testosterone in the dominance of rhesus macaques. When rhesus males or females are given DHTP (dihydrotestosterone proprionate) their dominance status increases and persists even when the DHTP administration ceases. When a male is defeated, his plasma testosterone levels decrease. Thus, hormones produce social changes, and social events produce hormonal changes (see Mitchell, 1979, for primary references).

In rhesus macaques, males are dominant over females. Males display dominance with branch shakes, yawns, mounts, strutting with crooked tail, chewing and gnashing, and barking. Males appear to be more aggressive in their dominance encounters than do females. Peripheral males, in particular, do the most to determine the relative dominance of two different troops (see Mitchell, 1979).

As female rhesus macaques achieve adulthood, they rank just below the rank of their mothers, while males gain or lose rank or leave the troop. A brother is dominant over a sister, unless the brother leaves the troop.

While males usually dominate females, occasionally old females dominate and adult males are kept out of the troop (Neville, 1968a). In addition, female choice is important in sexual behavior. Females prefer certain males for reasons other than their dominance. Numbers of ejaculations in males do not differ from the top third of the dominance hierarchy to the bottom third. Similar results are obtained when one looks at female hierarchies in the wild. These findings are *not* true for females in captivity, however. In captivity, low-ranked females experience high stress levels and hence get pregnant less than do high-ranked females (see Mitchell, 1979). On the whole, however, it is true that while dominance in rhesus macaques may lead to power and control, it does not necessarily lead to reproductive success.

Japanese macaque males are also dominant over females but male sex hormones seem to be somewhat less involved in their dominance than in rhesus dominance. Despite this, male dominance displays do seem to influence female choice of males. In Japanese macaque males, age and rank are correlated. High-ranking males mate with high-ranking females, low-ranking males with low-ranking females. Dominant males can and do interfere with the courtship activities of lower ranking males, however.

As in rhesus females, the "principle of youngest ascendancy" applies to Japanese macaque females. The youngest sister ranks just below the mother. Almost all males leave the troop eventually, but for those who stay, age and length of time in the troop are correlated with dominance rank.

Dominant male Japanese monkeys tend to remain in the center of the troop, near females. They play a "group focus role." A male learns dominance by being the son of a dominant and central female who associates with dominant males (Imanishi, 1965).

As in rhesus, occasionally there are troops of Japanese monkeys containing no adult males. In these troops, an old female dominates and *female* rather than male infants learn dominance behaviors. Thus, monkey "matriarchal" societies seem to produce sex roles which are different from those of "patriarchal" societies. Obviously large canines are not needed in Japanese monkey dominance relations (Alexander and Hughes, 1971). Despite data such as the above, however, Japanese monkeys, like rhesus, are *usually* characterized by male dominance.

Other macaques display male dominance over females just as rhesus and Japanese monkeys do. The pigtail macaque status hierarchy remains very stable only if a dominant male is present. The dominant male pigtail displays a "control role" in which he defends the group and prevents internal disturbance. In pigtail macaques in captivity, females low in dominance show low frequencies of sexual behavior and rarely conceive.

Bonnet macaque males are more tolerant of one another than are rhesus or pigtail males but bonnet males are dominant over bonnet females. In the bonnet group there may be several males that play the "control role" by cooperating in a "central hierarchy."

Stumptail macaques show the "principle of youngest ascendancy," high-ranking individuals are attracted to one another, and an alpha male is the focus of attention. Plasma testosterone levels in both males and females are related to social rank. A female's dominance increases after she delivers an infant.

Factors other than hormonal or biological ones are important in the dominance relations of still other macaques. In one captive group of crab-eating macaques, an old "control role" male was bitten and injured by his son (also an adult). There had been prolonged tension between the two and, after the bite, the elder male showed signs of submission. With no clear leader, aggression broke out in the rest of the group, particularly in the males. The older control male then appealed for help from others and *especially* from his son (who had wounded him). He received the aid and he and his son restored order until the son learned to play the control role by himself. Such respect for aging leaders, be they male or female, is not unusual among the more advanced nonhuman primates (See Mitchell, 1979, for primary references).

Baboons do not differ much from macaques in their dominance relations. Male dominance is the rule. Male baboons having longevity in the troop and a high rank at the start of their reproductive careers hold an edge over other males in regards to reproductive success, but the most aggressive *and* dominant males are not necessarily the leaders in all situations. Some baboons, unlike macaques, live in one-male groups. In these, the male is dominant over the females.

In other Old World monkeys, the macaque-baboon dominance system definitely does not prevail. Adult female talapoins rank above males and their status and aggressiveness relative to males increases still more during the breeding season. Female talapoins in captivity have been known to kill males. They also sometimes mount them. Males *prefer* the most dominant females as partners (Dixson and Herbert, 1974; Rowell and Dixson, 1975; Wolfheim, 1977; Dixson, et al., 1972; Dixson, et al., 1975; Keverne, 1976).[2]

APES

Common chimpanzee adult males are usually dominant over adult females. However, when a female is at the height of her sexual swelling, there may be temporary reversals in dominance between the male and the female. The administration of *estrogen* increases female dominance (see Mitchell, 1979).

As in monkeys, dominance and leadership are not the same thing. In fact, in chimpanzees the *least* preferred leader is sometimes the *most* dominant male (Menzel, 1973).

In the gorilla, the silver-backed male is the most dominant, but again, not necessarily the leader in every activity. Chest beating and many vocalizations are correlated with gorilla dominance. Chest beating is seen in females when they are sexually swollen (swelling is slight in gorillas) (Keiter, 1977; Hess, 1973; Nadler, 1976).

Adult male orangutans are definitely dominant over adult female orangutans. Occasionally the male even takes the female sexually by force. Among immature orangutans, however, dominance is more a matter of size than of gender. Also, in captive situations where adult

---

[2]Because the talapoin seems to be the Old World monkey exception which makes the rule, we have included a number of references on this particular species which readers may consult on their own.

male and female orangutans are housed with each other, the female may actually be more assertive in sexual relations than is the male (Maple, 1980).

In summary, most nonhuman primate social systems involve male dominance over females. Exceptions include some lemurs, some New World monogamous primates, perhaps one New World monomorphic but not monogamous primate, one Old World monkey (the talapoin), and perhaps the lesser apes. Dominance over males is seen in females of all species under certain circumstances. Dominance is situation specific. In females, dominance increases during estrus and following delivery of a baby.

ALLIANCES AND COALITIONS

Alliances in prosimians have not been studied very thoroughly but some female prosimians will come to the aid of another female and protect her from a male, especially during delivery of an infant. The two females together overcome male dominance.

In monogamous New World monkeys, alliances and coalitions are usually cross-sexed. The adult male and female form a monogamous united front against outsiders.

Among nonmonogamous but sexually dimorphic New World monkeys, females engage in more affiliative behavior than do males. Female-female bonds are more cohesive than are male-male bonds, and females do occasionally form alliances against males. Two females in coalition can overcome the individual dominance of a male.

Nonmonogamous but monomorphic New World monkeys are different. Male spider monkeys assist other males in attacks on either males or females. Coalitions between females against males never occur. Most of the coalitions seen are alliances of males against females (see Mitchell, 1979, for primary references).

Old World monkeys are more like the sexually dimorphic New World monkeys. That is, female Old World monkeys form more coalitions than do males. However, there are peripheral male subgroups that operate in coalition. Males are able to form new groups partly because they have formed an alliance with another male in the past.

On the whole, female Old World monkeys are more adept at eliciting the aid of dominant others than are male Old World monkeys, particularly in adulthood. Sex differences in alliances then depend upon age as well as upon gender. Old World monkey sex differences in coalitions also change with familiarity. Females prefer familiar females but unfamiliar males as allies. Males prefer unfamiliar females, and peripheral males. Females have closed, within-group ties. Males, particularly young adult males, initiate between-group alliances. Even adult talapoin females, who are quite male-like in their dominance, form more like-sex coalitions than do adult talapoin males (cf. Mitchell, 1979).

The situation is much different in the lesser apes. Most alliances are across sex. The monogamous unit allies itself against intruders. Great apes, on the other hand, are much like Old World monkeys: female-female alliance is stronger than is male-male alliance. Mother-daughter chimpanzee associations last for many years. Kinship, of course, is important in alliances at all levels of the primate order (see Mitchell, 1979).

LEADERSHIP

Nonhuman primate leadership is a quality which appears in different individuals in different situations. Also, as we have already seen, dominance and leadership are not the same thing. One individual is usually not a leader in all situations. Initiating group movement is often, although not always, the role of an adult male.

Very little is known about prosimian leadership. Among New World primates, as usual, monogamous primates differ from non-monogamous primates. Female titi monkeys lead the family group in exploratory movements and throughout the group's daily range. In nonmonogamous howler and squirrel monkeys, mature males lead the group when moving or when exploring.

In Old World macaques, a basic group of old females is the most stable portion of the band. While males usually control internal strife, females return information about feeding areas and travel routes. They also have a large say in mating choices. However, leader males also guide troop migrations. In fact, in most macaques, it is usually a male that leads a progression and there is usually a male as a rear guard. When starting off, it is usually a male who moves first and, when leaving a feeding area for a resting place, the male may emit a special vocalization and others follow him (cf. Mitchell, 1979).

Baboons show a pattern much like that of the macaques. In movement there is usually a male at the lead, and one at the rear. Getting and keeping the group together (troop mobilization) for movement is almost always a male's job. Adult male baboons also usually enter a forest clearing first, although there are some occasions in which females *do* lead troop movements (see Rowell, 1972; Bramblett, 1970). In general, among Old World monkeys, it is probably safe to say that it is the adult females who hold the troop's valuable long-term knowledge and perhaps the decision of where to go. In the final analysis, decisions on where to feed and rest come from this stable female core. The male appears to actually lead the troop in its movements, however (see Mitchell, 1979).

The travel order for lesser apes is usually: adult female, infant, adult male, weaned infant or juvenile, and subadult. Thus, as in the monogamous New World monkeys, male leadership in movement is not typical in the monogamous lesser apes, whether they be siamang or gibbon.

As Menzel (1973) has shown, chimpanzee leadership is variable and situation specific. In one group, any of five different chimpanzees served as a leader, at least in terms of getting others to follow her or him.

In gorillas, the silver-backed male leads group movements, but no single individual is *the* leader. Leadership in the orangutan has not been studied.

In the next chapter we will discuss status, alliances, and leadership in people.

REFERENCES

Alexander, B. and Hughes, J. Canine teeth and rank in Japanese monkeys *(Macaca fuscata)*. *Primates,* 1971, 12, 91-93.

Bramblett, C.A. Coalitions among baboons. *Primates,* 1970, 11, 327-333.

Dixson, A.F. and Herbert, J. Gonadal hormones and aggressive behaviors in captive groups of talapoin monkeys *(Miopithecus talapoin)*. *Journal of Endocrinology,* 1974, 61, 46.

Dixson, A.F., Herbert, J., and Rudd, B.T. Gonadal hormones and behaviour in captive groups of talapoin monkeys *(Miopithecus talapoin)*. *Journal of Endocrinology,* 1972, 57, 41.

Dixson, A.F., Scruton, D.M., and Herbert, J. Behaviour of the talapoin monkey *(Miopithecus talapoin)* studied in groups in the laboratory. *Journal of Zoology* (London), 1975, 176, 177-210.

Fragaszy, D.M. Contrasts in feeding behavior in captive pairs of *Saimiri* and *Callicebus.* Paper presented at the *Animal Behavior Society* meeting, Denver, Colorado, March, 1976.

Hess, J.P. Some observations on the sexual behavior of captive lowland gorillas, *Gorilla g. gorilla* (Savage and Wyman). In Michael, R.P. and Crook, J.H. (Eds.) *Comparative Ecology and Behavior of Primates.* New York: Academic Press, 1973, pp. 508-581.

Hinde, R.A. *Biological Bases of Social Behavior.* New York: McGraw-Hill, 1974.

Imanishi, K. Identification: A process of socialization in the subhuman society of *Macaca fuscata.* In Imanishi, K. and Altmann, S. (Eds.) *Japanese Monkeys.* Atlanta: Altmann, 1965, pp. 30-51.

Keiter, M.D. Reproductive behavior in subadult captive lowland gorillas *(Gorilla gorilla gorilla).* Paper presented at the *American Society of Primatologists* meeting, Seattle, Washington, April, 1977.

Keverne, E.B. Dominance, aggression and sexual behaviour in social groups of talapoin monkeys. Paper presented at the *International Primatological Society* meeting, Cambridge, England, August, 1976.

Maple, T. *Orang-utan Behavior.* New York: Van Nostrand Reinhold, 1980.

Menzel, E.W. Jr. Leadership and communication in young chimpanzees. *Symposia of the Fourth International Congress of Primatology.* Basel: Karger, 1973, pp. 192-225.

Mitchell, G. *Behavioral Sex Differences in Nonhuman Primates.* New York: Van Nostrand Reinhold, 1979.

Nadler, R.D. Sexual behavior of captive lowland gorillas. *Archives of Sexual Behavior,* 1976, 5, 487-502.

Neville, M. A free-ranging rhesus monkey troop lacking adult males. *Journal of Mammalogy,* 1968a, 49, 771-773.

Rowell, T.E. *The Social Behaviour of Monkeys.* Baltimore: Penguin, 1972.

Rowell, T.E. and Dixson, A.F. Changes in social organization during the breeding season of wild talapoin monkeys. *Journal of Reproduction and Fertility,* 1975, 43, 419-434.

Shields, S.A. Functionalism, Darwinism, and the psychology of women. *American Psychologist,* 1975, 30, 739-754.

Wickler, W. Socio-sexual signals and their intraspecific imitation among primates. In Morris, D. (Ed.), *Primate Ethology.* Chicago: Aldine, 1967, pp. 69-147.

Wolfheim, J.H. Sex differences in behavior in a group of captive juvenile talapoin monkeys *(Miopithecus talapoin). Behaviour,* 1977, 63, 110-128.

15
Status, Alliances and Leadership in People

Children have been directly compared with immature chimpanzees and orangutans with regard to dominance. In the childhood of all three species, males are more assertive than are females (Braggio et al., 1976). In other studies, however, children up to 4 years of age have been studied and both boys and girls appear at high, middle, and low dominance ranks. Dominance in preschool children is situation specific. When a preschool child is subordinate at school she/he may still be dominant in her/his own home. Preschool boys, however, appear to show more dominance both at home and away from home than do girls. In most studies they tend to be at the top of the dominance hierarchy, with preschool girls at the bottom. There *is* substantial overlap between the sexes, however. When in *isosexual* preschool situations, it is as important for a girl to be tough as it is for a boy; and, girls and boys develop similar hierarchies (see Mitchell, 1979, for references).

In preadolescents, females tend to submit when with males more than they do when with other girls. Even boys who *readily* submit in all boy games will compete in mixed-sex games. In high school, boys are dominance-ranked by their peers on the basis of athletic ability and physical attractiveness rather than on the basis of intelligence. These rankings begin some six years before high school. High school boys are dominant over high school girls (Weisfeld et al., 1977).

Despite sex differences in dominance in middle childhood, children of both sexes *perceive* the same-sex parent as being the most dominant and the most punitive. Recall that, in our chapters on infant care, parents were less tolerant of children of the same sex than they were of children of the other sex. This may be evidence of already well-formed and somewhat separate like-sex or same-sex dominance systems in humans (Goldin, 1969).

On the basis of what we know about nonhuman primates, sexual dimorphism and male dominance tend to go together. Humans are intermediate between baboons and marmosets in the degree of physical sexual dimorphism they display. While baboons usually show male dominance over females and while marmosets frequently show female dominance over males, humans show some dominance of males over females, but extensive overlap between the sexes (cf. Mitchell, 1979).

Despite significant overlap in dominance between the sexes in humans, religion, the schools, government, and business all tell us that men are dominant over women. Advertising for men's products and the products themselves suggest male dominance. A large share of this advertising is sexist and not based upon "real" group differences. Our society is not a subsistence society and is requiring less and less in the way of sexual differentiation of roles. To the extent that we are like baboons in regard to dominance, if in fact we are like them at all, we are still capable of changing away from that style.

Scientific studies of adult human dominance of today do not always report greater male dominance. Answers given on the College Self-Expression Scale in 1977, for example, indicated that female college students were *more* assertive than were male college students. (As in children, each sex was more assertive toward members of their own sex than toward opposite-sex persons.) Of course, this is but a scale. What college women actually *do* may be different from what they say they do (Stebbins et al., 1977).

Also among college students, there is evidence in females that the status of a male affects their evaluations of the female in that male's company. If the man is attractive and has high status, college women evaluate the female in his company as being intelligent, self-confident, and friendly. Evaluations of the same woman by college men are unaffected by the status of her male partner (Sheposh, et al., 1977).

People are *often* rated stereotypically, and dominance ratings of other people are also sometimes stereotyped. Nonmarried human males and females are usually rated stereotypically, regardless of the dominance roles they typically display. However, marriage seems to change this somewhat. Married women are rated somewhat more dominant and married men somewhat less dominant than their single counterparts (Gerber and Balkin, 1977). But this rating difference may be more than stereotype. Recall that, in monogamous nonhuman primates, males and females are closer in dominance than they are in nonmonogamous nonhuman primates (see Mitchell, 1979). In addition, Maccoby and Jacklin (1974) have concluded that wives become more equal in dominance the longer the marriage lasts.

As in nonhuman primates, aggression and dominance in humans are independent phenomena. While Maccoby and Jacklin (1974) may admit that human males are more aggressive than human females, they conclude that whether or not human males are more *dominant* than human females is an open question.

In any case, both adult human males and adult human females use dominance displays. We need only go to a baseball or softball game to see the victors of both sexes assume erect postures, leap, clasp hands, shake arms and fists, and dance. The losers sit or walk with shoulders hunched and head down as they walk with slow movements. Female athletes and fans emit the same behaviors as do males, although somewhat less aggressively (Maple and Howard, 1977). Dominance is by no means the domain of men alone.

ALLIANCES

Prior to going into a discussion of the more political and social psychological aspects of sex differences in dominance and power, we will first examine alliances and leadership in people. Among human children of three to five years, cooperation is more frequent in girls than in boys (Sanders and Harper, 1976). By seven years of age, same-sex preference for peers has developed. Seven-year-old children prefer to smile at and touch same-sex peers (Travis and Fontenelle, 1977). Between five and twelve years of age girls have higher altruism and cooperation scores than do boys (Skarin and Moely, 1976). Results such as these suggest a greater potential for alliance or coalition in dominance for girls than for boys.

Girls associate in pairs or small groups of age-mates, boys in gangs or in large groups of playmates. It is probable that girls and women make closer friends with one another than do boys and men (Maccoby and Jacklin, 1974). Among college students and older adults, for example, females are more deliberate than are males when they select a friend and their friend must more closely approximate their own ideals as far as intelligence is concerned than must a man's friend (Bailey et al., 1976).

In cross-cultural studies (Whiting and Pope, 1973), girls (age 3-11) tried to control a person in the interest of social welfare or of that person's welfare, whereas boys were more individualistic, even egoistic, in their dominance interactions. In addition, in same-sex interactions, as we've seen, girls and women get closer to one another and look at each other more than do boys and men (Exline, 1971). It is interesting that, even in monkey-human contact, female monkeys and female humans engage in more eye-to-eye contact than do male monkeys and male humans (Thomsen, 1974).

ALLIANCES WITH STRANGERS: HELPING STUDIES

In instances staged to look like a person was in minor trouble and needed help, men were much more likely to volunteer their services to a stranger than were women. A female in minor trouble was helped more than was a man. *Both* of these sex differences were greater in Atlanta, Georgia than in Columbus, Ohio. A man in Atlanta with a flat tire was not likely to get help; a woman in Atlanta was. Overall, however, women were much more likely to get help from a stranger than were men and men were much more likely to help than were women. However, a lost child may produce different results, as might other situations potentially less dangerous for a woman interacting with strangers. In addition, we already know that young boys and men are taught all their lives to be initiators and actors. Girls and women are not (Deaux, 1976).

Aside from the overall sex differences in helping behavior alluded to above, there is also evidence that in *stranger* helping situations, cross-sex helping is more common than is same-sex helping (Deaux, 1976).

Moreover, when the task is to help a stranger, a distinction must be made between those cases where the helper must take the initiative and those cases where the one in need of help requests it. In the first case, men help much more; in the second case, the results are more variable (Deaux, 1976).

Cultural norms and expected rewards are also important in helping a stranger. Potential rewards for helping someone of the opposite sex are often assumed by the helper to be greater. In addition, cultural norms are important. In some areas of the United States, women almost never help strangers at all (Deaux, 1976).

COMPLIANCE

Women have often been labeled more conforming and compliant than men. But, on "feminine" topics, men are more conforming than women. Women are, not surprisingly, more conforming on "masculine" topics. As Deaux (1976) has said, "both sexes show independence in familiar areas and conformity when the territory is unfamiliar." (p. 96)

COMPETITION

Men are often labeled as being more competitive than women. But on games devised by social psychologists, some women are more competitive than men. Men are more competitive against other men and against highly competent people of either sex. Women tend to be more competitive against other women and against low achievers of either sex. Women are less competitive against *attractive* men, men are not less competitive against attractive women (Deaux, 1976).

During competition, men talk about strategy, women about friends and their *general* interest in the game. Men are more oriented toward the game itself, women toward the players in the game (Deaux, 1976).

COALITIONS IN GAMES

With three men in a game men play competitively in order to win. In order to do this they try to form alliances. Three women try to find the best outcome for everyone. In mixed-sex groups, men still try to form alliances to maximize their own gains. Women form alliances to minimize everyone's losses. In most games which are not gender biased, men and women do equally well. Women are less competitive in style but their strategy works as well as does that of men. Women show a greater interest in the interpersonal variables, in friendships rather than in alliances to win (Deaux, 1976).

SHARING ACHIEVED INCENTIVES

Dominance in primates is defined in terms of priority of access to desired incentives. What if some achieve the desired incentive? Will they share it?

In human adults, both men and women claim that the most equitable situation is the fairest. But what people say and what they do are often different. In *both* winning and losing situations, however, women are more humble than are men. Women are more likely to more equally share the rewards of work. Women share more whether their partners are male or female. Men, on the other hand, tend to share less overall but more with women than with men. When women lose, however, they are more likely to be harder on themselves than are men. In an employment setting, women *voluntarily* accept lower salaries. Typical or traditional women's jobs do not pay a salary. They may be more easily satisfied by less than are men. When directly asked, women say that money is not important more than do men. In the reward allocation situation, or in employment, women again seem more concerned with interpersonal than with financial aspects of the job. Financial reward is not as important to them as social reward (Deaux, 1976).

Data such as the above do not lead us to believe that men are simply dominating submissive women, who, in turn, are simply more compliant than the men. Things are more complex than that. Men and women have different objectives. Men want to win; women want to establish social relationships. Dominance differences may be as much a function of the females particular desires as the males. Females may simply be somewhat disinterested in the dominance games men play. Priority of access to them may mean priority of access to interpersonal interaction in general (see Deaux, 1976).

LEADERSHIP IN HUMANS

Human children of six and seven years believe that men are larger and more powerful, yet they perform better in learning tasks with women models as leaders than with male models. This is true even in building with wooden blocks (a so-called masculine activity)

(Bartlett, 1977). Thus, for children, power and efficient leadership qualities in adults are not the same thing.

In human adults there are probably few job-related differences in male and female leaders, although they may differ in other ways. It has been said that females respond more intensely to authority and particularly to female authority figures than do men (Wright, 1976); however, female leaders may employ less authoritarian methods than men (Maccoby and Jacklin, 1974) and show more consideration, tolerance of uncertainty, and satisfaction with co-workers than men (Bartol and Wortman, 1976). Thus, even if there is a more intense response in female-to-female authority relationships, these would be tempered by the less authoritarian nature of the female leader. To the extent that iron-fisted tycoons are anachronisms, women leaders are extremely valuable in today's society. They are, perhaps, less likely to impose their own wills on others (Maccoby and Jacklin, 1974).

If we list the leaders of the world, we see that most of them are men. Women make up 20 percent of the labor unions but hold less than 5 percent of the leadership jobs. Foremen of juries are almost always males. When any group contains both sexes, it is likely that the leader chosen will be a male. Even in dyads of one male and one female where the woman is clearly dominant and the man submissive (as measured by personality tests), in 80 percent of the pairs the man becomes the leader. The high-dominant woman makes the decision; *she* decides that the male partner will be the leader. Women are unlikely to become leaders at least partly because they *choose* not to be the leaders (Deaux, 1976).

When women fail as leaders they are often not blamed as much as are men.[1] After all, women are not supposed to be good leaders (Deaux, 1976).

REFERENCES

Bailey, R.C., DiGiacomo, R.J., and Zinser, O. Length of male and female friendship and perceived intelligence in self and friend. *Journal of Personality Assessment,* 1976, 40, 635-640.

Bartlett, L. The effects of sex of model on task performance in young children. Paper presented at the *Western Psychological Association* meeting, Seattle, Washington, April, 1977.

[1]Of course, Gandhi, Meir, and Thatcher have had their share of criticism.

Bartol, K.M. and Wortman, M.S. Jr. Sex effects in leader behavior, self-descriptions and job satisfaction. *Journal of Psychology,* 1976, 94, 177-183.

Braggio, J.T., Nadler, R.D., Lance, J., and Myseko, D. Sex differences in apes and children. Paper presented at the *International Primatological Society* meeting, Cambridge, England, August, 1976.

Deaux, K. *The Behavior of Women and Men.* Monterey, CA: Brooks-Cole, 1976.

Exline, R.V. Visual interaction: The glance of power and preference. *Nebraska Symposium on Motivation,* 1971, 19, 163-206.

Gerber, G.L. and Balkin, J. Sex-role stereotypes as a function of marital status and role. *The Journal of Psychology,* 1977, 95, 9-16.

Goldin, P.G. A review of children's reports of parent behaviors. *Psychological Bulletin,* 1969, 71 (3), 222-236.

Maccoby, E.L. and Jacklin, C. *The Psychology of Sex Differences.* Stanford, CA: Stanford University Press, 1974.

Maple, T. and Howard, S. The thrill of victory and the agony of defeat: Ethological correlates. Paper presented at the *American Society of Primatologists* meeting, Seattle, Washington, April, 1977.

Mitchell, G. *Behavioral Sex Differences in Nonhuman Primates.* New York: Van Nostrand Reinhold, 1979.

Sanders, K.M. and Harper, L.V. Free-play fantasy behavior in preschool children: Relations among gender, age, season and location. *Child Development,* 1976, 47, 1182-1185.

Sheposh, J.P., Deming, M., and Young, L.E. The radiating effects of status and attractiveness of a male upon evaluations of his female partner. Paper presented at the *Western Psychological Association* meeting, Seattle, Washington, April, 1977.

Skarin, K. and Moely, B.E. Altruistic behavior: An analysis of age and sex differences. *Child Development,* 1976, 47, 1159-1165.

Stebbins, C.A., Kelly, B.R., Tolor, A., and Power, S.M. Sex differences in assertiveness in college students. *The Journal of Psychology,* 1977, 95, 309-315.

Thomsen, C.E. Eye contact by nonhuman primates toward a human observer. *Animal Behavior,* 1974, 22, 144-149.

Travis, C.B. and Fontenelle, G. Nonverbal signals of affiliation in children. Paper presented at the *Animal Behavior Society* meeting, University Park, Pennsylvania, June, 1977.

Weisfeld, G.E., Omark, D.R., and Cronin, C.L. Brains or brawn? A longitudinal study of dominance in high school boys. Paper presented at the *Animal Behavior Society* meeting, University Park, Pennsylvania, June, 1977.

Whiting, B. and Pope, C. A cross-cultural analysis of sex differences in the behavior of children age three to eleven. *Journal of Social Psychology,* 1973, 91, 171-188.

Wright, F. The effects of style and sex of consultants and sex of members in self-study groups. *Small Group Behavior,* 1976, 7, 433-456.

16
Further Examinations of Status and Power in Women

In social psychology, there is a growing realization that understanding the behavior of women is of importance in understanding human behavior in general. Many behaviors traditionally presumed to show biological sex differences now appear to be affected by social learning and social values. Sex differences are not immutable.

Grady (1979) has said that sex differences may emerge from at least two sources: (1) From within the individual, and (2) from others as a response to the sex of the individual. The first is called a *subject* sex difference, the second is called a *stimulus* sex difference. Sex as a stimulus variable is very much at the center of attention in social psychology, particularly in the social psychology of power.

If people are asked what the members of the other sex think of their own sex, they believe that the opposite sex wants them to be more different from the opposite sex than they believe themselves to be (O'Leary et al., 1979). Thus, there is apparently a social pressure felt by both men and women to be more "male-like" or "female-like" than they actually are.

What does this have to do with status and/or power? Power is traditionally a male domain. To be more male than one actually is, one needs more power. To be more female than one actually is, one needs to at least give the appearance of having *less* power.

But as women enter the realm of power, status, leadership, and control, the entire area itself changes (Carlson, 1976). Power involves at least three things: getting one's way, getting things done, and getting along with others. Men are traditionally identified with the first, women with the third. The second is not gender related (Goodchilds, 1979). Once the emphasis in power is shifted to getting things done, conflict felt by women and men concerning their femininity or masculinity disappears. Goodchilds (1979) wishes we would focus our research on power and leadership on getting things done rather than on gender-related variables.

Both women and men are questioning the traditional *macho* methods of wielding power. "Being nice," however, can also be given too much weight. Women (or men) in power may sometimes have trouble getting things done because they try to be nice, try to avoid confrontations, and try not to appear to be pushy and controlling. According to Johnson (1979), some re-education of women is needed to permit them to break outside of their straightjacket of overconcern for personal harmony. One way out of this straightjacket is to concentrate on getting things done, to put power in terms of *accomplishments,* rather than in terms of relationships (Johnson, 1979).

There is a popular notion that women have a greater tendency to yield in power relationships, that they are more easily influenced, compliant, and conforming under social pressure. We have discussed data from a few laboratory experiments in the previous chapter which suggested that this was not necessarily true. In fact, in traditionally "feminine" areas, men are more compliant and conforming than are women. In real life, however, men *are* concentrated in positions of power and authority. The laboratory setting artificially removes the real-life bias. Because the compliance differences disappear in the laboratory, *bias* is assumed to be responsible for the differences in real life. But practice in *not* conforming is also important for women. From this perspective, bias may go away only when the real-life situation changes, that is, only when women are found more often in positions of power and authority (Eagly, 1979).

Female attitudes are evidently quite different from those of males in several areas, most especially in ideas concerning mastery, work orientation, competitiveness, and concern for the self. High concern with all four of these areas does not necessarily lead to the greatest achievement, however. In one study, for example (Spence and Helmrich, 1978), it was found that male graduates of a business school who scored high in work and mastery, but *low* in competitiveness actually made more money than did males high in all three. It is interesting that in the discipline called the psychology of women, there has been a great deal of research on *achievement,* probably reflecting the *values* of the high achievers doing the research (Wallston, 1979).

Sex differences in groups in regards to power, coalitions, and leadership have been reported for some time. Male performance is more exploitative and competitive, female performance more accommodative and tension-reducing (Bond and Vinacke, 1961; Strodtbeck and Mann, 1956). As we already know, however, sex bias in this regard can be eliminated in the laboratory by selecting more or less feminine tasks (Deaux, 1976). It is the conviction of Hollander (1979) that the sex bias (competitive vs. accommodative) is a reflection of the distinctions made between father and mother roles, public vs. private orientations, and work roles vs. domestic duties. Women, even when in the work force outside the home, have been unable to shake the stereotypes of the home. Because of these stereotypes male leaders in small groups generally fare better than do female leaders. Even when a female leader *is* successful, it is likely to be attributed to luck. Not so with males (Deaux, 1976).

In sexual relationships, too, feelings of power are affected by sex biases. Jealousy is not experienced equivalently by the two sexes. Females tend to respond to jealousy-evoking situations with devastation, anger, and with a need for social support, while males are more likely to show reactive retribution or to move toward a confrontation. Males are also more likely to engage in behaviors which maintain their own self-esteem, whereas females are likely to try to maintain the relationship. For example, males respond by breaking up or becoming sexually involved with others, while females emphasize dependency on their partner and try to make themselves more attractive to their partner (Rodgers and Bryson, 1978). Bryson (1979) believes that these differences may reflect socialization experiences. Females are taught to define their well-being in terms of *relationships* rather than in terms of self-concern. In addition, in the United States, males are permitted more sexual freedom than are females, hence they have more alternatives open to them. Thirdly, females are more likely to associate love with sex, so female infidelity may be more threatening to the male, leaving him nothing to save but his self-esteem (Bryson, 1979).

The masculine pattern in power situations is termed *agentic* (Bakan, 1966). The agentic pattern promotes the individual, glorifies individual achievement, *creates* status distinctions, and separates the individual from the group. The feminine pattern in power situations has been conceptualized as being *communal* (Bakan, 1966). The communal pattern promotes the welfare of the group and relationships with others. Both of these patterns have positive and negative aspects (also see Kahn, 1979). However, one can avoid a sexist orientation by concentrating on neither of them, but instead emphasizing the accomplishments themselves, not the individuals who accomplish them. Getting things done should come before getting one's way *or* getting along (Goodchilds, 1979). If either getting one's way *or* getting along gets things done, fine. Otherwise one should probably concentrate on the task, not on the self or on social relationships.

In regards to the feminist reaction to male power, Jesse Bernard (1975) believes that emphasizing socialization differences between the sexes does not help at all. She proposes that feminists attack the institutions which preserve the differences. Even in marriage there is evidence that the higher the husband's status, occupational prestige, and income, the greater his power in family relationships. If women work outside the home, they have higher self-esteem, fewer psychological and physical symptoms, and greater *power* in family decision making (Tavris and Offir, 1977). Within every society of the world, however, men have more power than do women. "In no nation are women 50 percent of the key politicians or leaders" (Tavris and Offir, 1977, p. 285).

Equality in sexual relationships seems to be very much correlated with equal participation in politics and work. The same underlying tendencies in men and women can be seen operating in both situations. Women have a real-world disadvantage in the home, in marriage, and in the outside work world. There is real social subordination of women, so much so that the sexes learn different styles of speech reflecting their relative degrees of power. Boys speak assertively, they curse, give more direct orders, etc. (Tavris and Offir, 1977). Nonverbal behaviors also reflect differences in power. In addition, the people near us, the roles we come to play, the work we do, the situations we are in, and the rules we are expected to follow all conspire to produce more power for males.

In business, a protégé system has made it very hard for women to succeed by direct efforts. This forces them to use indirect methods including occasionally manipulation and seduction. Men can "get their way" by reasoned argument, women have traditionally had to bargain, deceive, or become emotional (Tavris and Offir, 1977). Even when women take over a formerly all-male occupation, the occupation itself loses status (Tavris and Offir, 1977):

> Real power means that the organization has given the person the authority to make decisions, institute them, and hand out important rewards and punishments. Power comes not just from job title or a fancy office but from membership in the informal inner circles of the company and from recognition by coworkers (Tavris and Offir, 1977, pp. 208-209).

Men do not welcome many women into their informal inner circles.

Getting back to marriage, husbands have much more power than do wives in most homes. Waller (1938) believes this is because women have a greater investment, are more involved in the marriage, and are more committed to a love relationship. Waller (1938) proposed "the principle of least interest" which says that the partner who is less involved has more power. This is probably an oversimplification. Economic and other factors are certainly of as much importance as degree of commitment to a relationship. Getting the woman out of the home and getting the man to share domestic and infant care responsibilities will do much in the way of producing a more equitable distribution of power in the home. Of course, such arrangements must always be the result of choice on the part of each couple; and, even more importantly, the result of the choice of each *individual,* woman or man.

It is interesting that in all other species of primates, the female is more powerful the more monogamous her relationship with a male. Only in the human primate is monogamy (i.e., marriage) more disadvantageous in terms of power for the female than is the non-monogamous relationship. Why are people unique in this way?

But even when in the work force, a woman's power is still negligible relative to a man's. Societal stereotypes do not change quickly. However, forces[1] alluded to earlier in this book may work together (*very* slowly, admittedly) to gradually provide women with more

---

[1]The forces referred to earlier were technology's making domestic duty easier, birth control, more open divorce and abortion laws, changing sexual morality, and the women's movement in general.

power. Whether they will ever acquire more power than men is debatable. If women in the United States do, in fact, achieve more power than men, they will be the first women on the earth at the present time to do so.

The male's advantage in getting out of the private, domestic sphere and into the public, working and political sphere is undoubtedly at the core of the sex differences in power. We will discuss the development of this advantage in our nonhuman primate cousins in the next chapter.

REFERENCES

Bakan, D. *The Duality of Human Existence.* Chicago: Rand McNally, 1966.

Bernard, J. *Women, Wives, Mothers: Values and Options.* Chicago: Aldine, 1975.

Bond, J.R. and Vinacke, W.E. Coalitions in mixed-sex triads. *Sociometry,* 1961, 24, 61-75.

Bryson, J.B. Sex and sexual jealousy. *Society for the Advancement of Social Psychology Newsletter,* 1979, 5 (3), 10-11.

Carlson, R. Understanding women: Implications for personality theory and research. *Journal of Social Issues,* 1972, 28 (2), 17-32.

Deaux, K. *The Behavior of Women and Men.* Monterey, CA: Brooks-Cole, 1976.

Eagly, A.H. Observations on the study of sex differences in social behavior. *Society for the Advancement of Social Psychology Newsletter,* 1979, 5 (3), 4-5.

Goodchilds, J.D. Power: A matter of mechanics? *Society for the Advancement of Social Psychology Newsletter,* 1979, 5 (3), 3.

Grady, K.E. Androgyny reconsidered. In Williams, J.H. (Ed.) *Psychology of Women: Selected readings.* New York: W.W. Norton, 1979, pp. 172-178.

Hollander, E.P. Sex roles in groups. *Society for the Advancement of Social Psychology Newsletter,* 1979, 5 (3), 9-10.

Johnson, P.B. Feminist people and power: Are we copping out? *Society for the Advancement of Social Psychology Newsletter,* 1979, 5 (3), 3-4.

Kahn, A. From theories of equity to theories of justice: An example of demasculinization in social psychology. *Society for the Advancement of Social Psychology Newsletter,* 1979, 5 (3), 12-14.

O'Leary, V.E., Wallston, B.S., and Unger, R.K. Women, gender, and social psychology. *Society for the Advancement of Social Psychology Newsletter,* 1979, 5 (3), 1-2.

Rodgers, M.A. and Bryson, J.B. Self-esteem and relationship maintenance as responses to jealousy. Paper presented at the meeting of the *Western Psychological Association,* San Francisco, CA, 1978.

Spence, J.T. and Helmreich, R.L. *Masculinity and Femininity.* Austin, Tex: University of Texas Press, 1978.

Strodtbeck, F.L. and Mann, R.D. Sex roles differentiation in jury deliberations. *Sociometry*, 1956, 19, 3-11.

Tavris, C. and Offir, C. *The Longest War: Sex Differences in Perspective.* New York: Harcourt Brace Jovanovich, 1977.

Waller, W. *The Family: A Dynamic Interpretation.* New York: Dryden, 1938.

Wallston, B.S. Values and social psychology. *Society for the Advancement of Social Psychology Newsletter*, 1979, 5 (3), 7-8.

17
Extragroup Behaviors: Protection and Predation

In Chapter 5, we noted an important sex difference in many non-human primates which appeared at or around the time of puberty and early adulthood. That difference was that in many species of nonhuman primates adolescent males become spatially peripheralized and, as they approach adulthood, may leave the group, join a temporary all-male group, become solitary, or change residence to another permanent mixed group. In Chapter 6, we likened this sex difference to the human sex difference in public vs. private orientation. Male humans have a more public, centrifugal orientation; females have a more private, domestic, and centripetal orientation. This difference may account for a large portion of the overall sex differences in political power in people.

In the current chapter we will be looking for additional evidence for an orientation outward from the group in our nonhuman primate cousins. Is the sex difference apparent *only* in group spacing, solitary living, and group change, or do males display *other* behaviors which indicate that they have a greater interest than females in the outside world? As we will see, the answer to this question is that there is an overall pattern of sex differences indicating greater involvement for males in extragroup orientation.

In previous chapters we have also discussed the "control role" of dominant members of primate groups. The "control role" in sexually dimorphic nonhuman primates is a role typically taken by an adult male. The "control role", however, involves two major activities: (1) the settling of internal strife, and (2) troop or group protection from outside danger. The former activity involves within-group leadership and intragroup control, the latter usually deals with extratroop or intertroop threats. Up to now, we have dealt only with dominance, leadership, alliances, and power in the context of internal organization, spacing, social structure, and within-group stability. In the present chapter, however, we will concentrate on the other major half of the power and leadership role which includes vigilance for possible danger from outside the group, group protection, territoriality, etc. In addition, we will discuss feeding habits, and in particular meat-eating and hunting. Hunting is, in its most important respect for our purposes, an extragroup activity. Thus, through our discussions of protection and hunting, we will be dealing both with primates as prey and with primates as predators.

PROTECTION: PRIMATES AS PREY

According to some primatologists, protection of the group is the male's most important contribution to primate survival (Hrdy, 1976; Rowell, 1974). In most species of primates, it is in fact the males rather than the females who are the group protectors. Let us now survey the primate order taxonomically.

PROSIMIANS

In lookout or vigilance behavior, male slow lorises climb twice as much as do females. In bushbabies, the adult male is the dominant figure in territoriality. Only the male emits territorial calls; and, alarm (warning) calls are also more frequent in males than in females (Doyle, 1974; Mitchell, 1979). In lemurs, however, males scent-mark more but females emit more alarm vocalizations. Thus, for prosimians, it is not always the male, but probably the male more than the female, that is the most protective, vigilant and territorial.

NEW WORLD MONKEYS

Monogamous primates show fewer sex differences in extragroup behaviors than do nonmonogamous primates. However, even in the monogamous marmoset only the male reacts to alterations in the environment with increased scent-marking and takes the leading role in territorial behavior. In some other monogamous species (e.g., *Pithecia* spp) only the male emits the loud territorial bark (see Mitchell, 1979).

In nonmonogamous New World monkeys, primarily males direct threats toward intruders. Even in spider monkeys, where sexual dimorphism is not marked, it is primarily the males who express hostile behavior toward intruders. In sexually dimorphic species, it is the males that protect the group from predators (see Mitchell, (1979).

MACAQUES

Four-year-old male rhesus are the most frequent participants in *intergroup* interactions of all age and sex groups of rhesus monkeys. Males are wounded more than are females in intergroup conflicts. Males definitely protect the troop from external enemies of the same species, but the response seems to be somewhat specific to *male* intruders. *Females* defend against female intruders. Males, however, climb to higher locations and spend more time passively alert or vigilant than do females. Because they are peripheral, they become a first alert to outside danger. There is a tendency for adult males to be more active in driving off predators and in coming to the source of an alarm than females. Adult males drop to the rear during flight from danger. They shake branches and make aggressive noises toward strangers (see Mitchell, 1979, for primary references).

If an infant is threatened from outside the group both males *and* females protect the infant but in somewhat different ways. The adult female picks up the infant, retreats from the danger and then may threaten the intruder. The male, on the other hand, moves directly *toward* the intruder, places himself between the infant and the intruder, and either attacks or threatens (see Mitchell, 1977).

OTHER OLD WORLD MONKEYS

Among most Old World monkeys, adult males act as sentinels, give alarm calls, and show defensive behaviors. Lookout behavior and group protection is seen in adult male vervets and guenons. Leader males are found at greater heights and emit more loud calls of warning and defensive displays than do females. Adult males of many species come to the aid of infants in danger. Patas males serve as lookouts and perform diversionary displays when near potential predators. There is some variability among langurs, but on the whole, in most of them, males are the watchdogs and group protectors (see Mitchell, 1979, for primary references).

Baboon males, sometimes in alliance, protect the troop from predators, serve as lookouts, and perform displays intended to intimidate the enemy. Chacma baboons are particularly inventive in troop defense; they throw rocks. The most frequent hurlers of rocks and stones are four-year-old (and older) adult males (Hamilton et al., 1975).

Even in the talapoin monkey where female adults are more dominant and more aggressive than male adults *within* the group, the usual sex difference in vigilance and group protection from intruders holds up. Adult male talapoins are more vigilant than are females (Wolfheim, personal communication; also see Mitchell, 1979). Vigilance, however, may be primarily a function of peripheralization tendencies in Old World monkey males.

LESSER APES

Even though monogamous gibbons show few sex differences in guarding the family group, males still surpass females somewhat. The main protagonists in interfamily conflicts are the adult males who continue to squabble (vocally) long after the females have gone back to feeding. Males also chase extragroup intruders more than do females and males guard against predators. Males also emit more territorial vocalizations (Tenaza, 1976; also see Mitchell, 1979).

GREAT APES

An adult *female* chimpanzee will charge a human being to protect her infant, but in mobbing a predator the dominant male takes the lead. On the whole, highly aggressive charging displays are seen more frequently in males than in females. Communal male displays and male alliances against intruders are common.

Gorilla males also make more bluff charges than do gorilla females, but the displays are individual not communal. Chest beating displays in response to intruders occur more in males than in females. Gorillas have been known to attack people if they are taken by surprise, are wounded, are defending an infant, or are trapped. Dominant adult males acting in defense of the group are responsible for most of the attacks on humans (Sabater Pi, 1966).

In the orangutan, it is not clear whether or not males protect the female and young, especially since the males do not remain close to them. Of the two sexes, however, males more frequently show threat displays toward intruders (see Mitchell, 1979, for references).

HUMAN CONSIDERATIONS REGARDING DEFENSE

People are to a degree territorial. They defend their homes, their towns, even their places in line. Moreover, there are undoubtedly sex differences in these behaviors. When it comes to defending the human family (or possessions for that matter), men appear to be the major protagonists. A man will readily come to the aid of a woman or a child if he knows them or is related to them. He will also aid them if he perceives that they are not in the company of another man (Shotland and Straw, 1976).

In almost *all* nonhuman primates, males surpass females in vigilance, protection, territoriality, and intertroop activity. Even in monogamous primates, monomorphic spider monkeys, and the rather unique talapoins, males show more of these activities than do females. This sex difference in extratroop orientation is one of the most consistent sex differences in the nonhuman primates. It would be very surprising to us if human males and females did not differ in a similar direction. It is interesting that in books and articles on human sex differences this potential sex difference is rarely, if *ever*, mentioned. Some extremely important research is apparently being overlooked by social scientists (see Mitchell, 1979).

PREDATION: PRIMATES AS PREDATORS

We have seen that the most consistent primate sex differences thus far occur in group protection or group defense. In humans, physical and cultural anthropologists have been interested in sex differences in hunting. Hunting is primarily an extragroup behavior. Since there is a tendency for males to be extragroup oriented, we might expect more hunting in primate males than in primate females.

In recent years, behavioral primatologists have described a large number of examples of nonhuman primates hunting, killing, and eating prey. Perhaps the best-known studies on primate predation have concerned baboons in Africa. Harding (1973) witnessed the catch and consumption of 47 different animals over a two-year period by one troop of olive baboons. Adult male baboons caught and ate all but three of these 47 animals. Adult female baboons captured three hares but two of these females lost their catch to males.

Strum (1975) reported definite hunting for game and sharing of the meat.

"Starting as an adult male activity in the olive baboon troop, this tradition rapidly expanded to include capture and consumption of prey by adult females and juveniles of all ages and both sexes" (p. 755).

Adult male baboons kill small gazelles, lambs, quails, hares, and guinea fowl, often moving *deliberately* through herds of grazing gazelles in a genuine hunting method. Initially hunting is an individual activity; that is, there is a single hunter. Eventually, however, there is cooperation (Harding and Strum, 1976).

In two years, the olive baboons of Kekopey studied by Harding and Strum (1976) doubled their predation rate. Females began to kill more frequently and even *infants* ate the meat. Juveniles began to hunt and kill. The baboons learned to chase prey *toward* other baboons. Some hunts lasted from two hours to *three days* and, in the males, for as far as two miles from the troop. Baboons do not share other foods, but they do share meat.

Predation in baboons results from population explosions in the prey species. It also increases in the dry season. Males almost always eat more meat than do females.

As for other species of primates, *both* male and female macaques kill and eat meat. In stumptail macaques, females may kill and eat more prey than males (Estrada et al., 1978).

Prosimians such as bushbabies will eat meat: males more than females. New World monogamous marmosets also sometimes eat meat, including, occasionally, nonviable offspring. Some marmosets kill and eat snakes, and it is usually the males that do the killing. New World nonmonogamous species like cebus also kill and eat snakes, but no sex difference has been reported in the literature as yet (see Mitchell, 1979, for primary references).

Both arboreal and terrestrial primates eat meat. Arboreal species kill and eat primarily snakes and birds. In southern Africa, some arboreal male monkeys of the genus *Cercopithecus* are often mobbed by birds as they rob the birds' nests. Arboreal lesser apes hunt and kill birds, even in captivity. House sparrows are frequently killed and eaten by primates in captivity. *Female* gibbons seem to kill and eat *more* than the males. In one group of captive gibbons in Bermuda, domestic hens were killed by females and the males and young helped to consume them (see Mitchell, 1979).

In summary, both males and females and sometimes immature animals kill game and eat it. Only in the monogamous gibbons and perhaps some macaques is there meager evidence of more predation in females than in males. A systematic study of sex differences in primate predation has not been made; however, in most species it appears that the adult males do most of the hunting, killing and eating of the prey (see Mitchell, 1979).

Teleki (1973) has noted that predatory behavior depends upon awareness of the prey's presence when it is near. As we know, males show more extratroop vigilance than do females and might therefore be more aware of prey. In addition, hunting sometimes requires travel and males of most primates are more loosely attached to their troops and travel further from it than do females. Finally, size of predator (and size of canines) relative to prey is an important facet of hunting and males of many primate species are larger in size and have larger teeth than females (see Mitchell, 1979).

As a final point, it should be noted that for some primates, other species of primates are the favorite prey. Chimpanzees and baboons, for example, eat smaller monkeys. What is more, chimpanzees eat baboons. Not only do chimpanzees eat their smaller primate cousins, they also practice cannibalism (Bygott, 1972). Adult males are the most likely to eat their own species. When they do, the victim is usually an infant of a strange female. Adult females apparently do this less often. In the great apes, only the chimpanzee has been known to hunt, kill, and eat prey in the wild (Teleki, 1973). Males do all three of these more than do females. Chimpanzee prey is usually caught by adult males, often with cooperation; and, adult males seem to eat much more of the meat than do females (see Mitchell, 1979, for primary references).

In summary, "Man the Hunter" is a phrase that is probably more correct for the gender (males hunt more than do females) than for the species (people are not the only primates which hunt). Cooperative hunting seems to be a proclivity displayed much more frequently by males than by females, although there are, as usual, exceptions to this rule in the primate order.

REFERENCES

Bygott, J.D. Cannibalism among wild chimpanzees. *Nature,* 1972, **238**, 410-411.

Doyle, G.A. The behaviour of the lesser bushbaby. In Martin, R.D., Doyle, G.A., and Walker, A.C. (Eds.) *Prosimian Biology.* London: Duckworth, 1974, pp. 213-231.

Estrada, A., Sandoval, J.M., and Manzalillo, D. Further data on predation by free-ranging stumptail macaques (*Macaca arctoides*). *Primates,* 1978, 19(2), 401-407.

Hamilton, W.J. III, Buskirk, R.E. and Buskirk, W.H. Defensive stoning by baboons. *Nature,* 1975, 256, 488-489.

Harding, R.S.O. Predation by a troop of olive baboons (*Papio anubis*). *American Journal of Physical Anthropology,* 1973, 38, 587-591.

Harding, R.S.O. and Strum, S.C. The predatory baboons of Kekopey. *Natural History,* 1976, 85, 46-53.

Hrdy, S.B. Care and exploitation of nonhuman primate infants by conspecifics other than the mother. *Advances in the Study of Behavior,* 1976, 6, 101-158.

Mitchell, G. Parental behavior in nonhuman primates. In Money, J. and Musaph, H. (Eds.) *Handbook of Sexology.* Amsterdam: Elsevier/North Holland Biomedical Press, 1977, pp. 749-759.

Mitchell, G. *Behavioral Sex Differences in Nonhuman Primates.* New York: Van Nostrand Reinhold, 1979.

Rowell, T.E. Contrasting different adult male roles in different species of nonhuman primates. *Archives of Sexual Behavior,* 1974, 3, 143-149.

Sabater Pi, J. Gorilla attacks on humans in Rio Muni, West Africa. *Journal of Mammalogy,* 1966, 47,123-124.

Shotland, R.L. and Straw, M.K. Bystander response to an assault: When a man attacks a woman. *Journal of Personality and Social Psychology,* 1976, 34, 990-999.

Strum, S.C. Primate predation: Interim report on the development of a tradition in a troop of olive baboons. *Science,* 1975, 187, 755-757.

Teleki, G. *Predatory Behavior in Wild Chimpanzees.* New Jersey: Associated University Presses, 1973.

Tenaza, R.R. Songs, choruses, and countersinging of Kloss' gibbons (*Hylobates klossii*) in Siberut Island, Indonesia. *Zeitschrift für Tierpsychologie,* 1976, 40, 37-52.

Wolfheim, J.H. Personal communication, 1977.

18
Communication

GROOMING AND TOUCH

Grooming is a favorite relaxing activity of many species of non-human primates. It is often taken for granted because it is so commonly seen (cf. Mitchell, 1979). It is extremely important to the social stability of a group, however, as we shall see.

Prosimian Grooming

In prosimians, grooming is done by the mouth more than by the hands. Bushbabies often direct grooming toward other-sexed individuals. Since some bushbabies live in groups which are somewhat like a serial monogamy or a spatial harem, this is not surprising. When bushbaby grooming *is* seen between liked-sexed individuals, it is almost always between females. In the slow loris, as well, grooming is predominantly a female activity. They groom 57 percent more than do males. In prosimians of both sexes, grooming increases with age (cf. Mitchell, 1979; Doyle and Martin, 1979).

New World Monkey Grooming

In monogamous New World monkeys, almost by definition, grooming must be primarily heterosexual in nature. During estrus, the male grooms more than does the female. In fact, male marmosets and tamarins groom quite a lot at other times as well. Overall, males *initiate* somewhat more grooming than do females:

> . . . a basic characteristic of monogamy may be the simple fact that a male and female sleep and groom together (Kleiman, 1977, p. 59).

Nonmonogamous New World species vary in regard to sex differences in grooming. Spider monkeys show no sex differences, in cebus and howler monkeys the females groom more than the males. Thus, sexually dimorphic species display more female grooming than male grooming, whereas species which are not sexually dimorphic do not show a sex difference. Monogamous males groom more than monogamous females (Mitchell, 1979).

Old World Arboreal Monkey Grooming

Old World arboreal females groom more than their male counterparts. In some of these species males have never been seen to groom other males. This is true of the genera *Cercopithecus* (guenons), *Presbytis* (langurs), *Colobus* (colobus), and *Cerocebus* (mangabeys). Even the unique talapoin shows the usual sex differences in grooming. Despite being more aggressive than her male counterpart, female talapoins groom more than do males (cf. Mitchell, 1979).

Old World Terrestrial Monkey Grooming

Rhesus macaque females groom, perhaps even *self*-groom, more than do males. Even isolate-reared (socially deprived) females display more self-grooming and invitations to groom than do their male counterparts, although at much lower levels than socially reared animals. A large share of rhesus grooming is done in kinship networks, particularly those involving mother and daughter (Mitchell, 1979).

Male rhesus increase their grooming of females if the female is in estrus. Grooming in consort pairs is extremely important for reproduction. Female-female grooming, on the other hand, is so much at the core of group behavior in free-ranging rhesus that Missakin (1973) has used cessation of grooming behavior between adult females as an index of group fission. That is, she uses intra*female* grooming as the definition of whether or not a group even exists!

Females also groom more than do males in pigtail macaques, crab-eating macaques, stumptail macaques, and bonnet macaques. In bonnet macaques, there is greater tolerance between males than is seen in other macaques, and male-male grooming does occur. However, even in this species, females groom more than do males (Mitchell, 1979).

Japanese macaque males will occasionally groom infants, however, females of this species groom them and each other more than do males. Vocal sounds play an important role in Japanese macaque grooming, but only in female-female grooming.

Most baboons are not much different from macaques when it comes to sex differences in grooming. Females groom more than males in yellow baboons, olive baboons, chacma baboons, and even gelada baboons who live in one-male groups. However, in the hamadryas baboon, which lives in a one-male, male-dominated harem, the male grooms more than does the female (cf. Mitchell, 1979).

Ape Grooming

Monogamous lesser apes groom heterosexually of course. The monogamous lesser apes groom much more overall than do the great apes (15-30 minutes vs. 10 minutes per day) (Kleiman, 1977). There are few, if any, sex differences in gibbon and siamang grooming (cf. Mitchell, 1979).

Chimpanzee males do give and receive heterosexual grooming but females give a lot more and receive a lot less. Chimpanzee grooming however, is primarily a *within*-sex female activity. As the degree of male sexual possessiveness of a female increases (degree of monogamy?) so does the male's grooming of the female. Most female chimpanzees receive and reciprocate more grooming from their mothers than do most chimpanzee males (Mitchell, 1979).

For gorillas, the sex difference in grooming is even greater than it is in the chimpanzee, females grooming more. In addition, female orangutans in captivity groom more than do males. Even in captivity, however, the great apes groom less often and for shorter durations than do Old World monkeys (Mitchell, 1979). Orangutans and gorillas groom much less than do chimpanzees (Kleiman, 1977; Maple, personal communication).

In summary, in nonhuman primates females groom more than do males unless the relationship is a monogamous one, or unless the female is in estrus. Other factors affecting grooming are dominance, reunions of old friends, changes in group composition, kinship networks, differential early experiences and social traditions (Mitchell, 1979).

Humans

Female humans are more adept at nonverbal communication than are human males. They seem to be more interested in social relationships, more interested in social stimuli, and more interested in reducing social tension. Grooming serves all of these interests in nonhuman primates and *female* nonhuman primates groom more than do males (if they are *not* monogamous) (Mitchell, 1979).

Questionnaire data on same-sex friendships in people show that women are more likely to just sit and talk than are men (Caldwell and Peplau, 1977). In decorating their rooms, college women use more personal and social items than do college men (Vinsel et al., 1977). Even in *cross*-species eye-to-eye and physical contact including close bonds with pets, female humans surpass males (Thomsen, 1974; Cameron, 1977). As we will see, this proclivity toward intragroup socialization in primate females, including humans, will show up in other areas of social communication as well. What seems to get in the way of *power* relationships for women, becomes a strong advantage in promoting social *stability*. It has even been argued by some researchers that there would be no permanent social groups at all without the females of most primate species, including our own. Recall however, that in grooming, monogamous primates do not show the female superiority in grooming. Recall also that people are probably more monogamous than are *most* primates. (Although there is still some dispute over this.)

If we look strictly at who touches whom in humans we get confusing results. Men are more likely to touch strangers while women are more likely to be touched by them. In a store or library, women who are briefly touched by a clerk feel more positive than do women who are not touched. Men are not affected by the touch (Deaux, 1976).

Women, however, have more experience in *being* touched than do men. Even at 13 months of age girls stay closer and touch their mothers more often than do males (Lewis, 1972). Same-sex touching is only permissible for females, unless in a football game or some other clearly masculine activity (Deaux, 1976).

Brown (1965) has proposed a "universal norm" for social behaviors including touching. The "universal norm" is that the form of a behavior which is used mutually between intimates (touching), is used by the superior person in an unequal relationship. The form of a behavior which is used between strangers (refraining from touching) is used by the inferior person in a relationship. In female-male stranger interactions, masculine touching means dominance. If the woman protests, howevers, she is accused of reacting unkindly to "friendliness." Using Brown's universal norm, it is *not* friendliness. It is friendliness only among intimates. Among intimates, women touch each other more than do men. As we know, most other non-human primates show the same sex differences.

VOCALIZATION

As we have seen, sex differences in nonhuman primates depend to a great extent on the degree to which the male of the primate in question is intra-or extragroup-oriented. Males are often more peripheral-ized, more vigilant, and more involved in predation and group change. Females, however, often tend to remain with the troop and concern themselves with grooming and other intragroup activities. Given these very general tendencies for the two sexes, we might expect differences in vocalization consonant with them. For ex-ample, we might expect fairly loud, distant or extragroup-oriented vocalizations in males and more quiet, intimate, or intragroup-vocalizations in females.

Prosimian Vocalizations

Vocalizations are as important to prosimians as they are to simians. Diurnal prosimians tend to be more social than do nocturnal pro-simians, but both types use vocalizations to communicate. Nocturnal prosimian vocalizations, however, tend to be more discrete or stereo-typed and contain fewer, graded intermediates (Petter and Charles-Dominique, 1979).

Petter and Charles-Dominique (1979) have reviewed the vocaliza-tions of 34 prosimian species. In solitary species, the mother often deposits her infant in a nest and leaves it. Mother-infant contact calls, with the mother calling first and the infant answering, are therefore common in these species. In more gregarious species, like lemurs, the infant emits faint calls when being carried on its mother's belly. The mother responds to these by providing comfort for the in-fant. The infant also emits louder calls (distress calls) when separated from its mother, and until reunited with her (Petter and Charles-Dominique, 1979).

Solitary, nocturnal primates have relatively loud, long-distance, mating vocalizations which have no counterpart in the more group-oriented diurnal prosimians. There are, however, group coordination calls, which help to maintain contact with the group, in diurnal prosimians. There are also territorial vocalizations and alarm calls in prosimians, both of which occur in *both* nocturnal and diurnal forms (Petter and Charles-Dominique, 1979).

In general, female prosimians utter the most infant-directed contact calls, sleeping-place contact calls, and mating calls. The sleeping-place calls often unite mothers and their adult daughters to sleep or to gather after sleep at night or in the morning (in some nocturnal species). Both females and males emit distant group-contact calls and few sex differences have been reported for alarm calls. In tree shrews and in some lemurs, female aggression is apparently more vocal than is male aggression, although males are more aggressive than females in some of these species. In the lesser bushbaby, there is a specific *male* call used in territoriality. However, there has been little or no interest in sex differences in prosimian vocalizations up to the present time, despite the fact that there have been several major publications on the vocalizations themselves (see for example, Doyle and Martin, 1979; and in particular, Petter and Charles-Dominique, 1979, in that volume for references).

NEW WORLD MONKEY VOCALIZATIONS

Monogamous marmosets and tamarins show few sex differences in vocalizations, but male titi monkeys emit more warning and territorial vocalizations than do females. Nonmonogamous New World monkeys do display gender differences in vocalizations. Howler monkey males emit more territorial and alarm vocalizations than do females; and, even Saki males emit more loud territorial barks than do their female counterparts (see Mitchell, 1979, for references).

MACAQUE VOCALIZATIONS

Not only rhesus males, but adult males of other wild macaques also emit alarm or warning barks more frequently than do their female conspecifics. Adult male macaques more often make aggressive noises near strangers than do females; and, they emit more vocalizations which apparently induce others to follow (cf. Mitchell, 1979).

Female macaques probably vocalize more frequently overall than do males. The only circumstances where male macaques vocalize more than females involve extreme aggressive contexts. However, as in most primates, there is a decrease in numbers of vocalizations as an animal passes puberty. One specific vocalization, the "coo" vocalization (a call for contact), is emitted more often by females than by males. Clear calls increase following social separations, particularly from familiar animals. Even in adults, who vocalize less frequently than do immature animals, females coo and girn (a sound of greeting) more than do males (Mitchell, 1979).

Although the above sex differences in macaque vocalizations are well established, the vocalizations are affected by many other factors besides gender. The differences attributable to gender can be lessened or increased according to: (1) The specific call or noise in question, (2) the degree of agonism or affiliation, (3) the degree of familiarity of the animals involved, (4) the age of the animals, (5) rearing experiences, (6) hormonal state, (7) the specific social situation, (8) social faciliation effects, (9) anticipation of, a witnessing of, or an actual social separation, and (10) discrimination learning of vocalizations (see Mitchell, 1979).

However, soft sounds are, in fact, often female-related. A gender difference favoring females, for example, has been noted for Japanese monkeys. When grooming, adult female Japanese macaques vocalize far more frequently than do males (they also groom more) (see Mitchell, 1979).

Other Old World Monkey Vocalizations

Adult male chacma baboons mobilize the troop by giving loud vocalizations. Mandrill males also have "rally calls." Harsh aggressive noises are more male-related; clear calls and squeals and screams are more female-related. Adult male langurs probably emit more whoop, territorial and alarm calls than do adult female langurs, although there are exceptions to this. *Cercopithecus* (vervets and guenons) species sex differences follow along similar lines. Only proboscis monkey males emit growls and honks of warning and only the angola colobus male voices the jump-*roar* display. In general, vocalizations involving territorial, defense, warning, and alarm calls are *male* sounds within the Old World monkey groups (see Mitchell, 1979).

In regards to soft social calls, a female patas monkey rejoining a troop will softly "moan." Adult female baboons, mangabeys, guenons, and langurs emit soft grunts when in female dyads. These are close contact calls. Only female and juvenile mandrills emit contact calls. Females, in general, emit more of those vocalizations which serve an intragroup function of holding the group together than do males (Mitchell, 1979).

Ape Vocalizations

The monogamous lesser apes show few sex differences when their brains are electrically stimulated to elicit vocalizations. Both male and female gibbons emit "morning calls" for spacing. In some species, however, females vocalize *closer together* than do males and males do more of the territorial singing than do females. On the whole, however, it is likely that the nonmonogamous lesser apes evince fewer sex differences than do the Old World monkeys (see Mitchell, 1979, for references).

The two- or three-toned roar is made only by the adult male gorilla, as is hooting during chest-beating. The adult silverback male also emits most of the alarm barks. Screams are emitted by females. Also, females tend to answer infant calls more often than do males (Mitchell, 1979).

Relative to chimpanzees, gorillas are quiet and seldom in communal chorus. Chimpanzees are very vocal, noisy and often in communal chorus. Long-range "pant-hooting" has no climax in female chimpanzees; it does have a climax in males. Female chimpanzees emit close contact soft grunts in female-female dyads. Their vocalizations tend to minimize rather than maximize intragroup tension. It is also interesting that female chimpanzees are less easily fooled than are males by tape-recorded chimpanzee loud calls played back to them in the wild (see Mitchell, 1979, for primary references).

Only the *male* orangutan has a "long-call," signaling a disagreeable mood. He wanders alone, giving loud bellowing vocalizations, apparently in vocal competition for females (Horr, 1972).

On the whole, the gender-related vocalizations of nonhuman primates suggest that female vocalizations often serve to hold the group together and to decrease tension. In field studies of nonhuman primates, there has been a preoccupation with warning barks, territorial calls, and agonistic vocalizations. Too little attention has been paid to softer vocalizations and their function. As in other areas of intellectual pursuit, female behavior has been slighted while male aggression and dominance has been glorified.

Implications for Human Vocal Behavior

There have been reports of a greater overall frequency of vocalizations in *female* human infants, of better development of syntax in four-year-old girls than in boys, but of a greater frequency of agonistic yelling in nursery school boys than in nursery school girls (Maccoby and Jacklin, 1974). Among close, same-sexed friends women are more likely to just sit and talk than are men (Caldwell and Peplau, 1977). These differences remind the behavioral primatologist of similar gender differences heard in the vocalizations of many nonhuman primates. We are not simply suggesting that women communicate while men display or just make noise. The male behaviors are obviously as useful to us as are the female behaviors. On the other hand, it is by no means impossible that some of these nonhuman primate sex differences may help to shed light on the evolution of the reported greater *verbal* and *nonverbal* communicative abilities of human females.

VISUAL COMMUNICATION

Nonhuman and human primates rely heavily upon vision in communication. Primate vision provides depth perception and excellent acuity. Instantaneous communication is a hallmark of the visual channel. In addition, through vision several signals can be received simultaneously.

Prosimians

Prosimian and simian primate vision differs in the fine analysis of color vision. Prosimians, in general, have less elaborate or nonexistent color vision. Many prosimians are nocturnal and this also makes them somewhat different visually than most primates. In some prosimians, the fovea is poorly developed or lacking (Pariente, 1979).

Some prosimians do not have very good depth perception. Prosimians, therefore, rely somewhat more on olfaction than do simians.

Nocturnal prosimians do not have a large variety of facial expressions. There is also probably less use of the face in diurnal prosimians than in simians. The mouth, the direction of gaze, and the mobile structures of the eye provide the main elements of prosimian facial expression. Male prosimians (e.g., *Lemur*) are prone to show the dominance yawn more than are females. Puckering of the lips and snout region in threat is also common in males (e.g., *Lemur*). There are few data on *sex differences* in visual communication in prosimians, however, despite the fact that an expansive volume on prosimian behavior was just recently published (Doyle and Martin, 1979).

New World Monkey Visual Communication

Relative to Old World monkeys, New World monkeys do not display many facial expressions. As we know, all South American monkeys are arboreal. They, therefore, *must* rely on audition as much as vision. Many primitive New World monkeys (marmosets and tamarins) also use olfaction to a larger extent than do Old World monkeys. Despite these differences from Old World varieties, all New World monkeys have steroscopic vision and sex differences in visual communication have been reported for several species.

In marmosets and tamarins, females are often more dominant and aggressive than males. Sex differences in aggressive or other facial expressions, however, are few. Monogamous titi monkeys, however, are different. Territorial threats in titis are primarily adult male behaviors. In terms of social looking, however, the adult female looks at her male partner more than he looks at her (Phillips and Mason, 1976).

In nonmonogamous squirrel monkeys, in agonistic contexts, touching of a partner and advancing the mouth towards the partner's neck can be elicited (by brain stimulation) from males more frequently than from females. Straightening of the body and thrusting of the chin toward the partner in agonistic contexts occur naturally only in males but these two behaviors can still be elicited in females if they are brain-stimulated (see Mitchell, 1979, for references). Territorial threats occur more in male howlers than in female howlers.

Macaque Visual Communication

Infant female rhesus look at their mothers' faces more than do infant male rhesus. Rhesus females have more eye contact, in general, even with humans, then do male rhesus. The affective behavior of males is more aggressive than is that of females. There are more threats in males than in females as early as 80 days of age. Branch-shaking is done mostly by males, as is chewing and gnashing of teeth. "Territorial" or intertroop threats are also usually made by males as are "crook tails" signifying dominance. Fear grimaces, on the other hand, occur significantly more frequently in females. These sex differences persist despite marked differences in rearing experience. Even in social isolates, males threaten more than do females (see Mitchell, 1979, for references).

During rhesus preadolescence, females look at tiny infants longer during each look than do males. They also direct lipsmacking and care-giving behaviors to infants. Male rhesus of similar age tend to threaten infants or play with them (see Mitchell, 1979).

In stumptails as well as rhesus, males predictably display more aggressively than do females. It is the *male* Japanese macaque who branch-shakes and emits "territorial" threats, while the female uses close visual signals and displays more fear grimaces. Sex differences in pigtail and crab-eater macaque visual communication resemble those seen in rhesus. In general, macaque males display distant, outgroup directed threats while females show more close visual contact and more fear grimaces (Mitchell, 1979).

Other Old World Monkey Visual Communication

Baboons resemble macaques in their visual displays. Branch-shaking is performed primarily by males. Young males are more inclined to imitate threat and attack patterns than are young females. In the arboreal langurs, males (but not females) tend to maintain a visual *observational tonus* in which they are more alive to more *distant* conditions and events than are females (Mitchell, 1979).

Vervet canine display, body bounce, and crook tail are limited to adult males. Head-bob, territorial threats, erect posture, eye-flash, and gape threat also occur more frequently in males than in females. Females on the other hand, crouch more than do males (Mitchell, 1979).

Even in the talapoin, males sit high in branches and visually survey activities around them. They also yawn more than do females. Females, on the other hand, seem concerned with close details within the group rather than with extragroup activity (see Mitchell, 1979).

Ape Visual Communication

In the monogamous lesser apes few if any sex differences in visual communication have been reported. In chimpanzees, however, males tend to imitate threat patterns more than do females and they look at distant events more than do females. Female chimpanzees are interested in close intragroup events, so much so that, as a consequence, they tend to develop myopia (nearsightedness) more than do males. In addition, it is the gorilla *male* who visually displays by branch-shaking and chest-beating.

Nonhuman to Human Extrapolations

Male nonhuman primates, at least those which are nonmonogamous and above the New World line, threaten more than do females, particularly outside of the group. Females show more crouching and fear. Dominance or tension yawns are emitted more by males than by females. Males occupy much of their time in vigilance-related activities and in protecting the group. Females seem occupied with infant care and with tension-reducing within-group behavior. Females, for example, groom more than do males and emit more soft vocalizations. Females do more observing of others from up close, in a positive social context, than do males.

With regard to people, Maccoby and Jacklin (1974) say that females are less aggressive, more competent at verbal tasks, and less competent at visual-spatial tasks than males. Our nonhuman primate review says that females are less aggressive, more competent at close vocal and visual tasks,[1] and less competent at distant visual and vocal tasks. If it is possible that the human sex differences are at least partly a function of our biological heritage, evolving over millennia, it would be interesting to check human sex differences in vocal and visual tasks at varying distances.

---

[1] It is interesting that human females as well as chimpanzee females develop *myopia* earlier and more seriously than do males (Young, 1977).

Human Vocal and Visual Communication

As Deaux (1976) has noted:

> While researchers in many areas have shied away from considera-
> tion of sex differences, students of nonverbal communication have
> not been able to avoid the question. Differences between men and
> women are pervasive in every area of communication (Deaux,
> 1976, p. 58).

As we noted, investigations have shown that girls are more vocal
than boys, more correct in their grammar, and more polite and cheer-
ful in their intonation. Boys display more agonistic yelling and men
speak more forcefully and swear more often.

If one looks at conversations already in progress, men talk longer,
initiate more topics, and interrupt more often than do women. Women, it is said, talk about men while men talk about business, sports,
and politics. On the other hand, women are more personal, more
willing to disclose information about themselves (Deaux, 1976).

In visual communication, women spend more time looking directly at another person than do men. They rely heavily upon close
visual contact; men do not. Men are actually *more* comfortable and
more talkative when they cannot see their partner. Women are better
interpreters of what the eyes and face have to say than are men. With
all possible combinations of males and females as senders and re-
ceivers of facial communication females are superior to males. This is
particularly true of senders. Women are very effective at *both* com-
municating facially *and* at reading the face (Deaux, 1976).

In front of a photographer a female will smile more than will a
male. Of course, they are both told to smile. Is this something like
a fear grimace? Do women "smile to affirm their inferior status"
(Deaux, 1976, p. 63)? Most photographers are men; does this account for the difference in smiling?

The smile may often mean something different for women than
for men. Children believe the verbal messages and ignore the smiles
of women; however, they *believe* the smile of a man. It may be that
women smile so often the message becomes unclear (Deaux, 1976).

Despite the fact that women, in general, are superior at nonverbal
communication, *some* men are clearly good at it. Men in acting, art,
and mental health are equal to or better than most women at reading

nonverbal cues. This skill may be what is referred to as "intuition," usually as "woman's intuition" (Deaux, 1976).

The women's movement has become involved with nonverbal communication in the last few years. Feminists have bemoaned the woman's obligatory smile, make-up, posture, clothing, and, especially, having to put up with being touched by a stranger. They see the male gestures of threat and physical abuse as symbols of male supremacy. Female psychologists in general, however, believe that female superiority in nonverbal communication should come to play a large *positive* role in the betterment of women's status. Studies of nonverbal behavior have provided information of great value to women. There *are* sex differences. One problem has been that they have been so unconscious that they are resistant to change. The female gestures of smiling, tilting the head, averting the eye, condensing the body, accepting touch from a stranger, and giving up space, are all functioning in a power/status dimension. Now that psychologists understand this, some of them are applying the understanding in assertiveness training for women (Henley, 1979). That many women need this becomes obvious when we consider how many of them become victims not only outside, but within their own homes. (Even wife beating is, to some extent at least, a question of a woman's inability to stand up for her own rights, and to seek help. In short, it reflects to a degree her inability to assert herself even at the expense of her own physical well-being. Unfortunately, however, even when she does seek help, there are usually no institutionalized means of providing it.)

REFERENCES

Brown, R. *Social Psychology.* New York: Free Press, 1965.

Caldwell, M.A. and Peplau, L.A. Sex differences in friendship. Paper presented at the *Western Psychological Association* meeting, Seattle, Washington, April, 1977.

Cameron, P. The pet threat. Paper presented at the *Western Psychological Association* meeting, Seattle, Washington, April, 1977.

Deaux, K. *The Behavior of Women and Men.* Monterey, CA: Brooks/Cole, 1976.

Doyle, G.A. and Martin, R.D. (Eds.) *The Study of Prosimian Behavior.* New York: Academic Press, 1979.

Henley, H.M. Women, nonverbal behavior, and social psychology. *The Society for the Advancement of Social Psychology Newsletter,* 1979, 5(3), 14-16.

Horr, D.A. The Borneo orang-utan. *Borneo Research Bulletin,* 1972, 4, 46-50.

Kleiman, D.G. Monogamy in mammals. *The Quarterly Review of Biology,* 1977, 52, 39-69.

Lewis, M. Parents and children: Sex-role development. *School Review,* 1972, 80, 229-240.

Maccoby, E.E. and Jacklin, C.M. *The Psychology of Sex Differences,* Stanford, CA: Stanford University Press, 1974.

Maple, T.L. Personal communication, 1979.

Missakian, E.A. The timing of fission among free-ranging rhesus monkeys. *American Journal of Physical Anthropology,* 1973, 38, 621-624.

Mitchell, G. *Behavioral Sex Differences in Nonhuman Primates.* New York: Van Nostrand Reinhold, 1979.

Pariente, G. The role of vision in prosimian behavior. In Doyle, G.A. and Martin, R.D. (Eds.) *The Study of Prosimian Behavior.* New York: Academic Press, 1979.

Petter, J.J. and Charles-Dominique, P.C. Vocal communication in prosimians. In Doyle, G.A. and Martin, R.D. (Eds.) *The Study of Prosimian Behavior.* New York: Academic Press, 1979.

Phillips, M.J. and Mason, W.A. Comparative studies of social behavior in *Callicebus* and *Saimiri:* Social looking in male-female pairs. *Bulletin of the Psychonomic Society,* 1976, 7(1), 55-56.

Thomsen, C.E. Eye contact by nonhuman primates toward a human observer. *Animal Behaviour,* 1974, 22, 144-149.

Vinsel, A., Wilson, J., Brown, B.B., and Altman, I. Personalization in dormitories: Sex differences. Paper presented at the *Western Psychological Association* meeting, Seattle, Washington, April, 1977.

Young, F.A. The nature and control of myopia. *Journal of the American Optometric Association,* 1977, 48, 451-457.

19
Aggression

As we have seen at many points in this book, males of most primate species appear to be more aggressive than their female conspecifics. Male aggressiveness is, to some extent, determined by prenatal androgen levels; and, this aggressiveness is further supported in sex differences seen in mother-infant interactions and in other social relationships between the immature male and members of his social group. Aggression is also learned through observation, imitation, and practice. From infancy males are more interested in and spend more time practicing aggression (Hamburg, 1974).

Of course, gender is not the only factor affecting aggression (see Marler, 1976). Ecological conditions, population density, and food supplies also affect it. Adult testosterone levels are correlated with changes in dominance rank that often involve aggression. The extra-group orienting tendencies of many males bring them in contact with strangers and/or intruders more often than would be the case for most females. Aggression is more likely to occur among strangers than among friends. Proximity and similarity in age, or in gender, are also correlated with aggression. So are pain, frustration, and being the object of another's aggressive display. All of these factors being controlled, however, males usually display more aggression than do females. Let us now review primate sex differences in aggression taxonomically.

PROSIMIAN AGGRESSION

Male tree-shrews appear to be more aggressive than females. There is more actual biting in male aggression. Among galagos (bushbabies), isosexual aggression is more common than is aggression between the sexes. Territoriality decreases wounding, since the animal in the home territory usually wins. Aggression is more frequent, more intense, and more reciprocal in male bushbabies than in females. This is true of most prosimian species but not of all of them (see Doyle and Martin, 1979).

New World Monkey Aggression

Marmoset males and females usually show equal amounts of like-sex aggression but in some species the *female* is more aggressive than is the male (e.g., *Saguinus fuscicollis*). Titi monkeys show less conspecific aggression than do marmosets and the male titi shows slightly more aggression than does the female (see Mitchell, 1979, for primary references).

In squirrel monkeys, males are more often the object of attack than are females. Females in *established* isosexual groups often fight, however, when a strange male is introduced. Also, when two strange groups are combined, *females* fight the most. Of course, in the wild, two such groups would probably never come together (see Mitchell, 1979).

In howlers, within-group fights often involve females. Most aggression directed toward outsiders is done by males. The same is true of spider monkeys but, in spider monkeys, males also account for most of the intragroup aggression, almost all of which is directed *toward* females. Degree of sexual dimorphism in New World cebids does not seem to be related to amount of out-group directed aggression by males. The spider monkey heterosexually directed aggression seems to be an exception to the rule that animals attack others of similar class (gender). Of course, spider monkeys are monomorphic; hence, males and females are similar in size, if not in gender (see Mitchell, 1979).

Overall, New World monkeys do not show a consistent pattern regarding sex differences in aggression. The kinds of sex differences seen are almost as numerous as the numbers of species studied.

Old World Monkey Aggression

Among most Old World monkeys, males are more aggressive than females but the form that this difference takes varies from species to species. In some species males threaten more, in others they attack more than do females. In aggression toward strangers, the sex of the stranger and the sex composition of the host group also make a difference. Males often show restraint when fighting females and they frequently lose in battles with coalitions of several females. Males, in general, show less submission than do females even though they are aggressed more (Mitchell, 1979).

Unfamiliar females in the laboratory show very high aggression, but the aggression is not reciprocal as it is in males. In addition, in the wild, unfamiliar females rarely encounter one another. Adult males usually do the aggressing while females support and instigate the aggression of the males. Female-female alliances are more stable than are male-male alliances (Mitchell, 1979).

Even among *infants,* males are more aggressive than are females. (Androgen injections increase female aggression, however.) Males remain more aggressive than females throughout the juvenile period (one to two years) and into adolescence and adulthood (cf. Mitchell, 1979).

Old World monkey aggression peaks during the breeding season. Redirected threats occur frequently in consort pairs, particularly in the female when her estrogen levels are high. However, aggressiveness cannot be said to be enhanced by either estrogen or androgen independent of an individual's natural behavioral predispositions and ongoing social factors. For example, when an old dominant male loses his position through physical aggression from a younger male, there is a transition period during which there is "joint redirection" of aggression, or a coalition between the two competing males, to maintain the social order (see Mitchell, 1979).

Old World monkey males are wounded more frequently and more severely than are Old World monkey females. Males with canines display more aggression than do males without canines (Erwin et al., 1976). In one captive group of Japanese macaques, full adult males accounted for almost all of the attacks on a neonate. Males are more likely to increase their aggression under crowded conditions than are females. Low-ranking males are especially susceptible to receiving attacks (Mitchell, 1979).

In some Old World monkey species which live in one-male groups, in which leaders change from time to time, the new male leader may systematically kill all of the neonates and youngest infants (Sugiyama, 1966). This infanticide has been said to advance the estrus of the females in the troop so that the new leader can more quickly sire his own infants. However, there is controversy over the reasons why males do this. Some researchers feel that infanticide by new males is related to crowding in the wild (see Sugiyama, 1966; Dolhinow, 1977).

In those males that form temporary all-male groups, aggression is rare in these groups. The males who come together without females are usually quite friendly toward one another and have often known each other from an early age (see Mitchell, 1979).

In summary, among Old World monkeys of most species, males aggress more frequently and with more intensity; they produce and receive more wounds; they show more extragroup aggression; their aggression is more reciprocal; their aggression increases during the breeding season; and, in species which live in one-male groups, new leader males sometimes kill the youngest infants of the group. Exceptions to these generalizations can be seen in patas and talapoin monkeys. In patas, females are often involved in extragroup oriented aggression. In talapoins, females are more aggressive as adults than are males. Some female talapoins have been so aggressive during mating periods that they have *killed* males (Wolfheim, 1977). This, however, is certainly not the usual state of affairs for Old World monkeys.

APE AGGRESSION

In the monogamous gibbons and siamangs, the male and female are about equally aggressive. In captive chimpanzees, males attack females more than they attack other males, but females are just as aggressive as are the males. Young males, however, tend to imitate threat and attack behaviors more than do young females. In the wild, bipedal swagger, sway walk, and charging displays are more frequent in male chimpanzees than in females. Wild males initiate many more attacks than do females (see Mitchell, 1979, for primary references).

Mature orangutan males cannot be kept together in captivity whereas orangutan females can. Orangutan males aggress one another more severely than do orangutan females. However, females often fight (Maple, 1980). In gorillas, bluff charges and chest-beating are seen in males more than in females. Attacks on humans are made primarily by males (see Mitchell, 1979, for references). But female gorillas are also antagonistic (Maple and Hoff, in press).

HUMAN AGGRESSION

Those species of nonhuman primates who show strong sexual dimorphism in size (e.g., baboon) tend to show more aggression in males than in females. Species low in sexual dimorphism (e.g., marmosets, gibbons, etc.) do not show this sex difference. We might expect humans to be somewhere between these two extremes. In terms of sexual dimorphism, human males seem to have evolved more physical equipment for aggression than have human females. However, human males do not have larger canines as in other more sexually dimorphic species.

In childhood, girls whose mothers received androgen during pregnancy show heightened aggressiveness. In preschool children, boys push, beat, chase and yell at others more than do girls. Later in childhood, boys are still more aggressive than girls. During puberty and adolescence we observe the maximum expression of aggression in people, and particularly for males. Crime rates are two to five times higher for males than for females. College-age males rate themselves more daring than do college females. In humans, adult males appreciate hostile wit more than do females. Aggressive abnormalities are far more frequent in males than in females.

Thus, in human as well as nonhuman primates, males are more aggressive than are females. The difference is seen in both physical and verbal aggression and it appears as early as two-and-a-half years of age and lasts into adulthood (see Mitchell, 1979; Maccoby and Jacklin, 1974).

Despite all of these data, women can be as aggressive as men on some occasions. In addition, in recent years it has become apparent that women in the United States are learning to be more aggressive or are more willing to be aggressive than in the past (Deaux, 1976).

When children are given an opportunity to witness aggression (toward a doll) and to repeat the observed behavior, boys show more aggression than do girls. When rewarded for imitating, however, girls aggress as much as do boys (Deaux, 1976).

When college students are asked to give shocks to people, males give significantly higher levels. Women are more reluctant to shock another person in this simple situation, but they increase their shock levels to that of the males if they are shocked back. Hence, women can be just as aggressive as men if they are provoked (Deaux, 1976).

Men and women appear to differ physiologically when they are aggressing. The heightened blood pressures of men recover quickly following aggression whereas those of women remain high. Aggression apparently produces some anxiety in women but not in men (Deaux, 1976).

In the real world, men who are behind an unmoving car honk their horns more than do women; but if someone steps in line in front of them, men are no more aggressive toward the intruder than are women. In this situation the women are particularly good at the angry glare (Deaux, 1976).

Men are, however, more consistently aggressive when they must initiate the exchange than are women. Women are more likely to equal men in aggressiveness when they respond to anothers' rudeness or aggression (as when someone steps in front of them in line). Thus, female reciprocation, seen so rarely in female nonhuman primates, is not something which female human primates shun. It is noteworthy that in *most* incidences of violence between husbands and wives aggressive acts apparently occur equally often for the two partners. Male aggression, however, can be more damaging (Deaux, 1976).

Human Victims

Boys and men receive more aggression than do girls and women. People show less aggression toward women than toward men. In the laboratory, people (of both sexes) will administer less shock to a woman than to a man. Women who cut in line or bump into others are less likely to provoke aggression than are men. The woman who looks and acts the most feminine (stereotypically speaking) is least likely to provoke an aggressive response after intruding on others. She is also less likely to receive shock in the laboratory. Interestingly enough, men who are for women's liberation are more likely to hit or attack a woman competitor with a pillowlike club than are men who are against women's liberation. "Traditional" men feel uncomfortable in this relatively harmless situation. This, a change in the attitudes of a potential aggressor *may* mean that women will receive a larger share of aggression of at least some kinds (Deaux, 1976).

Witnessing Aggression

While competing in an artificial laboratory situation in which shock is involved, males are much more aggressive in the presence of a male witness than they are in the presence of a female witness. Thus, the presence of a woman does *not* appear to increase aggression between two males. The presence of a man *does.* A man is more supportive of aggression than is a woman, particularly if the male witness is dressed in aggressive garb himself. Even the presence of a woman witness will encourage aggression in a man if the man knows that the woman supports aggression. Without knowledge about the witness, men fall back on stereotypes. They believe that a male witness will support further aggression and that a female witness will not.

In summary, as *initiators* men are more aggressive than women. Given provocation, however, women can be as aggressive as men. With stereotypes aside, the sex differences are lessened still further (Deaux, 1976).

OTHER CONSIDERATIONS

In humans, aggression can take many more forms than it can in other primates. In all of its forms, however, human males seem to surpass human females, at least as initiators. This is true across many if not all different cultures (Whiting and Pope, 1973). The most popular explanation for this sex difference attributes it to sex differences in *socialization.* There is the belief among many psychologists that the underlying biological potential for aggression is the same for both sexes. On the whole, however, the evidence is *not* good that sex differences in aggression are completely the result of differential socialization practices. In other words, there is probably a biological substratum accounting for a part of the sex differences. Consider the following evidence:

1. Males are more aggressive than females in *all* societies studied.
2. The sex differences appear early in life and continue throughout life.
3. There is little evidence for differential socialization.
4. The same sex difference is seen in other primate species.
5. Aggression is related to levels of sex hormones (High levels of aggression can be both a cause and an effect of, for example, higher testosterone levels). (See Williams, 1977, pp. 152-154.)

Of course, there is considerable overlap between the sexes in aggressiveness and some forms of aggression are socially acquired. The threshold for aggression *does* seem to be lower for males on the average, however. The evidence does not contradict the biological substratum hypothesis.

REFERENCES

Deaux, K. *The Behavior of Women and Men.* Monterey, CA: Brooks-Cole, 1976.

Dolhinow, P.J. Normal monkeys? *American Scientist,* 1977, 65, (letter).

Doyle, G.A. and Martin, R.D. (Eds.) *The Study of Prosimian Behavior.* New York: Academic Press, 1979.

Erwin, J., Anderson, B., Erwin, N., Lewis, L., and Flynn, D. Aggression in captive pigtail monkey groups: Effects of provision of cover. *Perceptual and Motor Skills,* 1976, 42, 319-324.

Hamburg, D.A. Ethological perspectives on human aggressive behaviour. In White, N.F. (Ed.) *Ethology and Psychiatry.* Toronto: University of Toronto Press, 1974, pp. 209-219.

Maccoby, E.E. and Jacklin, C.M. *The Psychology of Sex Differences.* Stanford, CA: Stanford University Press, 1974.

Maple, T. *Orang-utan Behavior.* New York: Van Nostrand Reinhold, 1980.

Maple, T. and Hoff, M.P. *Gorilla Behavior.* New York: Van Nostrand Reinhold, in press.

Marler, P. On animal aggression: The roles of strangeness and familiarity. *American Psychologist,* 1976, 31, 239-246.

Mitchell, G. *Behavioral Sex Differences in Nonhuman Primates.* New York: Van Nostrand Reinhold, 1979.

Sugiyama, Y. An artificial social change in a Hanuman langur troop (*Presbytis entellus*). *Primates,* 1966, 7, 41-72.

Whiting, B.B. and Pope, C.P. A cross-cultural analysis of sex differences in the behavior of children aged three through eleven. *Journal of Social Psychology,* 1973, 91, 171-188.

Williams, J.H. *Psychology of Women: Behavior in a Biosocial Context.* New York: W.W. Norton, 1977.

Wolfheim, J.H. A quantitative analysis of the organization of a group of captive talapoin monkeys (*Miopithecus talapoin*). *Folia primatologica,* 1977, 27, 1-27.

20
Vulnerability and Pathology

In the present chapter we will discuss sex differences in vulnerability in general, whether it be to infectious diseases, to accidents, to congenital disorders, to early social deprivation, to stress, or to crowding. Aging and mortality are also responded to differently by the two sexes. We will review sex differences in vulnerability in the nonhuman primates first, then examine sex differences in vulnerability in people.

NONHUMAN PRIMATES

Diseases and Mortality

Travel in areas not frequented by the natal group can lead to the acquisition of disease. As we know, male nonhuman primates seem to travel more than do females. In addition, competition and aggression is accompanied by stress and wounding. Males surpass females in these qualities as well. Activity differences may lead to differences in the frequency and number of accidents. Males, being more active in play, for example, might be expected to suffer more accidents (Mitchell, 1979).

Old World Monkeys. Old World monkey vulnerability to disease is almost always higher in males than in females. Even prior to birth, the rhesus and other macaque male embryos and fetuses are more vulnerable to abnormal development than are the females. Congenital malformations of the limbs occur more in males than in females.

Among free-ranging rhesus, bone fractures (e.g., of clavicle) are found more often in males. At age four, male rhesus have a higher mortality rate than do females. By eight years of age, only 26 percent of the males but 60 percent of the females are still living. Mortality among reproductively mature males is greater than is mortality among reproductively mature females (see Mitchell, 1979, for references).

Even in those situations where females receive more wounds than males, the males' wounds are more likely to impair locomotion and threaten survival than are the females' wounds. Males receive more serious bites. On the other hand, with regard to myopia and eye enlargements, female rhesus are more susceptible than are male rhesus (see Mitchell, 1979).

For prematurity and low birth weight, males are more susceptible than are females. In some species (e.g., pigtails) female mortality is higher for short portions of the animal's life (e.g., between 30 and 180 days postpartum) but by four to five years of age, female mortality rates become low and male rates surpass female rates. High early female mortality has been related to exclusion from food whereas male mortality has been related to disease and fighting. There is usually a slight preponderance of males at birth and in infancy, but females outnumber males as adults. Senile females are more numerous than are senile males in most Old World monkey groups.

It is interesting that, at water holes, heterosexual groups have priority of access over all-male groups (and over solitary males) in some species (e.g., in patas). There is also a differential mortality in these species in the dry season, with all-male groups having higher mortality rates (see Mitchell, 1979).

But males are *not* more vulnerable than females in all situations. Remove an adult Old World monkey female from her stable group of female friends and put her in a new group and she suffers much more than does the male. The male pattern in Old World monkeys is to meet strangers, to change groups, to live a solitary existence. From this he suffers from wounds but not from chronic physiological stress. The female may suffer great stress in such a situation (see Mitchell, 1979).

A fearful, stressed animal crouches, moves rigidly, looks quickly, frequently—even furtively—bares its teeth in a grimace, and responds physiologically with increased adrenalin (epinephrine). If the stress is prolonged there is an increase in blood levels of adrenal corticosteroids. The adrenal glands enlarge and produce more steroids.

Sassenrath (1970) has shown a sex difference in response to stress in rhesus. Estrogens stimulate the adrenal response, androgens inhibit it. Increased stress in females interferes with their reproductive capacities. In the quarantine period following capture, female rhesus and baboons show amenorrhea and low conception rates (see Mitchell, 1979).

It may be that females experience more stress than do males when they are removed from their stable kinship groups, but that males experience more stress *within* the stable groups themselves (because of higher aggression, etc.). Further data on Old World monkeys may answer this question.

It does appear that estrogen levels prime females to respond to the stress related to strange places and strange new animals. Subadult females, low in estrogen, do not respond to such stresses as well as do adult females. The adrenal response increases as the subadults approach maturity (see Mitchell, 1979 for references).

Under artificially crowded conditions, male Old World monkeys respond by aggressing one another. Females seem better able to tolerate crowding, at least with regard to *not* showing as marked an increase in aggression as do males (see Mitchell, 1979).

The reverse condition, social isolation, particularly when it occurs early in life, seems to affect males more adversely than it affects females. If an Old World monkey is raised apart from its own kind, it develops behavioral abnormalities. During the first year, the isolate animal develops self-clinging, stereotyped rocking, self-mouthing, crouching, and excessive fear in social situations. At puberty, continued pacing replaces rocking, self-biting supplants self-sucking, and social aggression develops as social fear wanes. In adulthood, the isolate-reared monkey becomes even more abnormally aggressive, self-mutilative, and sexually incompetent (see Mitchell, 1968; 1979).

All of these symptoms are more severe in the male than in the female. Self-mouthing, self-clasping, and rocking occur more frequently in young male isolates than in young female isolates. Adult male isolates display more self-biting, higher levels of abnormal aggression, and more abnormal sexual behaviors than do adult female isolates. Parental behavior is seriously abnormal in isolate-reared animales of both sexes. In social behavior, male isolates are more disturbed than are females isolates (Mitchell, 1968; 1979).

When sixteen isolate-reared rhesus monkeys were placed into a free-ranging environment with a wild troop, only two of six isolate males survived whereas seven of nine females survived (Sackett, 1974). Most male isolates are incapable of executing an appropriately oriented sexual mount. While isolate females do not often present appropriately, occasionally some of them do present well enough to conceive. The female Old World monkey is less seriously handicapped than the male by early social deprivation.

Apes. As in Old World monkeys, among chimpanzees, females are more susceptible to visual myopia than are males (Young et al., 1971). With regard to diseases, wounding, and other abnormalities, male apes seem to be more vulnerable than females. Even in regards to susceptibility to alcoholism, male apes are more vulnerable than females (Fitzgerald, Barfield, and Warrington, 1968).

Sex roles are not as sharply differentiated for chimpanzees as they are for many Old World monkeys but, even in the great apes, early social deprivation has more severe and lasting consequences for males than it does for females (Mason et al., 1968). For the chimpanzee, deprivation during *puberty* seems to be particularly devastating as far as sexual behavior is concerned; and, this is especially true for males. Chimpanzee males, however, seem to be more capable of recovering from early social deprivation than do Old World monkey males. But female chimpanzees recover even more than do males. Infant care-giving behaviors are seriously affected by early isolation in both males and females of all the great apes.

Summary of Nonhuman Primate Vulnerability. Nonhuman primate males are more vulnerable than females to prenatal and congenital abnormalities, to many diseases, to accidents, to wounding from fighting, to color blindness, and to the effects of early social deprivation. Females are more susceptible to stress as a result of loss of a stable social group. They also develop myopia more than do males. Each of these sex differences in vulnerability can be related to overall gender differences discussed previously in this book. The male's tendencies toward peripheralization, group transfer, and extratroop behaviors are associated with increased aggression and with increased exposure to disease, wounding and accident. The female's proclivities toward *within*-group socialization and close communication, including grooming, can be related to susceptibility to stress in strange places and with strange individuals as well as to myopia (close work leads to myopia).

Comments on Human Vulnerability. Girls appear to be more resilient than boys to the effects of early social interactions. Boys seem to be more permanently affected than girls by the emotional climate of infancy, whether warm or rejecting (Bayley, 1968). According to Bayley (1968), the months 13 to 36 are critical for boys, whereas adolescence may be more disruptive for girls. Yet, the number of boys with childhood schizophrenia surpasses the number of girls by eight or ten times throughout childhood and *particularly* at puberty and beyond. In children's clinics, three times as many boys as girls display head-banging and other self-injurious behaviors. Male suicides outnumber female suicides by three or four to one (Bender, 1946; Lester, 1972; Jackson, 1954; Peters and Hammen, 1977).

Prior to birth, human male embryos are more vulnerable to teratogens than are female embryos (Taylor, 1969). There are three to four autistic boys for every autistic girl (Wing, 1976). There are more perinatal, neonatal, and early childhood disorders in boys than in girls (Luce and Wand, 1977). In sexual behavior, human males again display greater vulnerability to disorder. Men also show more alcoholism than do women (Luce and Wand, 1977).

Once past puberty, as noted by Bayley (1968), human females begin to show higher referral rates for mental or emotional problems than do males. Depression may also be higher in females. *However,* clinical judgments often parallel cultural stereotypes (Broverman et al., 1970). There is undoubtedly sex bias in the helping professions. If a woman shows stereotyped male-role behavior she may be judged unhealthy. Like female monkeys and female apes, however, female humans *do* show more myopia than do male humans (Young, 1971, 1977).

Finally, in all species of primates, including humans, females live longer than do males. The sex difference in longevity may be attributable to the biological substratum, not just to differences in pressures to succeed, to smoking, to socialization differences, to ulcers, or to other disorders of stress.

CROWDING IN HUMANS

Overpopulation and crowding in the cities have become important ecological and psychological topics in recent years. But what is crowding? We must distinguish between social density and spatial density. In increasing *social density* the number of people are increased in the *same* amount of space. In increasing *spatial density* the amount of space is reduced for the same number of people. Using these two types of density we can discriminate between the effects of *crowding* and *group size*. In general, people feel better about each other and the group when the group size is small (Deaux, 1976; Erwin, 1976).

Men prefer a larger personal space than do women; and, *in general* men find crowded conditions more unpleasant than do women. In small crowded like-sexed groups of seven to eight people, men react more negatively than do women. Women actually see this high-density situation as being more pleasant. In mixed-sex groups of the same *small* size, there is no sex difference with regard to the effects of crowding. Thus, it has been said that men are more uncomfortable than women in highly crowded conditions (Deaux, 1976).

But what about larger groups? In college classrooms of from 10 to 300 people, college men *report* feeling increasingly aggressive as density increases. College women report no changes in aggressive feelings with increased density but they do report being more *nervous* under crowded conditions (Deaux, 1976).

But other factors are involved besides density and group size. The time that a group has been together is also of importance. Being in a crowded elevator from floor to floor is unpleasant but forced confinement for a matter of hours (not in an elevator) can be fun. During New York City's blackout, people who were so confined had parties (Deaux, 1976).

With regard to group size, as noted above, people like small groups better than they like large groups, but this tendency is greater in men than in women. For example, four persons vs. 16 persons is preferred far more in men than in women. Men also prefer mixed groups to all-male groups. Based upon the primate literature one might suspect that this difference might change with the age of the males. Women prefer *both* men and women in large groups but all women in small groups. Both men and women prefer mixed company in crowded groups. Initially over a *short* period of time men react more negatively to crowding than do women. They appear to need more personal space and to show a kind of territorial behavior. Women do not find cramped conditions as uncomfortable at this stage as do men. Over a period of time, particularly if a problem needs to be solved, men come to feel less hostile and less uncomfortable. Women, who tend to enjoy the more personal and socioemotional aspects of crowding more than do men, may sometimes get irritated by a problem-solving requirement under extremely close conditions. The problem solving may be incompatible with their socioemotional tactics. According to Deaux (1976), greater stress on social and emotional skills would increase pleasure among women and decrease pleasure among men in crowded conditions.

ABNORMAL BEHAVIOR AND CRIME IN HUMANS

Biology and socialization conspire to give girls the edge over boys in the early years of life. Additional genetic material on the female's second X chromosome conveys protection to females against sex-linked disorders. At least partly as a result of this, girls show fewer congenital abnormalities, lower rates of mental retardation, and fewer cases of schizophrenia. Different developmental rates for girls and boys may also give girls some unseen advantage in coping or in interpersonal skills. Girls are also cared for by same-sex models, boys are not. Finally, girls are less aggressive and hence probably less antisocial (see Williams, 1977).

Boys usually show delinquency by acting out aggressively. Girls often show delinquency by seeking love through sexual acting out. Boys are significantly more delinquent than are girls, however. Girls are more likely to be punished for offenses which violate sexual mores and parental authority (nonadult crimes), boys for larceny, car theft, etc. ("adult" crimes). Women are remarkably under-represented in crime statistics relative to men. Much of female crime is masked, however, because of the woman's protected role (in the home, etc.) (Williams, 1977).

However, female crime is growing. Whereas the male to female arrest ratio was 8 to 1 in 1960, it was only 6 to 1 in 1973. (The ratio in prison in 1973 was 25 to 1, however.) As society becomes less protective of women, less patriarchal, female criminals will be dealt with more severely.

Women put into prison are people removed from more salient social roles than are men put into prison. To compensate, women in prison set up social networks which simulate those outside. The networks are often systems of informal nuclear families made up of homosexual alliances and so-called "kinship ties." A "couple" starts a "family" by getting other inmates to be their "children." This system helps solve feelings of alienation and isolation (Williams, 1977).

Even in prison there is discrimination against women. Programs do not prepare for later potential employment but merely help in prison maintenance. Work-release programs (work during day, prison at night) are less available to women. Educational and therapeutic programs are not as frequent for women. Conjugal visits are being introduced for men only, the implication being that a woman's sexual needs are less urgent than are a man's (Williams, 1977).

MENTAL ILLNESS

Single, divorced, and widowed women have fewer mental problems than do their male counterparts. Married women account for most of the mental illness among adult females. Men with serious mental problems are more likely to stay single than are women with serious mental problems. Female schizophrenics, unlike males, are spread quite evenly among the single and the married. The change in marital status from married to divorced is more devastating for the man than for the woman (Luce and Wand, 1977).

SUICIDES

While men commit suicide three or four times as often as women, women make four times as many attempts at taking their own lives. Men use more violent methods, women are more inclined to use pills. Women also use the attempts to make appeals to others. Professional women account for a larger portion of the suicides than one would expect by chance.

PUBERTY

The female's advantage regarding vulnerability begins to be lost at puberty and during adolescence. Men are probably overall at greater genetic risk for mental disorder than are women, *but* the effects of socialization into sex roles become more obvious at puberty. Girls and women whose selves are not autonomous but are maintained through relationships with others, may be especially vulnerable to changes in their social-affective lives. The achievement of intimacy is paramount for many women. If they do not achieve it, it is often devastating for them. "Research on problems that typically affect women and on the ways women cope with them is only beginning to appear" (Williams, 1977, p. 355). Thus, even in the area of treatment for female emotional problems, psychology has been negligent.

REFERENCES

Bayley, N. Behavioral correlates of mental growth: Birth to thirty-six years. *American Psychologist*, 1968, 23(1), 1-17.

Bender, L. Schizophrenia in childhood: Its recognition, description, and treatment. *American Journal of Orthopsychiatry*, 1946, 26, 499-506.

Broverman, I.K., Broverman, D.M., Clarkson, F.E., Rosenkrantz, P.S., and Vogel, S.R. Sex role stereotypes and clinical judgments of mental health. *Journal of Counseling and Clinical Psychology*, 1970, 34(1), 1-7.

Erwin, J. Aggressive behavior of captive pigtail macaques: Spatial conditions and social controls. *Laboratory Primate Newsletter*, 1976, 15(2), 1-10.

Fitzgerald, F.L., Barfield, M.A., and Warrington, R.J. Voluntary alcohol consumption in chimpanzees and orangutans. *Quarterly Journal of Studies on Alcohol*, 1968, 29(2), 330-336.

Jackson, D.D. Suicide. *Scientific American*, 1954 (Nov.), pp. 1-6.

Lester, D. Self-mutilating behavior. *Psychological Bulletin*, 1972, 78, 119-128.

Luce, S.R. and Wand, B. Sex differences in health and illness. *Canadian Psychological Review*, 1977, 18, 79-91.

Mason, W.A., Davenport, R.K., and Menzel, E.W. Jr. Early experience and the social development of rhesus monkeys and chimpanzees. In Newton, G. and Levine, S. (Eds.) *Early Experience and Behavior*. Springfield, Illinois: Charles C. Thomas, 1968, pp. 1-41.

Mitchell, G. Persistent behavior pathology in rhesus monkeys following early social isolation. *Folia Primatologica*, 1968, 8, 132-147.

Mitchell, G. *Behavioral Sex Differences in Nonhuman Primates*. New York: Van Nostrand Reinhold, 1979.

Peters, S.D. and Hammen, C. Differential rejection of male and female depression. Paper presented at the *Western Psychological Association* meeting, Seattle, Washington, April 1977.

Sackett, G.P. Sex differences in rhesus monkeys following varied rearing experiences. In Friedman, R.C., Richert, R.M., and Vande Wiele, R.L. (Eds.) *Sex Differences in Behavior*. New York: Wiley, 1974, pp. 99-122.

Sassenrath, E.N. Increased adrenal responsiveness related to social stress in rhesus monkeys. *Hormones and Behavior*, 1970, 1, 283-298.

Taylor, M.A. Sex ratios of newborns: Associated with prepartum and post-partum schizophrenia. *Science,* 1969, 164, 723-724.

Williams, J.H. *Psychology of Women: Behavior in a Biosocial Context.* New York: W.W. Norton, 1977.

Wing, L. (Ed.) *Early Childhood Autism.* New York: Pergamon, 1976, pp. 67-71.

Young, F.A. The nature and control of myopia. *Journal of the American Optometric Association,* 1977, 48, 451-457.

Young, F.A., Leary, G.A., and Farrer, D.N. Four years of annual studies of chimpanzee vision. *American Journal of Optometry,* 1971, 48, 407-416.

21
Aging

CHANGE OF LIFE

After puberty and into adulthood, sex hormonal levels stay high in both male and female nonhuman primates. If the female primate lives long enough she experiences a menopause. In the rhesus monkey, menopause occurs at around twenty-seven or twenty-eight years of age (van Wagenen, 1970). In the chimpanzee, regular menstrual cycles continue until death. Breeding is unsuccessful at around forty years of age, however. While menstruation still occurs, ovarian senescence is obvious and the female chimpanzee becomes infertile (Graham and McClure, 1977).

Women, like rhesus monkeys, but apparently unlike chimpanzees, experience a true menopause. Estrogen and progesterone secretions decline, starting some time in the woman's forties and progressing more rapidly in the fifties and sixties. The ovaries fail to respond to FSH and ovulation stops. With reduced estrogen and progesterone, menstrual cycles disappear and the woman becomes infertile (Williams, 1977).

The entire sequence is a very gradual one, but eventually the woman may experience physical symptoms like a hot flash. Her vaginal tissues become thinner, and less lubricated, she loses hair and muscle tone and her breasts and other tissues droop and become flabby. The hot flash includes perspiration and sometimes dizziness. Insomnia, headaches, and anxiety may also occur. Synthetic estrogen administration can help relieve the symptoms if they are serious (see Williams, 1977).

Men do not experience these physical things. There are psychological changes in men, however. Mood swings, changes in self-concept, and changes in life style are common in men. Sperm production decreases only slightly. Men remain fertile throughout their lives, although testosterone levels gradually decrease as men age. Consequently, the sexual capacity to sustain erection declines somewhat with age (Williams, 1977).

Stereotypes regarding middle-age abound. Middle-aged women are often cast as wicked stepmothers or witches, or as people with relatively bland personalities. Women are not encouraged to develop qualities that improve with age (e.g., intellect, problem-solving, etc.).

Women of 50 often report feelings of depression and uselessness as a result of these stereotypes. Loss of children, loss of physical attractiveness, loss of purpose, produce the despair. But the despair is often *socially*, not biologically, caused. It is still, of course, possible that *some* depression is biologically determined.

BIOLOGY OF AGING

As people age there is an increase in connective tissue between the body cells, a loss of elasticity in the skin, an increase in fat, a decrease in muscular strength, and a decrease in sex hormones. In general these changes reduce the person's ability to recover from illness and trauma.

In the brain, there is cell death, oxygen deprivation, and chemical changes. Nerve cells do not reproduce. Reaction time slows in most people. However, those with high intellectual ability to begin with decline hardly at all in performance. Some even continue to improve at least to age 50. There is no precipitous decline in intellectual ability as a function of age (Kimmel, 1974).

The average life span of people has increased, but the upper limits of the life span have not. They appear to be genetically fixed for each species. Longevity is a sex-linked trait. Females live longer than do males. Female primates, but not males, out-live their reproductive capacities (Williams, 1977).

The female's ova are present at birth and remain as old as she is throughout life. Older ova are more likely to produce unhealthy offspring than are young, healthy ova. The risk of Down's syndrome (mongolism) increases with a woman's age. The male's sperm are continuously produced in the testes throughout life and are not subject to aging. One can immediately see why males are more expendable, hence more vulnerable than females.

The climacterium is a developmental phase, like puberty, becoming an adult, etc., in which reorganization of the personality is made necessary. It is another challenge of life. Most women respond to the challenge in terms of a life stage. The absence or presence of menstruation usually does not bother them. More than 50 percent of women report concerns of widowhood, of disease, of children leaving home, or of just aging in general. Some report better sexual relations *after* menopause than before. Most women do not report many serious physical problems associated with menopause. Only 10 to 15 percent seek medical assistance (Williams, 1977).

Depression, apathy, loss of energy, are occasionally reported at menopause. The more a woman has fit society's stereotypes, the more she reports feelings of despair. To her, she no longer has a purpose. Depression in menopausal women is probably *not* due to hormonal changes but to a loss of self-esteem. Overprotective and overinvolved mothers are particularly prone to show depression in the menopausal period. Housewives suffer more than working women, Jews more than Catholics and Protestants, whites more than blacks (Williams, 1977).

Depression develops when either parent believes that personal needs have been subjugated to those of the children, and rewards for selflessness will be reaped only later. Children, however, "do their own thing." They do not recognize the parental contribution, but they do *expect* it.

Depression in middle age, whether for women or for men, may be a result of being confined, or confining oneself, into too narrow a range of life styles, choices, or opportunities. It is cultural, social and *personal*, not biological. It is worthwhile to make certain that one has more than one justification for living. We must all have alternatives.

But the most confused and depressed reactions of all come from women and men who are in the social transition group, in that group which has not yet adapted to the changes brought on by the women's movement, and other factors. Both completely "traditional" women and men and "liberated" women and men adapt better than do "transitional" women. In the latter, the maternal role is often not available but neither does she have the required skills for the "liberated" role (Williams, 1977).

In modern studies of the so-called "empty nest syndrome," new results have been coming in. In one door-to-door study of 49 middle-aged people 22 of them said that this was the *best* stage of their lives so far. Only *three* people (all women) gave negative evaluations of middle age. However, *twice* as many wives as husbands said that life without the children was *better* than it was with the children. Clearly, a well-defined female menopausal and/or empty-nest syndrome was lacking (Williams, 1977).

SEXUALITY

There is no discontinuity in sexual desire or behavior in middle age. Beliefs and expectations regarding sexual decline are exaggerated; attitudes toward sexuality in older people are negative. The aging person is not asexual. Sex in older people is not unnatural.

Strength and energy are reduced when age and body responses slow down. The frequency and intensity of sexual behavior also wane, but orgasm still occurs. The female's orgasm develops somewhat less fully and orgasmic contractions are fewer and less intense, but clitoral response is unchanged into old age. In males, attaining erection takes longer, but the erection can be maintained longer because of both greater experience and changing physiology. Thus, the male's performance and effectiveness from the female's point of view, if not from his own, may actually improve. The aging male also experiences fewer orgasmic contractions and less vigorous ejaculation.

Estrogen is not directly responsible for the sex drive in women. The availability of a partner and regularity of sexual behavior maintain a woman's sexual interest. Freedom from fear of pregnancy, financial problems, the children, in-laws, etc. often lead to greater satisfaction in sex. Women actually have a more stable sex drive than men as they age. In men, impotence occasionally occurs in later age (Masters and Johnson, 1968; 1970).

The ratio of men to women declines with age. From 65 to 74 years of age there are only 72 men to every 100 women. This ratio, plus the fact that there is a double standard of aging wherein older men may marry younger women but older women rarely marry younger men, results in many women without partners. Getting older tends to operate in favor of men.

A woman over 65 still seeks erotic encounters, still reports erotic dreams, and still experiences multiple orgasms. Masturbation becomes her outlet if she has no partner (Williams, 1977).

Despite the obvious presence of eroticism in older women (over 65) they do not have as active a sex life as do men of the same age. The percentage of women having no intercourse jumps sharply for females over 55. At age sixty, 94 percent of the men but only 80 percent of the women are still sexually active. Societal attitudes toward sex in older females accounts for most of the sex differences (Williams, 1977).

MARITAL STATUS

More than 60 percent of the women over sixty-five in the United States are not married. The percentage is even greater for blacks than for whites (Williams, 1977).

When a woman is widowed—and most married women are—she needs to express her grief, find companionship, solve immediate problems produced by the situation, and re-engage herself into the social system. Black women, in particular, seem to have little social support when widowed, but most widows lead lonely lives. Many widows remarry, usually for companionship, although adult children are often obstacles to this. Seventy-five percent of late life re-marriages are highly successful ones (McKain, 1969).

PERSONALITY

There is both stability and change in personality with age. General adaptation, cognitive ability, and style of social interaction remain stable. Emotional stability and the degree of hostility and passivity also remain consistent. There is, however, a decline in ego-energy and a shift in sex-role perception. Emotional energy for the outer world declines, and there is increasing avoidance of self-assertiveness and of challenges. In general, there is a change from active mastery to passive mastery. In addition, there is a gradual shift toward sex-role reversal. Older men are frequently seen as being more submissive, older women as more aggressive and dominant. Older people are less sexist. Women become more tolerant of their own aggressiveness, men of their own nurturant and affiliative tendencies (Williams, 1977).

Aging appearance affects women more than it does men. This, along with societal attitudes, helps produce a double standard in regard to the way people respond to the two sexes of people as they age.

Our society values youth, particularly in women, but also in men. The self-actualized person, however, is less affected by the appraisal of others. As women in general become stronger, more independent, and freer to grow they will be less affected by societal stereotypes. The education of society in general with regard to aging could be of great value in promoting greater acceptance of aging and a larger contribution by old people to our society. Because our society as a whole is aging, and since a large portion of these old people will be women, education in both sex differences and aging appears to be necessary.

REFERENCES

Graham, C.E. and McClure, H.M. Ovarian tumors and related lesions in aged chimpanzees. *Veterinary Pathology*, 1977, 14, 380-386.

Kimmel, D.C. *Adulthood and Aging.* New York: Wiley, 1974.

Masters, W. and Johnson, V. Human sexual response: The aging female and the aging male. In Newgarten, B. (Ed.) *Middle Age and Aging.* Chicago: University of Chicago Press, 1968.

Masters, W. and Johnson, V. *Human Sexual Inadequacy.* Boston: Little, Brown, 1970.

McKain, W.C. *Retirement Marriage.* Storrs, Conn.: Storrs Agriculture Experiment Station, University of Connecticut, 1969.

Van Wagenen, G. Menopause in a subhuman primate. *Anatomical Record,* 1970, 166, 392.

Williams, J.H. *The Psychology of Women: Behavior in a Biosocial Context.* New York: W.W. Norton, 1977.

22
Ability and Achievement

We have seen that male nonhuman primates are more vulnerable to the effects of early experience than are female nonhuman primates. This information regarding differential vulnerability has sometimes been used without objectivity. The argument has been that if males are more susceptible to early environmental effects, they must be less prewired in their nervous systems than females. There is little or no evidence to support this latter assertion.

Underlying these behavioral sex differences, however, are sex differences in the brain, especially in the hypothalamus and connected areas, which are, in turn, related to the amount of prenatal androgens. The development of the prefrontal cortex, for example, may be sensitive to the effects of androgen. In object discrimination reversal tasks 46-day-old rhesus male infants perform significantly better than do females of similar age. Neonatal injections of androgen, however, improve female performance. Lesions in the prefrontal orbital cortex decrease object discrimination reversal ability in infant males, but *not* in infant females. If the infant females are androgenized, however, such lesions *do* decrease performance on object discrimination reversal tasks. Normal male rhesus monkeys with orbital prefrontal lesions are impaired at two-and-a-half months of age. Normal females are not impaired by orbital prefrontal lesions until 15 to 18 months of age. There are apparently gender-specific "critical periods" for this particular brain area (Goldman et al., 1974). Since this area is implicated in delayed response and reversals, it is of some interest to us, for our current topic, to know that there are sex differences in its maturation. There is thus no doubt that early differential levels of androgen change the rhesus nervous system, even outside the hypothalamus. There is little evidence of a general differential plasticity based on gender, however (also see Goldman, 1976).

Looking at the data on sex differences in learning rather than in the brain, we find that greater susceptibility to the effects of early experience does *not* necessarily mean greater overall plasticity in learning situations. Higher order learning abilities such as delayed response and reversal learning are well-developed in both male and female primates. Let us look at these abilities in nonhuman primates, with an eye out for sex differences.

DELAYED RESPONSE IN OLD WORLD MONKEYS

In rhesus monkeys, as noted above, 46 day-old infant males perform better on reversal tasks than do 46 day-old infant females. At later ages, however, females are more adept than are males. Blomquist (1960) found that adult female rhesus were superior to adult male rhesus in delayed response performance. McDowell et al. (1960) reported similar data. How are such abilities used in the wild?

A task related to delayed response is the sand-digging task. In the sand-digging test, a reward is buried at different depths in the sand. At the greater depths it takes longer to reach the reward through digging and there is therefore a longer delay. In such situations, macaque females show more enduring attention and greater persistence in digging to the reward at the greater depths than do macaque males. Female macaques, therefore, perform better on such tasks than do males (Tsumori, 1966; 1967).

Tsumori (1966, 1967) has argued that the sex difference has more to do with the female's enduring attention to the task, to her motivation, and to her prolonged attentiveness to close detail than to any superiority in attention to cue production or in cue retention. Males attend to distant events, in their roles as troop protectors, guardians, look-outs, and wanderers. Females attend to close events within a troop. Perhaps a delayed response task involving more distant cues and incentives might produce a different sex difference (see Mitchell, 1979).

DELAYED RESPONSE IN APES

As in the macaque-delayed response studies, female chimpanzees surpass males in delayed response performance. In delayed matching-to-sample, a sex difference is seen which extends over a considerable period of time and over different retention intervals. Females are superior to males (Grilly, 1975).

TOOL USING IN NONHUMAN PRIMATES

Most studies of tool using and the development of new skills in Old World monkeys find either no sex difference or else the results vary from study to study (see Mitchell, 1979). The same applies to the great apes. When it comes to using or inventing ladders, swings, or weapons, males (macaques or chimpanzees) seem to have the edge. However, when tools are made and used to obtain food or to groom the self or another animal, females seem to excel (Menzel, 1972; McGrew, 1974). McGrew and Tutin (1973), for example, found that female chimpanzees use tools to groom the teeth of other chimpanzees more than do males. Nadler and Braggio (1974) noted that female chimpanzees and female orangutans in captivity play with inanimate objects more overall than do their male counterparts.

SOCIAL LEARNING AND PROTOCULTURE IN PRIMATES

In social learning, there may be grounds for believing that female Old World monkeys have an advantage over males. Males (particularly peripheral males) are often the last to acquire new food-eating habits (Kawamura, 1963). In addition, since males often leave the troop to travel alone (or with other males) or to change troops, the older females and their younger close kin (usually also females) must retain most of the information regarding social tradition. This may be less true of the great apes, however.

RELATED HUMAN CONSIDERATIONS

In anthropological writings, the evolution of human tool use has been classically related to decreased canine size in *Homo sapiens* and to the consequent greater need for weapons or tools in defense, a *male* role. However, the role of women in the evolution of tool use has recently been the center of attention. Tanner and Zihlman (1976 a, b) emphasize the mother's innovative economic roles involving *gathering* with tools and *sharing* food with her infants. Because of her central role, socially speaking, she has been the primary socializer and the primary teacher of new skills, including tool-using. According to Tanner and Zihlman (1976a, b) males developed smaller canines not as a function of the use of tools for defense and hunting, but because females chose less aggressive males to help them with child rearing.

The integration of the male into the family, and the development of cultural transmission, required a nervous system of well-developed social-emotional systems as well as of well-evolved intelligence, learning capacity, and tool-using ability. Symbols, plans, and tools evolved in a social context, and the female was central in that social context (Etkin, 1963).

According to Tanner and Zihlman (1976b):

> While gathering plants, speech would add little, although do no harm; during predation or hunting, anything as noisy as speech would likely frighten away the prey (p. 475).

With this statement, they suggest that even language developed first in the female of our species. It is certainly true today that human females are superior to human males in verbal learning. At two to six years of age, girls have higher scores on syntax maturity, sentence length, and on specific grammatical categories. Boys seem to be better at visual-spatial tasks, at the discrimination of forms, and at mathematics. Overall, however:

> . . . there is no difference in *how* the two sexes learn. Whether there is a difference in *what* they find easier to learn is a different question (Maccoby and Jacklin, 1974, p. 62).

Just as one brain contains mechanisms for both male and female basic behavior, it also contains mechanisms for both so-called male and so-called female skills. On the other hand, the important determinants of sex differences in people are almost certainly:

> . . . cognitive templates in the brain built up through experience (Beach, 1976, p. 473).

Prenatal and hormonal effects must be seen as limited and diffuse, as setting a bias on the neural substratum which predisposes the individual to acquire and express one set of sex-related skills yet does not preclude the acquisition and expression of the behaviors and skills of the "other sex" (Reinisch, 1974, p. 51).

HUMAN ABILITIES

According to Tavris and Offir (1977), there are no sex differences in general intelligence. On most tests, females excel in verbal ability, particularly after the age of 10 or 11, males excel in visual-spatial and quantitative ability from the start of adolescence, and females excel on verbal creativity tests. There is no general sex difference in cognitive style.

There are no sex differences in the average IQs of human males and females because the IQ tests themselves are designed to minimize sex differences. In specific abilities, however, there are differences.

Verbal Ability

It is not really clear whether infant girls talk sooner than boys or are more skilled with words. However, measures of attentiveness and subsequent vocalization are more closely related in infant girls than they are in infant boys. Infant girls who listen attentively to an auditory stimulus are more likely to vocalize when it ends than are girls who do not listen attentively. No such relation is seen in boys (Williams, 1977). The absolute amount of vocalization does not differ, only the *significance* of the vocalization. Absolute differences in verbal ability are not demonstrated before the age of two (Williams, 1977), but throughout most of the school years girls outscore boys on tests of verbal skills. Among the underprivileged, girls have an even greater advantage in the verbal area because of greater male vulnerability to early deprivation. From ages two to ten, boys have more reading problems and, at age ten, girls are clearly superior in verbal ability. They maintain their advantage throughout high school (Tavris and Offir, 1977).

Quantitative Ability

Two- to four-year-old girls can count as well as can boys of similar age; and in the early school years, there are few sex differences in quantitative skills unless there is early deprivation. Under deprived conditions, girls surpass boys in quantitative ability in the early school years. At puberty, boys show greater math ability than do girls and the sex difference persists through high school, college, and into adulthood. Women also often *fear* math (Tavris and Offir, 1977).

Spatial Ability

According to Tavris and Offir (1977),

> . . . There is reason to believe that males are better, on the average, at visual-spatial tasks (p. 41).

Visual-spatial ability is "the ability to see the relationships between shapes or objects or to visualize what a shape would look like if its orientation in space were changed (Williams, 1977, p. 136). Very few studies report sex differences during childhood, although some results favor boys. From adolescence on, boys clearly surpass girls (Maccoby and Jacklin, 1974).

General Abilities

Overall, we know that three myths long held to be true are really *not* true:

1. Girls are *not* better at rote learning and simple repetitive tasks, and boys are *not* better at higher-level cognitive processes;
2. Boys are *not* better at analyzing and selecting elements needed for solution of a problem; and
3. The intelligence of girls is *not* more affected by heredity than is the intelligence of boys.

(see Maccoby and Jacklin, 1974; Williams, 1977).

Performance Evaluations and Gender

Because of myths like the three mentioned above, girls and boys are often evaluated differently. Even when we are aware that such beliefs are myths, our evaluations are not objective. We all have stereotypic beliefs. Often these beliefs lead to the devaluation of women, but not always (Deaux, 1976).

If an article is said to be authored by a man it is rated more favorably than if it is said to be authored by a woman. This is true whether men or women are doing the rating. Women, too, are prejudiced against women (Deaux, 1976). When a woman has the same credentials as a man she is typically rated lower in competence, has a lower position, is hired less frequently, and gets paid less.

If some recognized authority approves a woman's work, the woman may then be given credit. Otherwise she is often not evaluated positively. In addition, the more clear the criteria for good performance, the less likely we are to be biased against a woman. In short, if we are an expert ourselves, we are likely to know a good performance when we see one (Deaux, 1976). Otherwise, we tend to fall back on stereotypes.

In some situations, a woman is seen as *more* deserving of a reward than is an equally qualified man. The circumstances here, however, must be those in which the woman is clearly not *expected* to do well; *and,* those in which some expert or authority must clearly see that the work is of high caliber (Deaux, 1976).

One's explanation of how a person succeeded or of how to evaluate performance may not be correct, but it still helps one to understand the event. A person might do well on an exam because they are bright, because they worked, because they are lucky, or because they cheated. If a woman does well at a man's work, she is usually evaluated as being lucky. "What is skill for the male is luck for the female." (Deaux, 1976, p. 30).

When a woman finishes medical school, however, it cannot be all luck. In this case, men say she had it easier or she tried harder. Women say she tried harder, but that she also *had* it harder. Australian high school girls might even say the woman cheated (Deaux, 1976).

People usually believe that men are more competent than women. Hence, success by a man is *expected.* This, too, can be a heavy burden. While a woman is expected to fail, a man cannot. When a man fails he is judged as being far more incompetent than a woman who fails. In addition, men get nothing for succeeding in a woman's world whereas women are lauded for succeeding in a man's world (in fact, they are often over-rewarded). Woman's work is seen as less important. As Deaux (1976) has said,

Our expectations for both men and women tend to limit our perspective, and as a result of our stereotyping we may too freely criticize or too sparingly praise (p. 34).

Achievement Motivation

The United States is achievement oriented. Even in the new feminist boom period of psychology, achievement motivation is the most popular area of research. As originally defined by McClelland in 1953, the need for achievement was a desire to accomplish and to do things well, to excel and to achieve success (McClelland et al., 1953). In men, one could arouse or increase the need for achievement by specific instructions, in women one could not. Men high in achievement motivation select tasks of moderate difficulty, and are willing to work longer at them. Such men work well in academic settings. Data like these on women and achievement have been lacking until recently.

Women have a stronger desire for affiliation than do men, but show no real difference in need for achievement. They therefore tend to attempt to excel in social situations more than do men. When experimental instructions prior to testing stress the importance of social skills for the test, women show the same increase in achievement needs as men do when success and leadership are stressed.

Women, it is said, may also fear success because it is "unfeminine" and because they may be rejected by men if they succeed. Horner (1970) has presented data which she believes show that women do in fact fear success. Even in the middle of the 1970s the percentage of women showing fear of success was not decreasing. This was partly because of the conflict they had between job and family. On the other hand, men were showing *more* fear of success in the 1970s than they showed in the 1950s. Among blacks, fear of success was higher in men than in women. If fear of success was measured for white men when they imagined themselves in a woman's shoes, the men showed more fear of success than did the women themselves. Apparently stereotypes accounted for much of the difference (Deaux, 1976). However, *both* men and women now believe that success can have negative consequences, especially if the success is in a nontraditional setting (e.g., men in nursing). Women are not necessarily more afraid of success than men. It depends on the situation.

A woman who fears success does not compete well against a man on a masculine task, but will, in fact, perform quite well in other situations. Performance is very often determined by the values of the person in charge of evaluation. People, men and women, perform in a way which leads to the most favorable consequences. If someone is praised for doing poorly, they do even worse the second time around.

If someone is critized for doing poorly, they do better on a second try. When the consequences of success are explicit, people select the good consequences (Deaux, 1976).

Women have probably been criticized for doing well in masculine areas. Men have been mocked for doing well in feminine areas. They may fear success in these situations, but not necessarily in all situations. The basic behaviors of men and women regarding achievement motivation are not really that different. The important point is that most success is defined in masculine terms.

For women, there are two possible threats from achievement: (1) That if her achievement is unfeminine, men may find her undesirable, and (2) that achievement requires time and sustained effort which requires putting off affiliative goals. Before puberty, neither of these appears to be a problem, although the roots of autonomy begin to grow long before puberty. After puberty, interpersonal competence, attractiveness to men, and children become important to many women. As Williams (1977) has noted:

> Freedom from crippling emotional dependence on the approval and good will of others and a sense of oneself as an autonomous person clearly underlie the kind of commitment and willingness to extend oneself to take risks that characterize the high achiever (p. 187).

The achieving female child needs a secure, warm emotional base as a child. She needs a nurturant parent who permits exploration, encourages independence, and is not too protective. Today's parents are more protective of girls than of boys. Strong mother-feminine identification is counterproductive. Baumrind's (1972) authoritative and harmonious parental types encourage female achievement. His authoritarian and permissive types do not (see Chapter 13 on infant care in humans, Table 13-1 in particular).

REFERENCES

Baumrind, D. From each according to her ability. *School Review*, 1972, 80, 161-197.

Blomquist, A.J. Variables influencing delayed response performance by rhesus monkeys. *Dissertation Abstracts*, 1960, 21, 1634-1635.

Deaux, K. *The Behavior of Women and Men*. Monterey, CA.: Brooks/Cole, 1976.

Etkin, W. Social behavioral factors in the emergence of man. *Human Biology*, 1963, 35(3), 299-310.

Goldman, P.A. Maturation of the mammalian nervous system and the ontogeny of behavior. *Advances in the Study of Behavior*, 1976, 7, 1-90.

Goldman, P.S., Crawford, A.T., Stokes, L.P., Galkin, T.W., and Rosvold, H.E. Sex-dependent behavioral effects of cerebral cortical lesions in the developing rhesus monkey. *Science,* 1974, 186, 540-542.

Grilly, D.M. Sex differences in delayed matching-to-sample performance of chimpanzees. *Psychological Reports,* 1975, 37, 203-207.

Horner, M.S. Femininity and successful achievement: A basic inconsistency. In Bardwick, J.M., et al. (Eds.) *Feminine Personality and Conflict.* Monterey, CA.: Brooks/Cole, 1970.

Kawamura, S. The process of sub-culture propagation among Japanese macaques. In Southwick, C.H. (Ed.) *Primate Social Behavior.* Princeton, N.J.: Van Nostrand, 1963, pp. 82-89.

Maccoby, E.E. and Jacklin, C.N. *The Psychology of Sex Differences.* Stanford, CA.: Stanford Univ. Press, 1974.

McClelland, D.C., Atkinson, J.W., Clark, R.A., and Lowell, E.G. *The Achievement Motive.* New York: Appleton-Century-Crofts, 1953.

McDowell, A.A., Brown, W.L., and McTee, A.C. Sex as a factor in spatial delayed-response performance by rhesus monkeys. *Journal of Comparative and Physiological Psychology,* 1960, 53, 429-432.

McGrew, W.C. Tool use by wild chimpanzees in feeding upon driver ants. *Journal of Human Evolution,* 1974, 3, 501-508.

McGrew, W.C. and Tutin, C.E.G. Chimpanzee tool use in dental grooming. *Nature,* 1973, 241, 477-478.

Menzel, E.W. Jr. Spontaneous invention of ladders in a group of young chimpanzees. *Folia Primatologica,* 1972, 17, 87-106.

Mitchell, G. *Behavioral Sex Differences in Nonhuman Primates.* New York: Van Nostrand Reinhold, 1979.

Nadler, R.D. and Braggio, J.T. Sex and species differences in captive-reared juvenile chimpanzees and orangutans. *Journal of Human Evolution,* 1974, 3, 541-550.

Reinisch, J.M. Fetal hormones, the brain, and human sex differences: A heuristic, integrative review of the recent literature. *Archives of Sexual Behavior,* 1974, 3, 51-90.

Tanner, N. and Zihlman, A. Discussion paper: The evolution of human communication: What can primates tell us? *Annals of the New York Academy of Sciences,* 1976a, 280, 467-480. (a)

Tanner, N. and Zihlman, A. Women in evolution. Part 1: Innovation and selection in human origins. *Signs: Journal of Women in Culture and Society,* 1976b, 1(3), 585-608.

Tavris, C. and Offir, C. *The Longest War: Sex Differences in Perspective.* New York: Harcourt Brace Jovanovich, 1977.

Tsumori, A. Delayed response of wild Japanese monkeys by the sand-digging method. II: Cases of the Takasakiyama troops and the Ohirayama troop. *Primates,* 1966, 7, 363-380.

Tsumori, A. Newly acquired behavior and social interactions of Japanese monkeys. In Altmann, S.A. (Ed.) *Social Communication Among Primates.* Chicago: Univ. of Chicago Press, 1967, pp 207-219.

Williams, J.H. *Psychology of Women: Behavior in a Biosocial Context.* New York: W.W. Norton, 1977.

23
Culture

Cultural propagation of habits (what Itani, 1965, calls protoculture) has been described for many nonhuman primates. French and Candland (1977), for example, have observed the acquisition of tool use for play in captive Japanese macaques. The habit of using a metal rod for a swing rapidly spread through their captive group.

Burton (1972) has described what he called "tradition drift" in Barbary macaques. In 1940 the population of Barbary macaques in Gibraltar showed an extensive participation on the part of subadult females in infant socialization. By the 1970s this same group of macaques displayed infant care by young males, not by young females. In contrast to other macaques it was the adolescent *females* (not the males) that were largely isolated from other troop members.

In Japanese macaques new habits acquired by infants are passed on to adults who care for them. There are some Japanese macaque troops in which there is no adult male care of infants. In these troops, none of the adult males pick up new food-eating habits (cf. Mitchell, 1969). Adult male leader Japanese macaques look after females and infants. When infants of dominant females reach ten months of age, male leaders care for them. Some infant males in turn succeed in becoming leaders themselves because they are able to interact with leaders when they are young. Japanese macaque males whose social positions are most rapidly rising show the most male care of infants. Infant care by males is seen as being primarily cultural rather than hormonal in nature (cf. Mitchell, 1979). There is field evidence for the existence of troops without adult males. Laboratory evidence suggests that such Japanese monkey "matriarchal societies" produce infant sex roles which are different from those seen in troops with males. In the matriarchal societies, a *female* infant of a dominant female manifests more dominant behaviors than does her male counterpart (a son of a dominant female) (Lorinc and Candland, 1977).

In regard to feeding habits, great ape mothers may actively feed foods to their infants and share food with them (cf. Horr, 1977). Even the use of tools in getting food is passed on from generation to generation (McGrew, 1974).

Hamadryas baboons live in one-male groups in which the male "herds" his females by biting the napes of their necks to keep them near him (Kummer and Kurt, 1963). Other baboons (e.g., *Papio anubis*) live in multimale groups. There is evidence from mixed group studies and from female hybrids (*P. hamadryas* and *P. anubis*) that the females modify their own behavior according to the social pattern imposed upon them by the males (Nagel, 1970). The two different baboon social structures can be developed either by genetics *or* by social tradition.

In two short years (1972 and 1973), male olive baboons (*Papio anubis*) in one area of Kenya doubled their hunting, killing, and meat eating. Females also began to kill gazelles and other game and even *infants* learned to take and eat meat from their mothers and close males. Juveniles also learned to hunt and kill; the baboons began to share meat; and, more systematic hunting developed. The baboons learned to chase prey toward other baboons and a hunt for a gazelle came to last for up to three days and extended to a distance of two miles from the main troop for groups of males (Harding and Strum, 1976). There is evidence among primates that males are usually more responsible for the passing on of between-group or between-troop traditions while females seem to hold the advantage for within-group cultural propagation (see Mitchell, 1979). This may be less true of the great apes than for monkeys, however.

McGrew et al. (1979) have recently published an article describing cross-cultural comparisons of chimpanzees in Senegal, Tanzania, and Rio Muni. They were particularly interested in tool-making and tool-using to get termites. Differences between cultures existed. While most of the differences resulted from environmental constraints in the accessibility of prey, others seemed to be truly cultural, arbitrary, and free of the demands of the environment. As McGrew et al. (1979) concluded:

It is difficult to see how differences in genotype could effect the sort of differences presented here at the other locations . . . we conclude that cross-cultural differences exist between the three populations of chimpanzees examined. (p. 204)

MARRIAGE AND SEX IN PRIMATES AND PEOPLE

According to a recent volume on the evolution of human sexuality, "anthropologists traditionally have been more interested in differences among peoples than in similarities, and they may be emotionally committed to cultural relativism" (Symons, 1979, p. 67). Yet, as even Symons admits, cross-cultural data do indicate aspects of human behavior that are highly plastic.

In Symons' book he reviews the sexual behavior patterns of four different societies: the Mangaians, the Trobrianders, the Muria, and the Kgatla. The Mangaians, the Trobrianders, and the Muria have frequent sexual intercourse with a variety of partners: from puberty on in the Mangaians, from six to eight years old and on in the Trobrianders, and from six to seven on in the Muria. The Kgatla, on the other hand, are somewhat sexually active before marriage but one of the reasons for their marriage is for sexual gratification. In the other societies, according to Symons, people do not marry for sex (see Symons, 1979).

Symons believes that marriage in *Homo sapiens* succeeds not because of, but in spite of, sexual obligations. Humans are not monogamous in the same sense that titis, marmosets, or even gibbons are. Nonhuman primate "families" exist because mated couples repulse other adults of the same species. In humans, "a *larger* social matrix defines, creates, and maintains the family" (Symons, 1979, p. 121):

For the great majority of humanity—and possibly for all of it before modern times—marriage is not so much an alliance between two people but rather an alliance of families and larger networks of people . . . among most non-modern peoples marriages are negotiated and arranged by elders . . . Marriage begins with a public announcement—and usually a ceremony—and can be said to exist only insofar as it is recognized by the community at large (Symons, 1979, p. 121).

As Symons admits, gibbons and humans *are* alike in that their "pair-bonds" are not particularly sexual in character. One of the characteristics of monogamous primates relative to nonmonogamous ones is that the overall level of sexual behavior is lower in the former. "In most pre-literate societies, marriage is not erotic, but economic" (Symons, 1979, p. 122). The most important emotion is not sexual lust but jealousy, especially male jealousy. The relevant behaviors are agreements among males about sexual rights to females (Symons, 1979).

Sex Differences in Human Preindustrial Societies[1]

In preindustrial human societies children were a major resource and women were valued for their reproductive ability. Males were valued for their authority over children. Three main kinship types probably existed in preindustrial times: bilateral, patrilineal, and matrilineal (Paige and Paige, in press).

Bilateral kinships occurred in hunting and gathering societies. In this system the child was assumed to be related to the relatives of both mother and father. Thus, there were large numbers of kin scattered over a wide area, an advantage for hunter/gatherers (Paige and Paige, in press).

The *patrilineal* kinship system was the next most common type. In this form the child was considered to be of one lineage, that of the father. Only 84 societies in the world are currently *matrilineal*, where the child is thought to be related to the mother's brothers (Paige and Paige, in press).

In addition to kinship systems, residence patterns have also been of some importance in human families. There have been five major types of residence patterns: patrilocal, matrilocal, neolocal, bilocal, and avunculocal. In the *patrilocal* pattern, people usually lived with the husband's father. Male-male bonding was of importance here. In the *matrilocal* model, individuals lived with the wife's family. Conflicts with lineages were common in this case. The *neolocal* systems involved people living wherever it was most expedient for work and food. In the *bilocal* pattern, half the people lived with the wife's parents and half with the husband's parents. In the more specific *avunculocal* system, people lived with the husband's mother's brother (a matrilineal kinship system) (Paige and Paige, in press).

---

[1]I would like to thank Greg Herek for help in summarizing and evaluating the material presented in this section.

These varieties of human kinship systems and residence patterns have always been overlaid with many different kinds of economic systems and marriage systems. Paige and Paige (in press) list eight different economic systems: (1) hunting and gathering; (2) fishing; (3) mounted hunting; (4) shifting agriculture; (5) hoeing agriculture; (6) plowing agriculture; (7) pastoralists; and (8) peasants.

Marriage exchange systems, determining alliances and resource exchanges, have also been quite varied. Paige and Paige (in press) list seven: (1) total absence of marriage gifts; (2) brideservice (labor or other services rendered by the groom to the bride's kin); (3) gift-exchange (reciprocal exchange between bride's kin and groom's kin); (4) token bride-prices (symbolic payment only); (5) bride-prices (groom's relatives pay the bride's kin); (6) dowry (bride's relatives give property to bride, groom, or groom's kin); and (7) exchange (transfer of a female relative of the groom for the bride).

This mere listing of the varieties of kinship types, residence patterns, economic systems, and marriage exchange systems in humans emphasizes the degree of complexity and variety inherent in human relationships relative to nonhuman primate relationships. Nonhuman primate families simply do not show the variety and complexity that human families show. It is not surprising, therefore, that human *sex differences* are also more complicated than are nonhuman primate sex differences.

One way in which humans differ dramatically from nonhuman primates is in the development of political alliances. *Political* resources determine reproductive capacities in humans. The ability to make bargains or to form alliances in order to use force are of great importance in human reproduction. *Fraternal interest groups* (males of a kin group working together) are determined in part by a society's economic organization. In some societies, for example, sons must rely on fathers for access to wealth. Herding societies are likely to form such kin-based factions. Hunting/gathering societies, however, are less likely to form fraternal interest groups (Paige and Paige, in press).

Humans also use *ritual* much more than do other primates. *Ritual* is magical, religious, scientific, or daily social custom. Ritual serves to convey information. It is also political in that it manipulates public opinion. Reproductive rituals are a form of psychological warfare. Paige and Paige (in press) discuss three kinds of reproductive ritual politics: (1) *Ritual surveillance* (e.g., circumcision to assure loyalty);

(2) *social mobilization rituals* (e.g., couvade, in which a male goes through labor when his wife is delivering a baby); and (3) *ritual disinterest displays* (e.g., ritual disinterest in a woman's fertility to convince others that support for one's claims to a woman will not disrupt power relations). In short, reproductive rituals are used to convince the community of the legitimacy of one's interests. The rituals, in reality, are attempts to control biological events relating to reproduction. Societies with strong fraternal interest groups, however, do not need social mobilization rituals and are also able to postpone the marriage age. Strong fraternal interest groups can protect their females. Power and politics are extremely important in human reproduction.

According to Tavris and Offir (1977), many of the principles discussed above come together to help explain conditions of war. When war appears to be adaptive in a society, the society typically needs more food and fewer people. With war comes male supremacy and rituals that glorify males and subordinate females. Wars are correlated with patrilocal residence, polygyny, marriage by capture, bride price, restrictions on women's sexual behavior, and strong fraternal interest groups. "No single human custom or attitude can be studied in isolation from the others." (Tavris and Offir, 1977, p. 244) Strong fraternal interest groups, for example, develop in a public domain.

As we have seen in Chapters 6 and 17, inequalities between the sexes evolve from differential participation in private vs. public domains (i.e., the home vs. work).

> The most egalitarian societies are those in which both roles are valued and both sexes participate in household activities and important public events. Women are oppressed and lack social worth to the extent that they are confined to the home, and are cut off from other women and the outside world (Tavris and Offir, 1977, p. 266; also see Rosaldo, 1974).

The systems discussed above (kinship systems, residence systems, economic systems, marriage exchange systems, fraternal interest groups, etc.) involve many factors that work together to produce male dominance in human societies. But just because the systems have survived does not mean they are good (Tavris and Offir, 1977).

An evolutionary (sociobiological) approach makes genetic survival the ultimate yardstick. But customs are born from environmental pressures as well as from genetic ones, and customs can be *changed* by environmental pressures. To answer a question posed by Tavris and Offir (1977), there *is* a place for human purpose in society. As Tavris and Offir (1977) themselves recognized,

> ... People, unlike cabbages and dinosaurs, have minds and language, which permit learning and communications ... Social groups can deliberately speed change up, slow it down, and alter its direction. Cultural and technological change can influence, even overcome, the impact of biological change (p. 268).

On the other hand, evolution itself can produce customs that are beneficial without our knowing why. It is often rational to follow religious rules one does not completely understand because many of them have stood the test of evolution and have thereby acquired historical wisdom (Campbell, 1975). Even nonhuman primates, for example, practice incest avoidance.

That humans are not pawns of evolutionary forces, that they have the capacity to control the environment rather than merely reacting to it (Tavris and Offir, 1977) should not be too surprising; neither are monkeys or apes simply pawns in evolution, nor are dogs. *Every* species is an active participant in its own evolution (Piaget, 1978). The active role of apes and, especially of humans however, is far more conscious and self-aware than is the active role of monkeys and dogs.

The sexual division of labor in humans persists because of differences in *all* of the following: biology, economics, sociology, and psychology. The development of the more active role of apes and, especially, of humans has been made possible because of the biological evolution of the nervous system. There may even be sex differences in the degree of awareness regarding how much human purpose may be possible. In Chapter 26, we discuss this possibility. It is interesting that one of the goals of those who have been most actively involved in social change is consciousness raising in those who are not so actively involved. The assumption, presumably, is that sexism is at least partly a matter of not being aware. We all know, however, that some sexists are quite aware of what they are doing. Economics (politics) and sociology, as well as biology and psychology, are obviously of some importance to this problem. The present book, of course, does not do justice to the complexities and interactions of any of these in human evolution.

REFERENCES

Burton, F.D. The integration of biology and behavior in the socialization of *Macaca sylvana* of Gibraltar. In Poirier, F.E. (Ed.) *Primate Socialization.* New York:Random House, 1972, pp. 29-62.

Campbell, D. On the conflicts between biological and social evolution and between psychology and moral tradition. *American Psychologist,* 1975, 30, 1103-1126.

French, J.A. and Candland, D.K. The genesis of "object play" in *Macaca fuscata.* Paper presented at the *Animal Behavior Society* meeting, University Park, Pennsylvania, June, 1977.

Harding, R.S.O. and Strum, S.C. The predatory baboons of Kekopey. *Natural History,* 1976, 85, 46-53.

Horr, D.A. Orang-utan maturation: Growing up in a female world. In Chevalier-Skolnikoff, S. and Poirier, F.E. (Eds.) *Primate Bio-social Development.* New York: Garland, 1977, pp. 289-322.

Itani, J. On the acquisition and propagation of a new food habit in the troop of Japanese monkeys at Takasakiyama. In Imanishi, K. and Altmann, S. (Eds.) *Japanese Monkeys.* Atlanta: Altmann, 1965, pp. 52-65.

Kummer, H. and Kurt, F. Social units of a free-living population of hamadryas baboons. *Folia Primatologica,* 1963, 1-2, 4-18.

Lorinc, G.A. and Candland, D.K. The primate mother-infant dyad: Intergenerational transmission of dominance in *Macaca fuscata.* Paper presented at the *Animal Behavior Society* meeting, University Park, Pennsylvania, June, 1977.

McGrew, W.C. Tool use by wild chimpanzees in feeding upon driver ants. *Journal of Human Evolution,* 1974, 3, 501-508.

McGrew, W.C., Tutin, C.E.G., and Baldwin, P.J. Chimpanzees, tools, and termites: Cross-cultural comparisons of Senegal, Tanzania, and Rio Muni. *Man,* 1979, 14, 185-214.

Mitchell, G. *Behavioral Sex Differences in Nonhuman Primates.* New York: Van Nostrand, 1979.

Mitchell, G. Paternalistic behavior in primates. *Psychological Bulletin,* 1969, 71, 399-417.

Nagel, U. Social organization in a baboon hybrid zone. *Proceedings of the Third International Congress of Primatology,* 1970, 3, 48-57.

Paige, K.E. and Paige, J.M. *Politics and Reproductive Ritual in Stateless Societies.* Berkeley, CA: University of California Press, Still in press.

Piaget, Jean. *Behavior and Evolution.* New York: Pantheon, 1978.

Rosaldo, M.Z. Woman, culture, and society: A theoretical overview. In Rosaldo, M.Z. and Lamphere, L. (Eds.) *Woman, Culture, and Society.* Stanford, CA.: Stanford University Press, 1974, pp. 17-43.

Symons, D. *The Evolution of Human Sexuality.* New York: Oxford University Press, 1979.

Tavris, C. and Offir, C. *The Longest War: Sex Differences in Perspective.* New York: Harcourt Brace Jovanovich, 1977.

24
Variability and Individuality

Up to this point in our book we have discussed the degree of variability shown by male and female nonhuman primates as related to hormones, socialization pressures, and culture. Variability in sex differences is also apparent in regard to both cyclical and noncyclical idiosyncratic factors.

CYCLICITY

With regard to cyclical factors, many sex differences in behavior are correlated with reproductive cycles. In fact, the hypothalamus of the brain is organized differently in females than in males, at least partly as a function of prenatal androgens. Thus, we expect female primates, particularly in strongly dimorphic species, to show periodicities in behavior not seen in males. Most nonhuman primate females, for example, have estrous cycles during which they change somewhat behaviorally. However, there are other kinds of behavioral cyclicities besides those associated with monthly estrous cycles. There are also annual and diurnal rhythms. Males as well as females display these kinds of cyclicity (Mitchell, 1979).

Prosimian Cyclicity

Among most if not all prosimians, mating is restricted to a brief period and coincides with vaginal estrus. There is little emancipation of prosimian sexual behavior from hormonal influences. However, the cyclicity of the breeding season may differ by as much as six months when lemurs, for example, are in Portland, Oregon instead of in their native Malagasy Republic. Lemurs are sensitive to photoperiod changes (Mitchell, 1979).

Reproductive turnover—a kind of cyclicity—is high in prosimians. They have short gestation periods, multiple births, and relatively brief interbirth intervals (Mitchell, 1979). With regard to diurnal cyclicity, it has been found that the vocalizations of ring-tailed lemurs show daily rhythms (King and Fitch, 1977).

New World Monkey Cyclicity

There appear to be no seasonal changes in the reproductive tracts of at least some marmosets and tamarins. Squirrel monkeys, however, have a mating season during which both sexes put on weight in response to androgen (the "fatted" condition) (see Mitchell, 1979).

Rhesus Monkey Cyclicity

The estrous (or menstrual) cycle of the rhesus monkey is twenty-eight days long. During this time there are apparently two peaks of female receptivity, one at ovulation and the other just before menstruation. In the summer, female cycles are irregular. They also become irregular when the females are moved from their stable groups (see Mitchell, 1979).

There are seasonal fluctuations as well as monthly cycles in rhesus monkeys. Grooming, molting, and breeding all show annual cycles. These annual rhythms do not depend on the presence of gonads. They are evidently rhythms mediated through the brain, perhaps in response to photoperiod, weather changes, or social factors.

Rhesus also display diurnal cycles. Testosterone levels in the blood, for example, reach a high point in rhesus males at 10 P.M. This cycle *does* depend on the gonads. There are also diurnal rhythms in female spontaneous uterine activity (lower at night) (see Mitchell, 1979 for references).

Cyclicity in Other Old World Monkeys

Japanese monkeys have menstrual cycles like rhesus, and they have a breeding season and a birth season. Stumptail macaques show an unusual pattern of three birth peaks during the year. Pigtail macaques apparently show a diurnal testosterone rhythm which is the *reverse* of the rhesus cycle.

Among mangabeys, some male vocalizations are cyclical. In other Old World monkeys, subadult males leave the group only during the birth season.

Ape Cyclicity

The hormonal cyclicity of chimpanzee females during pregnancy is more like the human female's than is that of the rhesus. Sexual behavior and dominance are correlated with female menstrual cycles. The pygmy chimpanzee is less tied to a cycle than is the common chimpanzee (see Mitchell, 1979).

Gorillas also appear to be somewhat more tied to a cycle than do pygmy chimpanzees; and, there is some evidence that orangutans are also (see Mitchell, 1979).

Human Cyclicity

In human sexual behavior there is continual rather than cyclical activity. Although Old World monkeys and the great apes show signs of emancipation from hormones, only the pygmy chimpanzee shows the continual pattern of the human (cf. Mitchell, 1979).

Despite the relative freedom from hormonal effects, people *do* show some rhythms in behavior. The stimulus value of female odors for men varies with the ovulatory cycle. Women are sensitive to musklike odors at menstruation and at ovulation. Women living together and seeing males fewer than three times per week experience a synchrony of their menstrual cycles. Environmental change often disturbs menstrual rhythm in human females. At the time of ovulation, some women do, in fact, feel a strong sex drive. In men, blood androgen levels peak early in the morning. This is unlike the rhesus pattern but is nevertheless often correlated with feelings of sexual desire.

NONCYCLICAL VARIABILITY

As we have seen, sex differences are not static, they vary with hormonal levels, socialization pressures, and with culture; and, they are sometimes cyclical. There are other sources of variability less easy to explain. Many of the sex differences we have covered in this book do not appear as consistently and predictably as we have suggested. How do they vary?

First of all, as we already know, there is species-to-species variability. In general, females show more infant care than do males but in some species males display more than do females. Second, there is troop-to-troop variability. Kawamura (1963) reported that each wild Japanese troop had a food list all its own. He also found great variability in culturally propagated male care. Third, there is individual-to-individual variability. In stumptail macaques, for example, there is extreme variability in sexual posturing. Some postures are quite idiosyncratic. Fourth, there is variability from situation-to-situation. In macaque sexual consorts, dyads of different males with the same female show remarkable variability in sexual behavior whereas dyads of different females with the same male show very little variability.

As Burton (1977) has emphasized, regardless of sex differences, the outstanding characteristic of all primates is *variability*. Behaviors are not just classifiable by age, sex, or season. They are also classifiable by individual animal and by individual animal in a specific situation.

Prosimians differ in the nature of their social structures, in the size of their territories, in diurnal and nocturnal rhythms, in duration of infant care, and in the presence or absence of binocular vision. Some New World marmoset and tamarin families live in large temporary aggregations in the wild. In some of the marmoset families, the *female* does most of the infant carrying. Some female squirrel monkeys without males respond to each other as mating couples. Some New World monkeys, and particularly males, cannot see the color red.

Among Old World monkeys, there is marked anatomical variability in macaques, including in the genitals. Individuals display different degrees of finickiness in sexuality. Rhesus raised in social isolation display more variability in behavior between individuals and within individuals than do rhesus not raised under deprived conditions. Mating seasons vary from troop to troop; so do sex ratios. Occasionally Old World monkeys hybridize in nature (e.g., some baboons). Lesser apes differ in pelage coloration. Different species of gibbons hybridize in nature. The hybrids emit atypical vocalizations and have different pelage colors. Thus, there is substantial genetic variability due to hybridization in the Old World primates (see Mitchell, 1979).

Great ape variability is also legion. For example, there is marked individuality in the voices of gorillas, and the sexual behavior patterns of the three genera of great apes could hardly be more different than they are. Even within one genus (*Pan*), the two existing species are extremely different from one another in sexual behavior. The words "always" and "never" have become rare words in the behavioral primatologist's vocabulary (see Mitchell, 1979).

In people, there is no question that heredity plays a large role in determining individual differences. There is so much individual variation within the sexes of human beings that there is a great deal of overlap between them. Classifying behaviors according to sex or age can therefore be quite risky.

In Chapter 1 we made mention of the variability hypothesis. Because of social myth and science's entanglements with myth it has often been proposed, unjustly at times, that males in general vary more than do females (behaviorally speaking). In some cases this appears to be true. In infant care behaviors, for example, males of many species are more variable than are females. In some species (e.g., vervets), males show more variability in play than do females. On several dimensions of anatomical development (e.g., dental development) human males vary more than do human females.

During the 19th century and continuing into the 20th, many writers promoted the idea that male humans are more variable than are females in intelligence and creativity (Shields, 1975). There are more mentally retarded males than there are retarded females, partly because there is greater male vulnerability. The difference at the upper end is also real (in spatial and quantitative skills) but may be a reflection of socialization, social pressures, and prejudice. Genius is rare and results from a good combination of factors such as genes, motivation, opportunity, training, and tools. Males have been more likely to receive this good combination of factors than have females (see Chapter 23 on ability and achievement) (Williams, 1977). Thus, the idea that females are less variable in cognitive ability than are males has not been well substantiated.

In terms of human variability, it is unfortunate that both men and women are responded to negatively when they deviate from the expectations for their sex. This is true for males who deviate more than it is for females. An example of this sex difference is seen in the response of people to homosexuality in males and females (see Deaux, 1976). It is interesting that nonhuman primates seem to be more tolerant of variability and deviance than do humans. Handicapped individuals are often well integrated into wild groups of primates. Berkson (1977) released blind and defective individuals into wild groups of macaques and found that these primates even tolerate, interact with, protect, and compensate for the behaviors of totally blind individuals. Would that people could be as tolerant.

Humans occur in two basic biological types, male and female. By concentrating on sex *differences,* however, scientists have emphasized the ways in which men and women differ. The fact is they are more alike than different. Sex *difference* further leads to categorization into *opposites.* Females are *not* the opposites of males. Even the genitals themselves differentiate from the same common tissues. A concentration on differences *between* the sexes should not let us forget that there are perhaps even larger and more important differences *within* the sexes (see Williams, 1977).

> ... taking into account individual differences ... would essentially refine the results and lead to the generation of more intelligent and interesting hypotheses (Williams, 1977, p. 400).

We hope that by concentrating on the immense variability seen from genus-to-genus, from species-to-species, group-to-group, individual-to-individual, and situation-to-situation in our nonhuman primate cousins we can help those primarily involved in human research to more clearly see the tremendous potential for individuality and plasticity in the human species. Surely we can be no less adaptable, versatile, or variable than the rest of the primates. Dichotomization of any kind, but particularly stereotypic dichotomization, fails to adequately represent either primatological or human psychological reality (see for example, O'Leary et al., 1979).

REFERENCES

Berkson, G. The social ecology of defects in primates. In Chevalier-Skolnikoff, S., and Poirier, F.E. (Eds.) *Primate Biosocial Development: Biological, Social,* and *Ecological Determinants,* New York: Garland, 1977. pp. 189-204.
Burton, F.D. Ethology and the development of sex and gender identity in nonhuman primates. *Acta Biotheoretica,* 1977, 28, 1-18.
Deaux, K. *The Behavior of Women and Men.* Monterey, CA: Brooks/Cole, 1976.
Kawamura, S. The process of sub-culture propagation among Japanese macaques. In Southwick, D.H. (Eds.) *Primate Social Behavior,* Princeton, N.J.: Van Nostrand, 1963, pp. 82-89.

King, G. and Fitch, M. Vocal patterns in captive ring-tailed lemurs (*Lemur catta*). Paper presented at the *Western Psychological Society* meeting, Seattle, Washington, April 1977.

Mitchell, G. *Behavioral Sex Differences in Nonhuman Primates.* New York: Van Nostrand Reinhold, 1979.

O'Leary, V.E., Wallston, B.S., and Unger, R.K. Women, gender, and social psychology. *The Society for the Advancement of Social Psychology Newsletter,* 1979, 5(3), 1-2.

Shields, S.A. Functionalism, Darwinism, and the psychology of women. *American Psychologist,* 1975, 30, 739-754.

Williams, J.H. *Psychology of Women: Behavior in a Biosocial Context.* New York: W.W. Norton, 1977.

25
Psychoanalysis and Sexism[1]

As Williams (1977) and others have shown, women have been seen as representatives of both the highest and lowest forms of life. Men have generated myths which provide them with "explanations" to help control women. For example, women have been seen as mother nature and mother earth, bringing forth food and life. Women linked men to the earth. They were closer to the mystery of it all and had the power of generation. To neutralize this power, men set up myths.

Women have also been symbolized as enchantresses or seductresses who lured men away from higher pursuits, causing them to abandon reason or even emasculating them. Along the same lines, women were often viewed as evil, inferior, insignificant or as a mystery. At another extreme, there was the myth of women, the virtuous, faithful, loyal, submissive wives; the dedicated, loving mothers; the supporters of moral and religious values in their society (Williams, 1977). The suffrage movement ran straight into the teeth of these myths. Women's vote was seen by some men as an assault on religion, the home, marriage, and the family.

In the beginning of scientific studies of sex differences there was a bridge made between these myths and evolutionary theory; and, the two, science and myth, served each other (Shields, 1975). Thus, the biological perspective got a bad name from the start among feminists. From this link of myth and evolutionary theory came such ideas as

---

[1]The present chapter is based upon the first three chapters of a book by Juanita H. Williams, entitled *Psychology of Women: Behavior in a Biosocial Context,* W.W. Norton Co., 1977.

the variability hypothesis, which proposed that males varied more than did females on important dimensions like intelligence. This also served to "keep women in their places," since genius was a uniquely male trait. Recent evidence on differences in variability, however, has been contradictory (Shields, 1975; Williams, 1977).

PSYCHOANALYTIC THEORY

Freud's psychoanalysis was deterministic. That is to say, it denied that people had complete control over what they did. Unconscious forces shaped human behavior. Psychoanalysis was also touched by the myths, stereotypes, and prejudices of its day. Freud himself was a conventional, conservative person who lived in a strongly patriarchal Central European society in which there was an assumption of male dominance and superiority. Freud was critical of early feminists.

Freud's psychoanalysis developed out of his interest in hysteria, a condition felt to affect primarily women. Hysterical symptoms included paralysis, loss of speech, etc. Freud borrowed the cathartic method, a talking cure, from Breuer. In the talking cure, Freud had patients practice free association, in which the patient talked about anything that came to mind. Using this technique, Freud came to posit an unconscious that was usually repressed yet was often revealed in dreams, selective forgetting, slips of the tongue, and other "mistakes."

Freud also developed a theory of psychosexual development in which he dealt with stages. He postulated an undifferentiated sexual energy called libido which was not focused anywhere early in life (i.e., it was polymorphous perverse). Eventually, however, libido (gratification and pleasure) became associated with feeding; and, the mouth became an erotogenic zone during the first of Freud's psychosexual stages, the oral stage. Following the oral stage were four more stages, each being related to a focus for libidinal energy: the anal, the phallic, the latent, and the genital stages.

In regard to sex differences, Freud's theory was primarily based upon male development. Female development was added almost as an afterthought. The two sexes diverged at the phallic stage. Whereas boys loved their mothers, resented their fathers (Oedipal complex), and suffered castration anxiety as a result, the development of girls at this stage always remained somewhat of a mystery to Freud. Instead of castration anxiety as in boys, girls supposedly developed penis envy and a permanent sense of inferiority and passivity (see how myth and science became linked here). Anatomy became destiny.

The girl, however, did not have to go through the Oedipal complex with its castration anxiety and hence did not have to totally abandon libidinal interest in the father as the male had to do with the mother. Thus, her personality did not have to develop a conscience (or superego) which gave rise to morality and other qualities which made people civilized. Again note that women were labeled uncivilized and hence inferior by Freud.

Early proponents of women's rights did not like some of Freud's ideas. His theories depreciated the female, female sexuality, and the female genitalia. The girl was supposed to envy the male's penis. Feminists also objected to Freud's ideas because his ideas implied that anatomy was more important than culture. He never stressed the effect of society on personality and behavior, an effect that obviously influenced Freud himself personally.

On the other hand, according to Williams (1977), psychoanalysis helped us to understand to some degree the oppression of women. In retrospect we can see clearly how Freud's patriarchal society became mentally represented in the society of the times and even in its brightest citizens. The fact that Freud stressed the role of the unconscious also helped bring unconscious prejudice to a conscious level. Psychoanalysis was history at several levels. Psychoanalytic theory is a record of the way it was in a male dominated patriarchal society (cf. Williams, 1977).

The term psychoanalysis refers to both the theory and the therapy used by Freud. Psychoanalytic therapy concentrated upon overcoming the patient's resistance to reveal unconscious material which was then interpreted by the therapist. During the therapy the patient went through transference in which feelings and conflicts once reserved for the parents were transferred to the therapist.

OTHER PSYCHOANALYTIC THEORISTS

Helene Deutsch was known as the "dutiful daughter" of Freud. She did not change Freud's ideas much except that she noted that the personality trait of envy (supposedly a residual of penis envy) was not peculiar to women. She, too, did not emphasize cultural factors; and, she too relegated female sexual experiences to a less important level than those of the male. To Deutsch the female experience was one of passivity. Even masochism was a normal condition for women, and so was narcissism. According to her, the combination of narcissism, passivity, and masochism produced, in balance, a normal woman.

Erik Erikson developed what he called the "eight ages of man," beginning in infancy and ending in old age. But his examples in each of the stages were all male. In his famous study of the use of space, Erikson invited children to construct on a table a scene from an imaginary motion picture using toys. He reported that girls built interior scenes in static positions while boys erected buildings and towers outside and had scenes with action in them. To Erikson these differences were analogous to sexual anatomy and were evidence that anatomy was destiny. This biologistic determinism conflicts with feminist ideology. Moreover, Erikson's view assumed that the male was the prototype of humanity, and it equated the word woman with mother.

Freud, Deutsch, and Erikson all said that the woman's body was a major determinant of her personality and behavior. In addition, all three used a double standard to explain behavior wherein the male was seen as the norm and the female as the deviation from the norm (Williams, 1977).

The ideas of other psychoanalytic theorists like Karen Horney, Clara Thompson, and Alfred Adler were better liked by feminists because they did not propose that the male was the prototype, that biology was destiny, or that females were deviant. In addition, as the latter three theorists were making their marks, cultural relativity began to become more well known, thanks to the early work of Margaret Mead.

Karen Horney agreed with Freud that the unconscious and early childhood were important; however, she also believed that a person could not be understood without considering his or her present environment and interactions. Horney took a holistic approach in which she viewed the person as a dynamic whole rather than as a mechanistic system of different parts. Using a clinical approach she emphasized the male bias of psychoanalytic observers.

The girl, said Horney, was exposed from birth to the suggestion of her inferiority; and, since women were barred from accomplishment they had a factual basis for inferiority feelings. She saw male productivity as a compensation for their inability to create life as women could. According to some, her views of male compensation were as sexist as were Freud's views, although they represented a reverse sexism.

Horney doubted that masochism was a psychobiological necessity for women. She believed that other theorists felt this to be the case because they excluded cultural and social factors from the picture. Social conditioning taught women to be passive, masochistic. Horney rejected Freud's libido theory with its emphasis on biological drives. Instead, she said the child was born with potential for growth and for self-actualization. Her basic principle for motivating people was the need for security. She saw Freud's philosophy as a pessimistic one and her own as optimistic (cf. Williams, 1977).

The person's relationships with others was seen as crucial in the mind of Clara Thompson. In her theory, the basic drive was the need to grow and master the environment. She saw humans as the least instinct-dominated of all animals. Libidinal urges were less important to the child than was the formation of the self. Only in adolescence did sex become important, but even here it was the cultural attitudes about sex which were important, not the urges themselves.

According to Thompson, women's feelings of inferiority were a reflection of their real position in society (not of biological lack). Having no models of their own, women copied men because the world rewarded masculine behavior. Clara Thompson felt that women would do better if they found their own way, noting that the competitive race for success did not enrich the lives of those trapped in it. Thompson was also in the forefront in rejecting the view that women's sexual needs were unimportant. She denied that woman, her body and her functions were inferior.

Alfred Adler was the only major psychoanalytic male theorist to reject sexism. It was not surprising that he and Freud did not get along, although this was not a major issue in their disagreement. Adler, too, rejected Freud's idea that behavior was biologically determined. He believed that people were social beings motivated by social interest, cooperation, and the common good. Adler paid attention to the person as a unique individual striving to enhance the self. The person was not the product of urges; the person created his/her own life by actions performed. What the person *did* was important. Adler also reinstated conscious thought to a prominent role. Adler felt that people were ordinarily aware of why they did what they did, and he strongly believed that people could plan. An important facet of Adlerian theory was that people were motivated more by expectations of the future than by experiences of the past. They developed fictional goals and personal ideologies.

Feelings of inferiority were experiences that *everyone* had. Behavior was driven by a need to overcome them. Each person would strive to become superior, to complete the self. The normal person would strive for personal goals that were in the service of the common good, to form interpersonal relations, to identify with the group. Rather than libido, social interest was an innate disposition.

Adler accounted for individuality with his "style of life" concept. Each life style was a way of striving for superiority and social interest. In these strivings a creative self resulted. Adler trusted in human potential, in human choice, in human ability. Adler restored freedom and dignity to personality theory. He too was optimistic.

With his emphasis upon freedom and choice, Adler, not surprisingly, believed that a system of socializing children into roles of dominance and submission based upon sex was an inefficient and immoral system. The girl lost self-confidence because of prejudice against women, because she had models which were inferior, because she was powerless. In this sense, Adler was not unlike Mead.

Margaret Mead concluded that human behavior as expressed in personality was malleable beyond anything previously thought. Differences in social conditioning were important and the form of conditioning depended on the culture. Idiosyncratic or individual differences in temperament were attenuated to some extent by the specific culture in which that person developed. Mead felt that a good society could permit the development of many different kinds of temperaments, could build on different potentials. Beneath the superficial category of sex the same potentialities existed. These potentialities could be encouraged in both sexes so that differences among individuals would be real, not artifically imposed according to the superficial category of gender. Her emphases, like the emphases of Horney, Thompson, and Adler, were on the person, the individual, the self—not on gender.

So what were the effects of psychoanalysis on the psychology of sex differences? Clearly, psychoanalysis helped us to understand to some degree the oppression of women. It helped show us how the values of a society, including its myths, could affect scientific study. Most importantly, however, it taught us the value of an objective approach to the study of sex differences. Continued arm-chair philosphy did not answer major questions.

In retrospect, the reactions of Horney, Thompson, Adler, and others to Freud's biological determinism are similar to the reactions of many contemporary social scientists to ethology and sociobiology. Freud's unconscious, Lorenz's hydraulic ethological model of instincts, and sociobiology's selfish genes have much in common at this philosophical level. Freud without the gene was much like Darwin without the gene, correct in principle but not in detail. Opponents of Freudian theory, on the other hand, were often much like the opponents of Darwinian theory. They sometimes tended to accept religious doctrine and to believe in *Homo sapiens* as an organism somehow beyond the forces of nature. Of course, *Homo sapiens* is *not* beyond natural control.

Still, there is a sense in which opponents of deterministic models of human behavior (including sociobiology) *are* correct. Not all forces governing the behavior of human beings are unconscious. People are very much aware of many decisions they make and of many things they do. As we will see in our next chapter, the roots of this awareness are present in our nonhuman primate cousins.

REFERENCES

Shields, S.A. Functionalism, Darwinism, and the psychology of women. *American Psychologist,* 1975, 30, 739-754.

Williams, J.H. *Psychology of Women: Behavior in a Biosocial Context.* New York: W.W. Norton, 1977.

26
The Self

In using the term *behavior* throughout this book we do not assume that the primate behaving is conscious of its behavior. The typical prosimian, for example, probably does not intend to perform a particular behavior before it behaves. Thus, the average nonhuman primate has no conceptual representation of its own actions (see Reynolds, 1976). On the other hand, *some* nonhuman primates seem to be conscious, seem to intend to perform given actions, seem to have a conceptual representation of their own actions, and in fact seem to be *aware* of their *own existence* (Gallup, 1977).

An animal's identity can be separated into at least three different types, species identity, self identity, and gender identity. Species-typical behavioral patterns, to the extent that they exist in most primates, depend upon an awareness by the organism that it belongs to the same species as does its partner (Roy and Roy, 1980). Early experiences with conspecifics are necessary for the development of this knowledge. Isolation-reared rhesus do not know that they belong to their own species. However, species identity is not *completely* dependent upon experience. Primates are born with some knowledge about their own species. Infant rhesus monkeys prefer rhesus monkey pictures over nonmonkey pictures. Even human infants show preferences for schematic human faces (Roy and Roy, 1980). Of course, neither is species identity completely exclusive. Cross-species affinities certainly occur. This means that: (1) Some of the inborn knowledge is held in common by many primates, and (2) there is some amount of generalizability of ontogenetic attachment processes within the primate order (Mitchell, 1976; 1979).

In the case of isolation-reared Old World monkeys, it appears that not only do they not develop a completely appropriate species identity, they also do not develop the usual rudiments of self-awareness typical of this level of primate. Isolation-reared rhesus, as we know, are behaviorally abnormal. Their abnormality usually, if not always, includes abnormal behavioral relations with the self. Exaggerated self-clinging, self-sucking, self-rocking, self-pacing, self-chewing, self-hitting, self-biting, and an assortment of other more idiosyncratic movements and postures involving the self as the focus of attention are common. Males show more of these abnormalities than do females (Mitchell, 1979).

Despite the appearance of such self-directed abnormalities suggesting that isolate-reared rhesus do not develop normal self-identities, no one has been able to demonstrate that normally reared rhesus even *have* a self-identity. In fact, Gallup (1977) has concluded that only the great apes and humans are capable of self-awareness or self-identity.

Identity of the self is operationally demonstrated when an animal displays self-directed behavior toward some object or mark on its own body that it cannot feel or see without a mirror. When chimpanzees and other great apes are anesthetized and marked with red dye they can take advantage of a mirror to locate, touch, or inspect the spot or mark. None of the following species show such self-recognition: rhesus, crab-eaters, stumptails, spider monkeys, capuchins, mandrills, hamadryas, baboons, and gibbons (Gallup, 1977). These species respond to their mirror images as though they were seeing another conspecific.

What is interesting in the apes' case is that at least some of this ability is acquired in early life through interaction with others. Isolation-reared chimpanzees show self-directed abnormalities like isolation-reared rhesus. They, too, have poorly developed species identities. Isolation-reared chimpanzees cannot recognize themselves in mirrors.

There are sex differences in species identity in that males are more disturbed by early social isolation than are females. While sex differences in the development of self-identity or self-recognition in the great apes have not been demonstrated, it would not be surprising if early social isolation interfered more with the development of self-recognition ability in males than in females. Isolate-reared males *do* show more self-directed abnormalities than do isolate-reared females.

It is interesting that only with the great apes[1] has there been any success in the teaching of sign language. There are some (e.g., Terrace and Bever, 1977) who say that self-recognition is *necessary* for the development of sign language. The animal *must* be able to refer to itself symbolically. Because there are sex differences in human language ability, females being superior to males, it might be interesting to study sex differences in ape sign language ability *and* sex differences in ape self-recognition.

The third type of identity is *gender identity.* Gender identity presupposes self-identity. First I am me, *then* I am male. This is, of course, the normal ontogenetic sequence for humans. The great apes, but not the lesser apes and monkeys, are capable of classifying other apes into male and female categories, they are capable of classifying *people* into male and female categories, *and* they are also able to conceptualize themselves into male and female categories (Shapiro, 1978). Whether there are gender differences in gender identity in apes is not known.

COMMENTS ON HUMANS

Amsterdam (1972) has traced the development of self-identity in humans using self-recognition studies and mirrors. She has also used videotape techniques (Amsterdam and Greenberg, 1977). She found that 20-month-old human infants were more aware of themselves than were 10- to 15-month-old infants. Self-consciousness begins after 10 months of age and becomes fully developed by age two.

Schulman and Kaplowitz (1977) found that somewhere between 21 and 24 months of age, self-recognition is evident in the human infant. No sex differences were reported. Recall, however, that there are also few, if any, sex differences in language ability up to the age of two. Recall also that language use may require the ability to symbolically refer to the self.

Beyond the age of two, self-recognition develops into self-concept. The self-concepts of people go far beyond anything an ape could conceive of. Our ideas concerning self continue to change, to grow, as we ourselves grow with the world we encounter. From the pre-

---

[1]*Pan paniscus,* the pygmy chimpanzee, has not been tested for these skills.

school years onward we have little in common with the apes when it comes to self-reflection. They are but infants relative to us.

In humans, knowledge of one's self also includes knowledge of one's sex. Gender identity involves not only knowing which sex one is, but what one's sex is *supposed* to do (sex roles). It is in the latter domain that society builds stereotypes and squashes variability and individuality.

As in the great apes, atypical rearing affects the development of the self in humans. Becoming human requires early social contact with other humans. Severely deprived and institutionalized children display abnormal self-directed behaviors seen in socially deprived monkeys and apes (self-rocking, self-biting, etc.). They also display abnormalities related to self-object differentiation.

In autistic children (not deprived) there are often extreme self-directed abnormalities. Occurring along with these are language failures and a complete absence of the use of the pronouns "I" or "me" (Wing, 1976).

In summary, awareness of self, as seen in apes and people, suggests that behavior is conscious, intentional, and purposive. The individual is aware of his/her gender and can act as he/she wants to (or thinks he/she *should*). The self-aware organisms (apes and humans) are *capable* of a wider range of behaviors than are the non-self-aware organisms (e.g., rhesus). It is no wonder that male and female humans are so difficult to categorize according to gender.

In effect, it seems, the evolution of self-awareness and language makes much of what we have learned about our primate heritage and sex differences somewhat trivial. To refer symbolically to the self is an amazing and wonderful capacity. To use this capacity individually, independently, or autonomously is to be truly human.

A biological perspective on sex difference does not need to be in opposition to feminists or with the woman's movement. The primates, too, tell us to be ourselves.

As we move toward the more advanced species of primates, we see the evolution of an increasing knowledge of the self—more self-awareness. As we progress through the development of a healthy individual human being we also see the emergence of an increasing knowledge of the self—toward more autonomy and individuality. As we move through the evolution of humanity we see an increasing self-awareness. People are still evolving and, more than likely, they are continuing to evolve in the same direction--toward greater consciousness, toward self-awareness; and, indeed, toward individual autonomy. Cultural evolution has fueled this development. We see the woman's movement as a continuation of this trend toward autonomy and individual freedom.

It is interesting that awareness of self *increases* the feelings that the self is having. In human adults, mirrors increase feelings of self-consciousness and tend to produce positive feedback to the self-viewer of his/her own affective state or feelings. When angered, for example, a highly self-conscious person will aggress *more* than will a low self-conscious person. A mirror increases anger in an already angered self-conscious person. The awareness of anger feeds the anger. "Increased awareness of one's affective state enhances the tendency to respond to that state." (Scheier, 1976, p. 643). Perhaps the horrendous acts of humanity are partly the result of inherent self-awareness rather than of inherent aggressiveness. Perhaps we can better serve ourselves by concentrating on our more positive affects or emotions. Self-love and self-knowledge are quite close to being the same thing. Again, the extrapolations from behavioral primatology tell us to like and *be* ourselves.

REFERENCES

Amsterdam, B. Mirror self-image reactions before age two. *Developmental Psychobiology,* 1972, 5, 297-305.

Amsterdam, B. and Greenberg, L.M. Self-conscious behavior of infants: A videotape study. *Developmental Psychobiology,* 1977, 19(1), 1-6.

Gallup, G.G. Self-recognition in primates: A comparative approach to the bidirectional properties of consciousness. *American Psychologist,* 1977, 32, 329-338.

Mitchell, G. *Behavioral Sex Differences in Nonhuman Primates.* New York: Van Nostrand, 1979.

Mitchell, G. Attachment potential in rhesus macaque dyads (*Macaca mulatta*): A sabbatical report. *Catalogue of Selected Documents in Psychology,* 1976, 6, MS. No. 1177.

Reynolds, V. *The Biology of Human Action.* San Francisco, CA: W.H. Freeman, 1976.

Roy, R.L. and Roy, M.A. Consequences of atypical rearing experiences in humans. In Roy, M.A. (Ed.) *Species Identification: A Phylogenetic Evaluation.* New York: Garland, 1980.

Scheier, M.F. Self-awareness, self-consciousness, and angry aggression. *Journal of Personality,* 1976, 44, 627-644.

Schulman, A.H. and Kaplowitz, C. Mirror-image responses during the first two years of life. *Developmental Psychobiology,* 1977, 10, 133-142.

Shapiro, G. Is an ecological understanding of sign language in apes necessary? Lecture given to the Ecology Group, University of California, Davis, California, February 9, 1978.

Terrace, H.S. and Bever, T.G. Project NIM: Progress report I. Unpublished manuscript, 1977.

Wing, L. (Ed.) *Early Childhood Autism.* New York: Pergamon, 1976, pp. 67-71.

Author Index

Subject Index